Praise for *Diary of a Drag Queen*

"Accessible and hilarious . . . If you want a true depiction of what it's like to balance a drag queen persona with an everyday self, look no further." —Lauren Sharkey, *Bustle*

"The book on everyone's desk at *Glamour* HQ right now . . . Hilarious." —*Glamour* (UK)

"A riotous portrayal of the contemporary queer experience." —Salma Haidrani, *Dazed*

"Hilarious and candid . . . A must-read for anyone interested in drag. Or anyone with a sense of humour. Or just anyone at all." —Connor Young, *Gay Times*

"Truthful, revealing and obscenely hilarious . . . Strident and unapologetic but really sweet, too." —*Attitude*

"Outrageously scatological, bacchanalian, and foul-mouthed . . . And yet—amazingly—it is precisely this radical honesty that means the book is never disgusting, or repulsive; far from it . . . Rasmussen's voice as a writer is poetic, idiosyncratic, and unbelievably funny . . . [A] fierce debut." —*The Prickle*

Crystal Rasmussen with Tom Rasmussen

Diary of a Drag Queen

Thurstan Redding

William Marsden

Crystal Rasmussen, global superstar, is a columnist at *Refinery29*. Crystal forms one-fifth of Denim, the drag supergroup, and is adored for her lazy demeanor and her powerful falsetto. Living in overdraft since the Wall Street Crash of 1929, she released the rights to her diary to pay back millions in overdue alimony. Crystal's sellout solo show was among the top twenty best-reviewed shows at the 2019 Edinburgh Festival Fringe.

Tom Rasmussen is a journalist, a queer performer, and a contributor at *The Independent*, *Dazed*, *i-D*, *Love*, and *Refinery29*. Their work has also been featured in *The Guardian*, *VICE*, *Broadly*, *Tank*, and *Gay Times*. They were named one of the 100 most influential young global voices by the British Fashion Council in 2019, and their first book, *Diary of a Drag Queen*, is being adapted for TV. Tom forms one-half of the radical queer punk band ACM.

Diary of a Drag Queen

FSG Originals

Farrar, Straus and Giroux

New York

Diary
of a
Drag
Queen

Crystal Rasmussen
WITH TOM RASMUSSEN

FSG Originals
Farrar, Straus and Giroux
120 Broadway, New York 10271

Copyright © 2019, 2020 by Tom Rasmussen
All rights reserved
Printed in the United States of America
Originally published, in somewhat different form, in 2019 by Ebury
Press, Great Britain
Published in the United States by Farrar, Straus and Giroux
First American edition, 2020

Library of Congress Cataloging-in-Publication Data
Names: Rasmussen, Crystal, author. | Rasmussen, Tom, 1991–author.
Title: Diary of a drag queen / Crystal Rasmussen with Tom Rasmussen.
Description: First American edition. | New York : FSG Originals, Farrar,
    Straus and Giroux, 2020. | "Originally published, in somewhat different
    form, in 2019 by Ebury Press, Great Britain"—Title page verso.
Identifiers: LCCN 2019054792 | ISBN 9780374538576
Subjects: LCSH: Rasmussen, Crystal. | Female impersonators—England—
    Biography. | Sexual minority community—Social life and customs—
    21st century. | Gender identity. | Drag shows.
Classification: LCC HQ76.98.R37 A3 2020 | DDC 305.30942—dc23
LC record available at https://lccn.loc.gov/2019054792

Our books may be purchased in bulk for promotional, educational,
or business use. Please contact your local bookseller or the
Macmillan Corporate and Premium Sales Department
at 1-800-221-7945, extension 5442, or by e-mail at
MacmillanSpecialMarkets@macmillan.com.

www.fsgoriginals.com • www.fsgbooks.com
Follow us on Twitter, Facebook, and Instagram at @fsgoriginals

10 9 8 7 6 5 4 3 2 1

*For my families, biological and chosen—thanks for
loving me.*

For my community—thanks for teaching me.

*For my thirteen-year-old self—thanks for
sticking with me.*

*And for my grandma Kathleen,
the truest queen of all.*

A Note from the Author, Tom

Diary of a Drag Queen is a work of non-fiction based on the life, experiences, and recollections of both Crystal and myself. In some cases names of people, places, dates, and sequences of events have been changed to protect the privacy of others, as well as to prevent more unfounded lawsuits being taken out against Crystal after she was rightfully acquitted for her supposed involvement in numerous major art heists throughout the nineties and noughties.

This book contains descriptions of sexual and physical violence, on pages 195–197 and 388–390.

Diary of a Drag Queen also delves into love, drugs, shame, joy, opulence, queerness, being non-binary, my mum, and what really killed Rasputin.

What an honour. What a thrill. Who'd have thought—after years of writing diaries, addressing my readers with the opening gambit "Dear World" at the start of every entry—that my diary would be made into a real-life diary-book.

I've had my ups and downs. You all know. You all remember the James Franco thing? Where he was found, shoulder deep, in my asshole and had to self-amputate after 127 hours? Well, I never thought I'd peak like I peaked then. But this.

I was riding the Bakerloo line, doing a photoshoot for *Time* magazine's one hundred most influential people (I was number one, again). I never usually take public transport—I mean the clue's in the name—but my hundred-strong team of publicists decided they wanted me to appear as a "real person" to promote my new movie, *Homecumming*. Initially I was in shock—I hadn't been a real person since that time F. [Scott Fitzgerald] wrote about me under the pseudonym Daisy in his mediocre book *The Greatest Gatsby*. Something like that.

So I was there, on a staged tube carriage that had been fumigated four times before my entrance onto it, nude, with my darling friend Annie [Leibovitz]. I was instructed to bring my most personal belonging to the shoot, and so, when asked, I pulled the Hope Diamond from my human-skin Birkin, and my diary must've fallen out onto that train, which, after my seven-minute shoot—I've always nailed the shot in less than five—would be filled by morning commuters and real people. Naturally, some savvy publisher picked it up, and now I'm here, dictating my prologue to six of my topless assistants-cum-lovers as the other four feed me warm Brie with their unwashed fingers.

And really this was inevitable. I've written 281 books—from my first, the Rosetta stone, to my most popular, the Bible, to my most boring, *War and Peace*, all the way through to my last literary hit, *50 Shades of Hay*, which is a profound look at the farming communities of regional Wales. It only made sense that my next book would be my diary. Perhaps better known as "the inner workings of a genius," as my dear friend Ashlee Simpson tweeted.

But here, in these pages, I wanted my fans—otherwise known as every living thing on earth, otherwise known catchily as the Crystal hive—to get a real insight into what it takes to be me. Into what it takes to live life outside the lines, in a place where many misunderstand you yet want to use you for your image. This book is about so much more than the face of drag.

December / décembre*

* I can't speak French, but Crystal thinks it's wildly chic so she insists on using Google Translate. "Who cares, darling, it's about what people see. Plus my good friend and colleague Belle de Jour did it in her *Diary*—and she bought a house with the royalties off of that. Trust me."

18th December / le 18 décembre

That was hot, baby, wanna go again?

Last night, about 4:00 a.m., wrapped in cum-soaked Calvin Klein Egyptian-cotton sheets, I realised I had to quit my first job in fashion.

It's a fairly usual First Job in Fashion: latte runs, bollockings for eating too much at a PR breakfast, being reminded I'll never make it in this business as I carry my boss, Eve, up four flights of stairs while she's blackout drunk in the late afternoon. That kind of thing.

But there, last night, the cummy sheets slowly solidifying around me like a glamorous mummy, it all twigged. A postclimax sext from Eve's boyfriend arrived on her personal phone, which was by my bedside at her request.

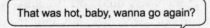

That was hot, baby, wanna go again?

My job title, personal assistant, turned out to be a fairly loose catch-all for a gig with a variety of responsibilities that I, an avid consumer of trashy, semi-abusive fashion reality TV growing up, totally expected. But boyfriend sexter never seemed to make the edit on those shows. That's right: Eve goes to bed at 10:00 p.m. on the dot every night and makes me stay awake to keep texting her boyfriend while he works a night shift. She told me, very specifically, that if I wanted to keep my job, I would have to "go with the flow with whatever Jared wants." So when he sexts, I sext back.

When I arrived in Manhattan, I was afresh with the naivety of a twenty-four-year-old drag queen and hopeful journalist on the hunt for a big break and a series of big dicks. Like Violet Sanford in *Coyote Ugly*, but fatter and not a dancer. I thought my evenings would provide the perfect set up for an hour or so of writing followed by seemingly endless hours out with my swathe of queer, cool, self-assured American gal-and-non-binary-pals. I'd given up on the idea of career drag upon arrival here, on account of not wanting to be broke for the rest of my life, but I'd thought I might have a little extra time for a few cash-in-hand gigs, and perhaps from there my contoured star would rise. A kind of accidental rise to fame, like those queers who populated the Chelsea Hotel some years before me.

Instead, I've spent my evenings trudging dutifully around a folder of my boss's nudes on Dropbox. Never fear, they don't run out—she constantly tops them up: buck-naked at the gym, an exposed tit in the bathroom of a Hard Rock Cafe (wtf?).* She once sent me a close-up of her vagina and told me to study it so when I tell Jared that I'm "touching my pussy,"† I actually know what a pussy looks like. Then she laughed. She doesn't pay me extra for this shit. If I'm going to do sex work, surely I should be remunerated.

---

* By "wtf?" I'm referring to the Hard Rock Cafe, not the bathroom tit, obviously.

† Her words, not mine. Apparently Jared likes it.

Well, if I'm not getting paid, I reasoned, I should at least use this opportunity as a sexual outlet for myself. Sex with strangers has always been a kink of mine anyway—probably something to do with the fact that, in my head, I've always imagined myself as someone famous, and thus having faceless, nameless sex is a rather joyous way to escape the paparazzi. Or it's something to do with shame. Frankly, I can't spend any more time on that subject, so I'm opting for the former.

As a result, then, I've transmogrified this traumatic sexual task into something glorious. Something hot, unadulteratedly sexual. I and many of my queer friends are quite skilled at this practice. So at night, instead of being this mistreated intern, I metaphorically drag up as my boss, my horrible boss, so horrible she could play a lead role in that horrible movie *Horrible Bosses*. And, no, my criticism isn't just that classic gay male misogyny rife among many parts of my community—she's just a categorically dreadful person. And, yes, if she were a man, I would think she was even worse, because men are, obviously, worse. So, terrified of losing my job by accidentally revealing myself as myself to Jared, for three months I've sexted like a boss: aggressive, power hungry, compulsively lying, with savageness coursing through my veins as I masturbate furiously in tandem with her unknowing partner, who is none the wiser.

I'm used to becoming a "her" after hours, but this is different. In my real-life drag I'm Crystal—full of love, laziness, sensitivity, with a subtly promiscuous edge and a penchant for hyperbole. As my new virtual drag character, Eve, I'm all about the power fisting—something

Jared has begun to love. I keep imagining Eve being shocked and confused as he requests these darker sexual arts in real life, but that only drives my pleasure more.

Anyway, I imagine Eve's boudoir persona can't be much different from her boardroom persona, and for this reason I stay, because I'm enthralled by the way she works. Like anyone else in fashion, her job is many things at once—she's part of the phenomenon of people who can do anything because they say they can, not because they actually can. She says things such as "unacceptable" and "foreclose" and "consequences" and "*Forbes* list" all the time, and it makes me feel powerful by proximity. Although she is the kind of white person who wears a Navajo-print poncho.

But, as is well-known to anyone who has been obscenely mistreated at work—anyone who's been shouted at, bullied, underpaid, criticised for doing things exactly as you were asked to—there forms a strange kind of Stockholm syndrome whereby you make hundreds of nonsensical justifications for staying despite knowing a day of work will end with a round of self-care triage as you pick up the shards and shreds of your confidence and stumble home.

I'd come to New York using what was left of my pitiful overdraft* because I had the chance for a first job that would help me break into the closed-off, elitist world of high fashion that I'd dreamed of since my

---

* That's when you've spent all your money, and you're living off the bank. Stunning.

grandma bought me my first copy of *Vogue* after church one Sunday.

Like any northern queer raised in the culturally barren land of the noughties, I dreamt of glamour, of fashion: the ultimate antidote to a childhood spent hiding. But after being here for four months it's become apparent that those things cost too much to acquire. The constant barrage of abuse and sexting amid near poverty, the mild PTSD, a recently re-excavated canyon of fat-phobia, and a ban from every Union Market in the city (I was caught stealing an orange and a wheel of Brie a few weeks back because I couldn't afford to eat—and now a picture of me is tacked behind the cash registers looking like the definition of *haggard*). It's just too high a price to pay.

> *"For glamour? For fashion?"* Crystal screeches into my head. *"Who did I raise you to be, young theydy*? I'm horrified. I sacrificed everything for glamour: I ran away from my gorgeous family palace in Russia in 1917 and was never found again, because I could live without my family, sure, but I couldn't live without my glamour."*

Maybe Crystal's right. A life of abuse for a big life in New York and a green card: a golden ticket to lift me out of my regular life and deliver me to a movie set, *the* movie set, upon which I can set the extraordinary life I've planned.

---

* *they* (my pronoun) + *lady* = *theydy*

With said green card I'll finally become Carrie but not annoying, Hannah but not a racist.* I will be the twenty-four-year-old who moved to New York, against all advice, and actually made it. It won't be long until I am one of those rich gays with a penthouse in TriBeCa who collects art and wears tortoiseshell glasses and goes to Miami Basel every year and gets a GLAAD award and still, somehow, despite all that success, remains politically radical.

Now it's officially Christmas break. In an hour or so Eve will be on a plane to Australia with Jared, so my nightly sext duties are suspended. I feel a little abandoned by him, to be frank.

Gonna go back to bed and wank over memories of sext conversations with Jared. Will go wash the sheets tomorrow.

21st December / le 21 décembre

Few things make a queen twirl like vintage Madonna. No, wait. I shouldn't be reductive, because then I'm just the same as pretty much every single media portrayal of anything LGBTQIA+ or aligned.† For some queens (and also some queers, femmes, butches, bull dykes,

---

* All white people are racist, but Hannah Horvath is the kind of racist who doesn't think all white people are racist.

† Lesbian, Gay, Bisexual, Transgender, Queer/Questioning, Intersex, Asexual, and + (others not listed but not heteronormative, i.e., not you, straight guy who loves glitter a bit but thinks bum sex is gross). Yes, it's a long acronym, yes, it's seven whole letters, but I learned the

trans women, transvestites, faggots, trans men, asexuals, leather daddies, fisting pigs, campy twinks, aromantics, bisexuals, and radical faeries) the ideal tonic might not be a Madonna: it could be a Judy or a Lady Gaga, a George Michael or a Beyoncé, the Cure or a niche riot grrrl group who should be way more famous than they are, or a Lou Reed or an Alaska Thunderfuck.

But for me, a proud cliché: Madonna. She's always been an escape route when things feel uncertain, going all the way back to this noise that set me aflame as a child. Generally I'll take all Madonna, but right now it's "Ray of Light," to which I've just finished spinning around in silver lamé boots that chafe my thighs, leaving them looking like uncooked bacon. I'm wearing a red wig and a lime-green muumuu that has dried sperm down the back from a story for another time. This kind of spinning has ignited a sensation I haven't felt for a while—a deeply sexual, emotional fury just south of my belly—and it reminds me of the first time I heard "Ray of Light," aged seven, sitting on my dog-hair-covered lounge carpet, at home in the north of England while my siblings fought over the remote. I didn't understand that deep-belly feeling, a naive me mistaking my genetically predetermined gay love for female icons for something more innocent, such as a strange reaction to food or nerves that one of my brothers might change the channel when I'd just discovered this thing that felt as if it were just for me.

---

national anthem even though borders are constructs, so you can learn seven letters.

I remember being terrified of myself. Terrified and desperate to spin so fast I would hurricane through the roof and onto a giant stage with thousands of people watching me the way I was watching Madonna. Spinning the way I am now.

So much of the queer experience is spent spinning.

I remember this song as the soundtrack to my teen years, blasting out on a yellow CD player that used to skip-skip-skip if you so much as inhaled, me sitting in my room flipping through *Glamour* or *Cosmo* or *Heat* with my one gay friend, Matt, who used to eat giant, curdled mounds of mayonnaise off a spoon—a whole jar on some occasions—with whom I was silently in love for most of those teen years. Humming along would be our best girlfriend, Beth, who would get so rampantly drunk she would foam at the mouth and try to kiss any and all of my brothers, revealing her giant, magnificent breasts at a moment's notice.

I remember, after fights with my parents—huge, hurtling rows full of terror and bile and homophobia and underappreciation being flung like shit from both sides— running up the stairs and climbing out of a skylight onto my jagged slate roof and whirring around to "Ray of Light," transmitted through the crappy earphones I'd kept from a flight my family took to Ibiza, our first abroad holiday ever.

I remember turning it up on the 555 bus home from Lancaster as homophobic, mean-spirited schoolkids pelted oranges at the back of my head or dropped fag ash into my hair from their endless Lambert & Butler Blues, me in a world light years away from the top deck of that bus, imagining being adored the way I had adored Madonna back when I first saw her.

I remember listening to it as I slowly built Crystal, or she built me, ritualistically piecing us both together— her backstory, her tastes, her look—in front of a shrine I'd built to (Her) Madge(sty) in my teenage bedroom. She wouldn't be called Crystal for another seven years, but her roots began to tangle around me way back when, listening to "Ray of Light."

I remember kissing a boy—who had a big beard that reeked of clever queer theory books and craft beers and vegan moisturisers, and who eventually moved to France with a much older guy to do a PhD in gender studies*—in my room at university while the song and my insides glittered and exploded like fireworks.

I remember all the times this song saved me as I twirl here now on my own, spilling discount rosé all over the dark wood floors of this apartment I'm illegally subletting in New York. I'm in half drag, a demi-lewk, about to go out to an infuriatingly glamorous club that once turned away Rihanna but lets my queer friends and me in so the rich people can gawp at something interesting. I might not be on the stage, with thousands of adoring fans looking up at me the way I looked at Madonna, but I am twice as wondrous as the me watching that Madonna video two decades ago ever dreamed. That me would be thrilled to be this me.

Sometimes it takes an old song, the old song, to lure

---

* Lol, who hasn't?

all the pieces back to yourself, back to your control, back to the same place at once.

22nd December / le 22 décembre

"I would totally die for you," Ace told me over FaceTime. We were chatting before he went down to Suffolk with his family for Christmas.

Ace is my "best friend," the kind of "best friend" for whom you use air quotations whenever you describe them because the truth, I am certain, is that we are both, dysfunctionally, in love. We met at university, and I spent months bitching about him behind his back because I didn't believe a gay could be both gay, attractive, and perhaps the kindest person I'd ever met after my very own mother. But he is.

That's one of many reasons I'm in love with him. Others include great hair, fucking hilarious, when he looks at me he sees a real person rather than a loud fag who must sing for their supper, a high, tight ass, and a smile so heartfelt you can feel pink flowers grow every time his lips crack upwards.

Before I arrived at this noisy apartment on the Lower East Side splashing around a tiny puddle of cash in a city where you can only survive if you're swimming in wealth, before I found a job in fashion that has me wanting to never pick up a magazine again, we drove around the southeastern coast of the United States together. We ate packs of biscuits and splashed out on a Cracker Barrel to break up the long drives between states. We did stereotypical gay-love-movie type things such as sit in fields full of long grass and smoke and talk about shit like Why Gay Men Love Female Pop Stars and Will Lady Gaga's New Album Be Any Good and Can Straight People Be Queer and Our Sexual History (testing the ground of our sexual future). Of course, we did not arrive at that sexual future by the end of the trip, and now our relationship is playing out in a blur of crackly pixels three times a week.

"I would totally die for you."

I'm not sure if it was a spontaneous expression of true love or a manipulative technique to check my allegiances after I was audibly bummed out and cold when he told me he had a date. Who goes on a date three days before Christmas?

"Sure. I would die for you, too, totally. But I wouldn't drown," I replied, edged by Crystal to smugly test his limits.

"Oh, charming. Although, to be honest, I wouldn't think to save you first if a plane was going down. Like, I'd affix my oxygen mask before yours and dive out onto the inflatable slide first. Removing heels, obviously. Dying in flight is just my idea of hell. But for the most part, I'd die for you."

Then we said goodbye. Then he hung up, bouncing offline to go on his date, which I decide is doomed. I also decide I'm being unfair because I'm the one who moved to New York "forever." Maybe finding someone who could love me enough to die for me in all but one scenario is a better promise than monogamy, which will inevitably fall apart if statistics are anything to go by. Especially among the gays: we're clearly allergic to intimacy.

Feeling bereft, I decided to take my sorrow onto the fire escape and smoke seven cigarettes, steeping in my loneliness. I miss Ace. I miss my friends at home, painfully, my casually confident demeanour of "I'm killing it out here" fading with every tabaccoey toke at the thought of them spread out across London, or Lancaster or Manchester or Newcastle, sitting outside bars in Soho, or at the Sun, our old Lancaster haunt, or on their couches watching *Gogglebox*, chain-smoking and talking about radical queer politics or whether they want pasta-pesto or a takeout for dinner, cloaked in colours and sequins, dressing gowns and slippers, no make-up, or make-up a few slicks too heavy.

I hope with a bursting wishfulness that they are thinking of me.

23rd December / le 23 décembre

I'm going out tonight so I spent the better part of the afternoon getting into a full face. Day to day I've been wearing less face than usual—a lip stain here, a highlight there—probably because Eve enjoys taking a verbal jab whenever the make-up gets a little cakey, which it does. But it's the big one tonight before the scene shuts down for Christmas, so I wanted to do full drag-queen-with-a-beard realness. I left myself three and a half hours, and for the first time in my life, I'm ready early.

So I'm sitting, staring at my make-up bag—messy,

glitter coated, jangled from four years travelling coast to coast, across the ocean, in and out of makeshift dressing rooms that are actually loos, up and down stairs, in the boot of countless cars. I love my make-up bag.

My make-up bag. The passport that contains a bunch of crèmes, potions, polyfilla, and over-the-counter drugs that diminish the muscles of an overbearing gender binary, allowing me to wrestle it down, even just for a night. These tools are the hardware that allows me to finally live out my childhood fantasies, every one. They're also margin comments in a history book, connecting me to the radical queens, queers, butch dykes, and trans folk who fought for me to be able to paint my face the way I want to paint it and wear it out in the world. In my make-up bag are thousands of tricks for me to cover the scars of my teenage acne, or the slice on my chin, from a homophobic attack, that has never quite healed. I love the scars in some ways, but having the devices to cover them allows me to dictate their mark upon me.

In my make-up bag are missing pieces and extra bits—given, received, and shared between my drag sisters and me like heirlooms, like gifts from Christmas crackers. We are reminded of one another whenever we use them. In my make-up bag are hairs cut from the long hair of a drag king friend to make a beard, strewn, unwanted, but so integral to the history this kit holds. In my make-up bag is a kind of self-care that makes you totally healed, a complete person, even if just for a night.

In my make-up bag is an ode to the women who gave me a femininity to explore but not to parody (that's just terrible, lazy drag). In my make-up bag is jewellery given to me by my friend who was so desperate for me to be kinder to myself that she found things to make me sparkle. And while it's so easy to talk about colours, powders, primers, highlighters (yum! fave!) with a kind of Zoella level of soullessness, make-up is—to me, to many of us—not an extravagant stockpile of excessive frippery but something that unveils my glory as it veils my face. In a world where power is usually taken from us, make-up lets us draw our battle lines.

Make-up is also a means to writing in a secret language, misunderstood and disregarded by boring dudes who think make-up is "gay," which allows us to communicate with one another silently or with floods of Facebook messages about Kat Von D's new matte lipstick. My make-up bag is a kit that allows me to create an illusion that is closer to the truth than the face I was born wearing. While people question whether wearing make-up is antifeminist (much like they question drag), make-up is, ultimately, about choice, about allowing yourself to choose how the world sees you. The same can be said for not wearing any, especially if you're expected to by society. People bandy about terms such as *fake*, but choosing how you want to look is the definition of authentic.

PERFORMANCE MEMO: Amanda Lepore said to me, in a club last night, "Most icons are dead and their image is frozen in time, so I froze mine—blond, red lips, body. Now when you see even this silhouette, you know it's me. And that's iconic."

24th December / le 24 décembre

Last night was glorious. We ran in a big bunch and circled the bars and the loos and the dance floor like a murder of spangled crows, ready to pick off anyone who shot us even the faintest hint of a stink eye. After I was dropped off by a few friends who were headed my way, I walked one block alone and instantly felt the real world prickle back into existence.

In a single block I was met with nearly every type of response a drag queen alone on a night-time street seems to invoke. From "Yassss, quaine!" to "Jimmy, check out that fag," from a popped tongue to a head shaken in disgust, I kept pacing, urged to safety by Crystal, who, through necessity, has become a pro at escaping attacks.

"Keys between the fingers, queen. And if one of them comes close, aim the stiletto heel for the eyeball," she instructs as my heart near tears through my red-sequinned dress.

A lot of things change when you're in drag. Of course, the way you feel about yourself changes. Yes, I feel empowered to take up space; I feel momentarily at peace with my gender; I feel emotionally in sync with other femme and non-binary bodies around me and before me; I feel grateful for my forebears. But perhaps, most prominently, I feel scared. Especially when I'm on the street.

The problem is that when you paint on this barrier, people no longer see you as a person: in drag you're either sub- or superhuman. By building a new face and transgressing binary lines of gender, you become a visible outlier. People assume many things that they wouldn't assume about other, plain-clothes folk. And they have the gall to comment on it. People assume we're all fabulous; we're all loud; we're all here for your consumption and entertainment; we're all here because we aren't good at other things, because we couldn't get a real job—yet they expect you to turn a show or a look better than any other person who enters the club.

People assume we'll take any sexual advance we can get, while also assuming that we're too freaky to be sexual with—often evidenced by men in cars who kerb-crawl you, then shout at you the moment you tell them to back off. People assume that we're a little dumb, an accessory, a stunning prop for a brilliant Instagram post. People think we want to go shopping, that we live in hovels underground (although, to be fair, given the economics of performance work, most of the queens I know do), and that we're self-involved—bitchy, even. Sure, the face of drag is resilience and strength. The face of drag is funny. The face of drag is powerful. It's critical and catty and mean and often problematic. But the heart of drag, in my experience, is something warm, kind, healing, and vulnerable.

I arrived home, make-up peeling off from one-block's worth of adrenalised sweat. I raced up the stairs of my Lower East Side sublet, terrified I'd meet an attacker in the stairwell. Keys, door, lights on. Check every single cupboard and cranny for potential attackers. Crystal has had many hits out against her, and that paranoia often creeps into my reality.

> *"When you've had eight high-profile divorces and have been through the witness protection program seven times, you know to check the cupboards first, darling."*

Text the others to tell them I'm home safe, and they all text back. Going out in drag is great, but getting back unscathed is even better.

25th December / le 25 décembre

Every year I think how funny it is that so many Christian denominations (not all, I know) hate gays but love Christmas. Like, aren't they basically the same thing? Tinsel? Gay. Gifting? We perfected it. A guy with major abs on a cross? That's gay BDSM 101.

It's a weird time for queers, really—the whole day, the whole tradition built around a religion that some use to perpetuate the idea that gays aren't chill. Love the sinner, hate the sin, you know. Add to this the fractious relationships so many queer and LGBTQIA+ folk have with their families, and the Christmas turkey tastes much, much drier for us 'mos.

Many of us don't even have family to go to on account of severed ties, chopped messily by the homo-, trans-, bi-, queerphobia that often abounds from the families of people like me. For something so camp, so apparently joyful, Christmas can be as emotionally tangled as the fairy lights you chuck in the bottom of the decorations box year on year.

I'm a lucky queer in that over the Christmases of recent years, after the spiral-of-existential-desperation-to-click-my-heels-and-disappear-dread that was my teens came to a close, I have developed a special relationship with my special family. I'm fortunate to be tight with my close relations, but the holidays proffer a different kind of loneliness, one brought on through everyone's misunderstanding of who you are. It's nobody's fault, but the more I progressed into life as a full-on queer, the more it became evident that some integral parts of me were not to be mentioned at the Turkey Table. While we all chat kids and weddings, we don't chat HIV activism or the powers of radical sex; we don't chat gender or whether RuPaul's transmisogyny renders her legacy obsolete.

All the burning queer politics or the nights spent in repeat motion—unsticking your wobbly heels or battered Docs from the Red Bull– and ecstasy-plastered dance floors of gay bars, hoping to suck anyone's dick—disappear around normative folk. A very Wizard of Ozzy kind of concussion. You feel infantilised and misunderstood, as if you've got a thousand secrets scantily concealed just under the surface, because even though everyone knows you're the things you are, they don't know the things that come with who you are.

But this year I'm here in New York and, like some kind of Christmas cliché, missing my family. I especially miss my dad, and my mum and her Christmas dinner.

Her four different types of potato, two types of carrot, parsnips, two types of stuffing, bread sauce, and, even the worst bit, the turkey. One time, when I worked on a farm for pocket money, I had to wank off tons of male turkeys (toms or gobblers, as we call them in the trade) to get them to spaff their loads into rubber tubes. Turns out fattened Christmas turkeys can't and/or don't have the energy to fuck, so we had to do it for them.* It sounds humiliating, but weirdly, once you've wanked off one turkey, you just feel proud to be part of the circle of turkey life, the wonder of the Christmas mass-slaughter.

I spent the day alone, watching bad Christmas movies and masturbating over Heath Ledger as the Joker, which is deeply unfestive and probably problematic. I facetimed my family while they ate Christmas dinner, but that just made me feel farther away, so I ate some fried chorizo and hummus and thought about home. I popped out to the diner on the corner of my street, Norfolk and East Houston, but it was closed, so I walked around the Lower East Side and chatted to two homeless women for about twenty minutes. They were genius, drunk and singing "Fairytale of New York," to which they knew none of the words except "faggot," "maggot," and "NYPD choir."

I got home and it was dark and I sat on my fire escape

---

* Other animals I have successfully retrieved sperm from include goats, horses, pigs, dogs, a cat, cows. Animals I have fisted or fingered include cows, goats, dogs. It taught me a lot about the art of masturbation and gave me no sexual pleasure whatsoever—in case you were wondering. Except maybe the horses. But they're so muscular!

for a good hour, thinking of nothing but thinking that if anyone could see me, they would think I was thinking about something big. I sent a few of my friends Happy Queermas texts, offering some queer solidarity on this strange old day. Glamrou, my sister in Denim, my drag troupe back in London—one of my best friends, and an Iraqi immigrant drag queen who hates Christmas more than me, responded with "Happy Queermas baby! It's such a fucking white queerphobic day. Have been feeling lonely throughout. Thinking of you xxx."

It made me feel less lonely knowing someone else was feeling lonely, too. Gonna go to bed and google *Tumblr big dick windmill.*

27th December / le 27 décembre

Sometimes when I'm on my own, I eat my bogies. Of all the things in my life, I think this is the thing I feel most shame about. And I once made out with my dog, in a genuinely sexual way, when I was eleven.

29th December / le 29 décembre

Laurie is this guy I've been fucking for the last two days—since yesterday morning, when I got so bored that I trotted right to Grindr and met this guy who's a "shoe designer" between seasons.

Everything about Laurie is everything I hate about

people: he's incredibly self-involved, he loves craft coffee and honestly has fifteen different ways of making it, he can't design shoes for toffee but describes himself as if he's as important to culture as Samantha Mumba or Jenny Holzer. He has loads of tattoos—none of which are ironic, all of which he describes as "pieces" with genuine earnestness—and he wears cycling hats even though he doesn't cycle. Pros, although few and far between, are that he's got a perfect six-and-a-half-inch dick with girth that seems custom-designed to tessellate with my once-tight (now tightish) bum hole; he has a nice dog* and an interesting collection of zines; he has enough money to order us takeout so we don't have to leave the house for literally two days; and he doesn't seem to take issue with my being a drag queen, even though it's clear he doesn't like me either.

But the fucking. Neither of us can deny that the fucking feels better than your parents telling you they're proud of you. It's all so base: pissy, cummy, sweaty, pounding, and both of us cumming a minimum five times a night. It's full of sexual aggression, to which we are both consenting: he asks, I say yes, he spanks me with a steel-toecap boot, and I push back in a way that reads "harder." I've lost count of the times he's choked me with his perfect cock and punched me in the face while doing it.†

Earlier this evening, the door clacked. It was Laurie,

---

* Although he watches us have sex and that's weird.
† My safe word is *goat*, btw.

wearing a pair of his own shoes—one of which featured an appliquéd picture of a screw and the other of which was appliquéd with a giant letter *U* (get it?). I looked at them trying not to gip, then looked him up and down, realising it was the first time I'd seen him dressed and he was wearing *boot-cut jeans*. "Get them off," I said, 20 per cent because we were about to fuck, 80 so I wouldn't have to look at them anymore.

We opened the wine he brought, a claggy red, and drank it on the bed from the bottle. Then things got weird. He undressed, I undressed, he asked if he could keep his shoes on. I said, "Ah, I'm worried about the sheets,"* so he flicked them off. I was hard, he was hard, and I was getting ready to take his wonderful gift in my wonderful gift receiver, when he put a finger to my lips and murmured, "Wait a sec," in his nasal Ohio accent, and dashed to the bathroom.

I waited, as told, with my finger pressing on my bum hole, in truth thinking about Ace and not even a bit about Laurie.

Lo and behold, Laurie reemerged in the doorway to my bedroom in a grease-smudged head-to-toe gimp outfit† in deep black rubber, a funnel and a tube to his mouth for me to—so he hoped—urinate into, and a zip from the belly button to the lower back offering access to all areas.

My first thought was that he hadn't brought a bag.

---

* I wasn't worried about the sheets.
† Like that guy in *Pulp Fiction* who lives in a box.

"How did you get that here?" I asked, to which I heard a rubber-muffled, "Hmm mmmmh cuhmmtp ppm-mmkt," which I translated as "In my coat pocket." I then wondered why that was the first thing I'd thought about—the practicalities of the transportation of the piss-funnel-gimp-suit he hadn't even taken the time to polish, rather than that he wanted me to get gimpy with him. Disclaimer—I'm not shaming gimps here; I love a gimp suit. What I'm shaming is his audacity in not even checking whether I was up for a good gimping.

> *"I lived as a gimp for fourteen years,"* Crystal reminds me, as I lie here in shock. *"For a president, actually. Won't say who, but let's just say . . . Watergate. What a wild ride."*

Before I knew it, Laurie had launched himself onto my sheets, which I was at this point genuinely worried about, and was holding both of my legs up in the air as if I were a roast duck hanging from a meat hook in a restaurant in Chinatown. How was he lifting half my body weight? Why was I thinking that? His cock started poking out of the zip, like a snail from its shell, and he was about to ram it in me, no lube or anything.

I asked him to stop—"It's all got a bit flustered"—but he carried on. I don't know if it's because he couldn't hear me through all the fucking rubber, but I asked him three times and he was still teasing my hole with his big purple bell-end, ready to thrust it in there quicker than you can say any safe word.

> *"Knee to the balls, baby! It worked on James Dean."* ⪦

Fourth time: "Stop." Fifth time and I was feeling edgy. Sixth time, "Stop," and I felt his bell-end beginning to push through the tightish resistance of my now totally clammed-up butt hole.

I swiftly jerked backwards and started slapping his cock hard while shouting, "I!" Slap. "Said!" Slap. "No!" Slap. "No!" Slap. "No!" I chased him across the room as he backed out of the bedroom door, the sticky rubber pulling the expensive Calvin Klein bed blanket—that's, frankly, scratchy—that I was entrusted with looking after at all costs with him as he went, his sight obscured by the two tiny holes in his gimp mask.

He left, quickly.

> *"How did he get changed in such record time? It's* ⪦
> *like that time I won the gold in the hundred metres*
> *for Bavaria."*

I have no idea, but I think we need to stop thinking about things that aren't immediately important, especially when I have a gimp coming at me.

Then, a good three minutes later, he came back, knocking at the door—I shit you not—to get the remnants of his wine.

Looking back on all my close encounters of the anal kind, I can't remember any of their faces, names, bodies—dicks, I can remember the dicks—or any of their defining features. Laurie's, too, will disappear in a week or so. What I can remember, however, is how I felt when I did the deed. Like when I was upset about this guy not texting back so I got hammered and swallowed the cum of three men aged sixty-plus, one after the other, in an alleyway near my house. Or the time I fucked a primary-school teacher in Hong Kong who offered me "ice" (which I declined even though Crystal was up for it), then took me into a custom porn-making room where we made a keepsake DVD of him fucking me doggy-style,* and I remember nothing about him or it; I just remember feeling particularly thin that day, and hence I jumped at the chance to make a DIY home porno.

I think about the straight boys at university, high school, even primary school, who took advantage of my evident gayness to try to solve the puzzle of their sexuality, how I just felt glad to be someone's receptacle, that someone would want me in that way even though once one of them spunked in my mouth and eye during lunch break, then told me, "I'll slit your fucking faggot throat," if what we'd done ever got out. I still don't remember much about him, just the pleasurable mix of shame, power, and terror he left in his wake—feelings that stayed at the forefront of my wank bank for years to come. Funny how shame can be pleasurable.

---

* It's still in my wardrobe at my family home, and I constantly have night terrors about my mum clearing it out and putting it on because it just says "Hong Kong" on it and she might think it's a DVD full of pics, omg.

"But then again, so can bathing an anal herpes sore,
and that's not good for you, is it, honey?"

My sex life is so rooted in shame: seeking acts that
will cause me some great feeling of pain or worthless-
ness because, I dunno, perhaps I think I deserve it. Then
I tell the story to friends who've lived similar things in
order not to internalise it.

But kicking Laurie out was growth, I think.

I went into the bathroom to wash my face and the
sweat off my butt hole, and there on the floor was Laurie's funnel, and for some reason the sight of it made me
instantly erect.

30th December / le 30 décembre

It was fucking freezing this morning so I smoked inside,
which was a terrible idea because I then had to leave
the apartment to buy air freshener, for which I had no
money. But then I found a fucking ten! In the corridor
outside the door. I thanked a God I don't even believe
in. Lily finally picked up the phone. She was getting
ready to go visit her "academic friend in Boston," who
is this Harvard PhD guy who's obsessed with her, and
who wants to take magic mushrooms with her and have
wild, trippy sex with her.

I first met Lily on the street outside the Natural History Museum uptown, just after I'd arrived in New York.
She'd just taken a bunch of mushrooms and was sliding
out on a bench just off Central Park, and I was getting

to grips with the city, which essentially meant walking around and thinking about all the gays who'd had sex here, what scene in *Sex and the City* happened where, and trying for the life of me to work out why everyone thinks Bloomingdale's is any good.

As we sat there on a bench just outside Central Park, Lily spilled the tea on everything New York. "The park is for rich people and tourists, unless you're a leather daddy who wants to bum or be bummed. Are you?"

"Maybe," I'd said.

"Ummm, fucking definitely," Crystal said.

I didn't know. I was just trying to seem chill about everything, up for anything, but, to be totally honest, I wasn't searching for leather daddies because I was burning for Ace. Turns out, some weeks later, I would find myself getting ravaged in the ass in the park: in an unexpected twist I found myself in the Ramble, where I picked up a leather daddy (Lily was right) who took great pleasure in "pounding that chub hole." I was pretty slighted by his liberal use of the word *chub*— "C'mon, chub, suck daddy's cock," "C'mon, chub, sit on papa's dick," "C'mon, chub, you want daddy's load?"— as I was feeling particularly thin that day, but I took it nonetheless because I was living for the whole Louis-getting-bummed-on-the-Ramble-in-*Angels-in-America*-degradation-realness-vibe. Thinking the whole time, "God, I'm so New York!"—as this chub-loving daddy worked out his baby issues on my booty.

I helped Lily pick outfits for her trip, over the phone.

"There's the black latex, which looks good with the purple marabou jacket?" she puzzled. At that, I told her I was having a slightly off moment with latex and explained what had happened with Laurie.

She insisted on coming over. I protested, but she insisted. We ate almonds and pears and split a Butterfinger (my favourite) and talked about different awful experiences we've had with sex—some hilarious, some heartbreaking—and what they each stem from in context for her as a heterosexual trans woman, and for me as a non-binary homosexual drag queen.

"For me it's this constant fetishisation," Lily complained. "People on these dating apps are always obsessed with what I've got down there—which is none of their goddamn business. Like, if you get that far, you should be so fucking lucky. And the number of men I've had call me a 'chick with a dick' or 'their fantasy' or approach me to do porn . . . is . . . it's fucking outrageous."

Lily is an incredibly beautiful woman. Today she was wearing thigh-high Balenciaga spandex boots in black, at which we both frequently stared in silence, interrupting our conversation. She has perfectly manicured nails, beautiful silky underwear, and her long black hair is always blown out, and each one has the width of a piece of spun silk. She's very aware of her passing privilege as a trans woman, explaining that she feels both overwhelming guilt and overwhelming pride at what her transition looks like. She has impeccable taste. I always wonder what it would be like to have grown up with impeccable taste—a wardrobe full of archive Margiela tabis and the lipstick-print skirts from Prada SS00. I guess to do so you need a little money, and my family was pretty cashless. I spent a good few years developing my personal style—but little money and less taste resulted in a kind of Only Gay in the Village style, there in my northern, not-quite-a-seaside town.

"I feel like a trick—like I'm either tricking men into sleeping with me, or like I'm a trick they can bring up with their friends to prove how kinky they are. It's fucked—I want intimacy, like, not just a shag and a to-ken pair of Miu Miu sunglasses as a thank-you; I want to be touched, like, emotionally."

"At least you get Miu Miu," I gassed, before asking her about Jeremy.

"He'll never leave his wife. She and the kids get Daddy for the weekend, and I get Daddy in the week—I get Daddy in the office, Daddy in the shower, Daddy in the bedroom, bathroom, living room, in the pussy and in the butt hole." Truth is Jeremy's a total arsehole, but he's good to Lily and so I let it lie.

We smoked a spliff. Then I was sick because we'd had wine and weed and I did what I always do, which is what they call a whitey. Last time I pulled a whitey was on my road trip with Ace, which was the first and only time I revealed that I love him, while vomiting into the lap of my drop-hem floral skirt, while he tried to find a place to pull over. We never talked about it again. After I vomited up all those nuts and Butterfingers, Lily lay down in bed next to me—asking with alarm why there were crispy patches on the sheets.

31st December / le 31 décembre

Woke up to a text from Ace:

> Hi my queen! Will have to miss FaceTime tonight
> as I'm going to a New Year's party with William
> of all people . . . ! Unsure whether it's a date,
> will report back tomorrow. Love you lots, Happy
> New Year beautiful xxxx

William is Ace's ex of four years ago, an ex who seems to crop up everywhere. He's an incredibly handsome, thin, floppy black-haired, very cool East London boy whose demeanour flexes towards the masc, and he's read a lot of books, which I, unless they're by Jackie Collins or another niche gender philosopher, haven't. He's essentially the polar opposite of me: a northern drag queen with a flabby Lancashire accent and an even flabbier belly. As I spiral into self-hatred, the following thoughts do backflips about my skull:

Maybe I've made this whole romance thing up? I've done it before.

Why would someone like Ace want to date me? He's got a six-pack, for God's sake.

Why didn't I take the chance to kiss him ages ago before I was, most definitely, friend-zoned?

Am I mad? I'm mad. Well, he doesn't deserve me.

Maybe I am just, at the heart of it all, completely unlovable.

"William is fucking boring compared to you, so Ace can make his bed and fucking suck a dick in it."

Crystal's advice is often terrible, or at least totally financially impractical, but in times such as these she smudges her drag lens across everything, reminding me I'm a star, I'm iconic, even if nobody else sees what she sees.

She's me, of course, all of these thoughts coming from the same place, but in my head are two distinct inner monologues, one of reason and one of stardom. When they converge, it's perfect, but when they don't, it's often because she'll be pushing me to do or say the thing I really want to say, and the "real" me doesn't dare say it. Drag is arduous, tiring, expensive, but I'm so glad I built that extra inner me.

January / janvier

1st January / le 1 janvier

Here's a comprehensive list of my New Year's resolutions:

- Sort out athlete's foot.
- Read *Communist Manifesto*, and Cherie Blair's *Speaking for Myself* to work out how she gets such bounce in that hair.
- Learn something new about drag every day.
- Be woke, but also stop using the word *woke* as it's been dislocated from communities of colour and isn't yours to use.
- Be better with money.
- Quit job.
- Buy Balenciaga boots.
- Wear Balenciaga boots while overthrowing capitalism / white male dominance.

I spent yesterday evening on the Upper East Side with the Beaumonts, which was a laugh a minute, if you enjoy feeling undermined by the rich. They're family friends of Cora's, whose family I know, love, and live for. They've fed me on mornings when I've had no money for food, they've bought me cocktails and connected me with people they know I might find common ground with. They're good people.

The Beaumonts are the worst. They live in one of those buildings that I thought was a myth—the kind

that has an elevator stocked with a waistcoated attendant. They're the kind whose interior décor you can't
place in any particular geographical region or historical period, but it all looks like what happens when you
have money. Expensive, and as if many things around
the house have been handed down through families for
generations. I've seen a few of these houses before, and
what links them isn't an eye for aesthetic—no, it's just
a lot of quite intense patterns and big statement pieces
and rooms you're not allowed to go inside, that are just
for show.

And there's always a lot of red and beige.

They have a Monet . . . in their loo . . . which I clocked
during a middinner shit. There are two Warhols, a Brâncusi sculpture, a Gauguin, and a family portrait shot by
Annie Leibovitz, before she got shit. Dinner was peppered by phrases like ". . . and that was how Barb got her
eighth skiing injury!" While I downed their amazing
Riesling, all I could do was cement my position as the
evening's entertainment by rolling out much-censored
stories of drag, which would be met with gasps and "Fascinating!" or "What a fabulous friend you have, Cora!"
said in the tone of someone who's just stepped in dog
shit.

Barb, the mother Beaumont, has a worryingly long
neck. Although I'm not here to pass judgment on women's
appearances, I'm just a little worried her head's going to
fall off. And she has this hair—a flat blond bob—that
kind of flops around as she speaks with a grimace and a
raised eyebrow that says both "I'm better than you" and
"You're stupid" at the same time. She's impossibly thin

and is wearing cashmere and a kind of lipstick that can only be described as frosty.

Daddy Beaumont is big in every sense of the word. A venture capitalist or something, he constantly tries to bring up the fact that he once had a ponytail, to provide some sort of proof that he is a Democrat. He's tall, wide, loud, and you can see Barb often visibly flinching as his voice booms into the conversations with some other dreadful anecdote from his past in banking.

Naturally, I want to fuck him. Even though he's the kind of man who speaks when he eats and gets food round his mouth and doesn't realise until Barb points it out, and he definitely has a fungal infection on his thumb, but if he asked me to suck his cock next to the Monet in the loo, I wouldn't hesitate for a second.

As they drink, they become looser, and the tension across Barb's cheeks, which seemed to lock in like rigor mortis every time she looked my way, began to ease.

The rich and the poor have little in common, but we can intersect on a few things when it comes to humour: repression, ubiquitous TV shows, things that are funny no matter your class background such as someone falling down, New York things such as the way the subway signs are impossible to navigate (even though they definitely have a driver), and the way we all hate fusion restaurants.

I'm not so bad at fading up into these wealthy spaces because time was this is where I aspired to be and where a lot of Crystal was born from. I learned much of the lingo, airs, and graces at university: one must sip the wine and use the knife and fork at the outside first. Once, when

I was eating my first meal with lots of posh people at uni, I sat aghast at what was in front of me, completely out of my depths and about to be busted for being a kid who loved to eat any and every meal with a spoon. Anyway, taking pity on me, this witch-like lady across from me slinked over and said, "Break the rules: eat with your hands, switch the order of your forks, anything, but do it as if you know exactly what rule it is you're breaking." The thing about rich people is that they love an eccentric—not like middle-class people, who are keen to homogenise. No, moneyed people love a wacko. Enter me.

The Beaumonts have a yearly tradition called DP Time. At the very mention the whole family moans with orgasmic glee. I thought it meant "double-penetration time," obviously, which Crystal and I found both hysterical and exciting, my mouth filling with saliva at the idea that things might get interesting. A cross-generational, cross-family orgy? Jackpot!

"Barb loves a good DP! When we got the house, we DP'd! When the girls were born, we DP'd! Every Thursday we DP! When Hanna turned thirty, we DP'd! When Gammy died, we DP'd to celebrate her life!" Daddy Beaumont almost foams at the mouth, explaining the family's history and its irrevocable tethering to the DP tradition. I couldn't stop myself, both Crystal and I were hysterical, weeping with laughter, and their fabulousing and fetishisation of me switched swiftly to disappointment at my strange behaviour.

I'm howling. I can't stop. I'm absolutely howling. I'm howling so much I'm weeping. Everyone is staring, even the eyes of the wonderfully grotesque Gauguin, and I weep with hysteria some more.

"Double penetration with Grandma. Hysterical! And not my first time . . . ," Crystal bulges forth, trying to excuse me by bringing everyone into the joke. "Come on!"

Cora immediately mouths apologies to everyone, my face lurches towards my pumpkin pie and coffee, tears of hysteria dripping into both. It's not even funny, but I'm doing that thing where you get yourself into an absolute state.

After much foreplay they brought out the "essential tool" for this impending DP session, and I had an erection.

Turns out a DP is a goddamn bottle of Dom Pérignon and they have been shortening the name to D bloody P for years.

I was swiftly—before I could snag even a drop of DP—escorted to the lift by Cora. I smiled at everyone, telling them I couldn't wait to see them again "for another DP extravaganza!" as Barb shook her head in silent, botoxed shock.

Cora gave me a can of seltzer, telling me to drink it, and to wait opposite the Met for her to come get me— she just had to "go DP with the Beaumonts," a sentence that she was now hysterically laughing at, out of earshot of the family.

As I flounced into the family lift, which casually opens out into their hallway, I'm greeted by the elevator attendant. We didn't chat, but he seemed amused as I stared closely at my face in the mirror trying to work out how someone this funny can be so underappreciated.

The attendant started to laugh at me, and only then did I twig that my inner Crystal monologue was actually coming out of my mouth. I cracked the seltzer and drank it and remembered that I hate seltzer.

Stumbling out onto Park Avenue, overjoyed to have left that suffocatingly rich and deeply snooty dinner, I emerged into the oddly quiet New York New Year's street. I considered, for a moment, that I might well be the best, funniest, freest person in the whole of Manhattan—a rare zing of pure arrogance fuelled by the booze-blurred line between Crystal and me. For a moment I believed I was both Patti Smith and Robert Mapplethorpe—one dragged up as the other, both me in my multiple forms. I didn't need Ace. My reality, which had been ebbing all day, flowed. I was right. Being lonely and far away from everything was all I ever wanted. I was valid and lovable and queer and non-binary and a drag queen and I looked amazing in red and I felt powerful because nobody on this whole continent knows me enough to make any decisions for me. For a moment I had new eyes and for a moment I felt that I was a whole person. For a moment.

4th January / le 4 janvier

I arrived at Eve's after walking from the Lower East Side all the way uptown as I had no cash for the subway. It dawned on me, only as I lay immobilised on the couch yesterday, preparing myself to go back to work by practicing my dissociation techniques, that my heart rate had considerably slowed over the Christmas holiday, my spots had near disappeared, and my desire to take shots of vodka through the eye had vanished. So I spent the trip psyching myself up to quit as I promised myself I would. I did the usual of listening to a bunch of power songs and imagining I were Madonna or Lady Gaga or Tina Turner or Buffy or a man.

But then, upon arrival, exhausted but ready to go full Britney Work Bitch, I heard Eve repeatedly smacking her cat hard for lying on her UGG boots* and I wondered if today was not the day to quit and be smacked like a cat.

I'm now sitting, still under her watchful eye, on my bed, holding her phone, ready to sext her boyfriend, and I desperately want to out her as a cat-beating, talent- and hope-sucking alien to this man I've weirdly become sexually intimate with.

But I decide not to. I'll just sext him unenthusiastically until 1:00 a.m.—

> oh big boy you are so big, oh big boy wow I'm tired, oh big boy I'm touching myself are you close?

—goading him to the finish line.

---

* A favour, if you ask me.

5th January / le 5 janvier

I was never not a drag queen. I shan't invoke the passé gay idea that I emerged dancing, in patent stilettos and glistening sequins, straight from my mum's vagina and onto the stage. Why? Well, first, because I was born via C-section. And second, a queer life can't be narrativised by a catch-all idea. To file it neatly in the "gay and fabulous" column erases the daunting task of getting from A to She, and all the ups, downs, tucks, and sucks it takes to be able to stand tall in front of people, while you lift the often-crushing weight of transgression, and the aggression that comes with it, up onto your padded shoulders.

But how does one get from A to She? I did all the comings out society requires of people like me: at the age of five, I acquired my first dress and was discovered lip-syncing to Celine Dion. At the age of thirteen, I came out as gay to an unprepared family while wearing a fluffy dressing gown, clutching a mug that read I LOVE SHOES!. At the age of nineteen, I stepped out in full drag for the first time. When I was twenty-one, my family attended their first-ever drag show—starring me.

These comings out might appear to be the defining moments in my journey to becoming a drag queen or, perhaps more appropriately, to becoming the realest version of me. Yet through all this, I was never not a drag queen. I was always inexplicably performative, lewd, flamboyant, feminine. There's a photograph of me in reception, aged five, in a black-sequinned dress and pearl earrings, holding court in front of an adoring crowd (of classmates most probably still in nappies). Growing up in Lancaster, flanked by farmland, I was engrossed by the trappings and signifiers of femininity and femaleness, by any crumb of glamour I could get my hands on. I was so deeply in love with my mum and my grandma, fascinated both by their appearance and their heady mix of northern savageness and warmth; and I was enchanted by the ways of the women of my quintessentially northern hometown.

While the women of Lancaster were magnificent, and often my only protectors, from primary school onwards, I was painfully derided for my likeness to these women I tried so desperately to mimic. From the age of nine, I was flooded with confusion. To me, I was these women, they were my idols, and yet—

There was my body. My male body, which in my teens grew and grew as I ate and ate anything I could get my hands on. Any food, all food, any men, all men, all to fill a hole inside me that, if left empty, would be flooded with terror, and fear, and self-loathing. The shame of my apparent moral transgression put me on a destructive path of obsessive overachieving and self-medication, both mechanisms employed to drown out the piercing noise of people telling you that your very existence is wrong. Coming out as gay didn't help; it merely reified everyone's suspicions, stocking the arsenal of my detractors with ever more deadly weaponry.

But I was still a drag queen. Though now I hid behind closed doors, tucked my maleness between my legs, and performed to that fragile shrine of my icons—Madonna, Celine, Tina—that I'd built inside my wardrobe. After a day of dodged rocks, hocked-up phlegm, and fragile masculinity shunted onto the nearest fag, I would come home, night on night, and perform the most affirming of survival rituals. I would gather up the scattered pieces of me and paint them with make-up I'd shoplifted or swiped from my sister's room. While in public I was an insecure, bitchy gay fourteen-year-old, in private I was an all-powerful diva.

As I hurtled through teenagerdom and into young adulthood, via comical sexual experiences that saw me drinking out of toilets (never again) and being asked to dress up as Snow White by a married man with young children, I continued to practise my nightly ritual, compelled by need, not necessarily by want. All I wanted was to be normal. But, with the imperceptible incremental shifts brought about by my nightly diva worship, normal stopped being an option. At seventeen I dredged up the courage to sing an Amy Winehouse solo at a school talent show, dancing onstage in all my femme glory. And (obviously, lol) I won.

Here was a taste of being adored for who I was. Like any born queen, I was hooked. I wasn't like the other boys, and as I grew up and left Lancaster, I was thrilled that this was so.

At university I slowly started to bring Crystal out, and after being spotted at a club in a stinking fake mink coat and plastic hair extensions, I was invited to audition for Denim. I got the part! Rapidly the wonder of being in (bad) drag, of finally feeling celebrated for a part of me that had incurred so much bullying, outshone my previously conventional path. My parents were furious.

To them, I'd chosen heels over financial stability. To me, I'd chosen profound happiness over mere survival; I'd chosen honesty, with myself and with those who would listen—but I still wasn't a fully fledged drag queen.

Together as Denim we found family, new family. Like a family, we are one another's mothers, sisters, bankers, brothers, drunken aunties, and personal assistants.

This queer family showed me not only how sublime and powerful drag could be, but how sublime, how powerful, I was. I hadn't realised until I met a clan of people like me that there, behind my bedroom door in Lancaster, I had been performing the Japanese art of *kintsugi*, in which you heal the cracks in broken pottery using lacquer dusted with gold, silver, or platinum. What was cracked by others, I put together and sealed with sequins and lipstick and feathers (because I couldn't afford precious metals). Once my queer siblings had brought her to life—like a glamorous, incisive, glistening Frankenstein—I carried Crystal into my everywhere.

Embracing her, I couldn't not shift my perspective: from a belief that I was in the wrong to a conviction of the wrongness in the structures around me, structures that cause so much hurt. This insight is the most precious gift that being a drag queen, and a queer, has given me.

Yet I'm here, barely in drag, never onstage—which is my second favourite place in the world after the loo—repressing my Crystal side all for some dud job. I'm far from my Denim family, and as I think about the next day at work with Eve, all the pieces I'd worked to put together feel as if they could crumble into nothing. All that time wasted. All that perspective shoved to the back of my mind.

6th January / le 6 janvier

Had lunch with Eve at a new Danish restaurant in TriBeCa and was intent on quitting. But before I could, she mentioned my green card over a sharing plate of tiny fish-centric starters. I was all ears, and she'd cooked up a bargain.

"I'm happy to sponsor you for a green card. Just look over this contract before you sign, then initial each page and sign the back one, and date."

I read, flicking pages, furiously, excitedly, forgetting Crystal and the stage and my intent to quit, instead steaming through the contract as if Eve had never told me I had no talent, or that I was useless, gullible gratitude outweighing hatred. I neared the end. The second-to-last page. All good. All in order. Then there, at the bottom, it explained that any earnings I made while under the sponsorship of Eve must be shared, in a 60:40 split, with her—including any wage she pays me, doubling back from my account to hers the moment it's sent.

It's hard to be young and to know your worth, but somehow I know I'm worth more than 60 per cent of a full salary.

"What? Oh, the sixty per cent thing. That's nothing to do with the green card side, it's just that you're an expensive assistant to keep—I mean, Jesus, you can eat, and I bought you those Club Monaco leggings last month. Totally normal. Sign it," she urged me, like Isabella Rossellini telling Bruce Willis to drink the potion in *Death Becomes Her*. "Sign it and soon you can stay here forever. There's so much opportunity here."

It felt strange for her to push so hard for me to sign this commitment to her when her whole approach to mentoring had been to explain over and over that I am never going to make it, that I'm untalented, and that I need her.

As my pen approached the paper, I remembered the time I went to a penthouse a few blocks over for a gay sex party. There were about forty men, all naked, the older ones magnanimously peering through an array of tortoiseshell spectacles, postcoitally enquiring about you after they'd just shot their load all over your back. It was all very civil, with actual fabric napkins on hand to wipe up aforementioned loads. These men were an acceptable kind of successful, conventionally interesting, had all lived in New York for twenty-plus years. It felt gay in that specific pink pound kind of way—not my scene, but good material for a story over FaceTime. There, I met this man called James who was born in Bolton—one city over from my hometown of Lancaster. His accent was international, lilting from continent to continent, and only as he'd growled, "Fuck me, you're tight," had I heard the northern weight of his vowels.

Sitting there in the restaurant, my eyes jittering around this clinical Danish box, I remembered something James had said to me after we'd left the party and strolled to get happy hour oysters in Chelsea. "Don't forget about England. Well, not England per se, but where you came from. Consider what you're running to and make sure that you're not running from. I've been running from things my whole life, and I missed my friends and their successes and my parents and their deaths. And for what? For the trappings of a life I'd cut and pasted in my head from movies and magazines when I was young? Always run to something."

In that moment I'd brushed off this advice as the mutterings of someone who had started off way more lost than me, someone who had had it harder and perhaps had more to run from on account of the combination of his age and his being gay in a northern working-class town, someone who had spent a lot of money on therapy and a lot of time escaping.

I definitely wasn't running from, I'd told myself. I had run to success, to respect from my peers. No way was being a drag queen ever going to pay the bills; no way was staying still ever right for me.

Although thinking about it now, it's not as if I gave staying still a chance. I've always had a feeling that because I was set aside as different when I was growing up, all the way through university, everywhere, that my life also needed to be different. A strange internalisation. Staying in Lancaster felt small to me, felt unremarkable to me.

But there's money in New York, I thought, there's respect in New York. People's lips would still flap about me, there in my hometown, but at least I'd always be the one so different they moved to New York. My quest hadn't until now been for peace or love or happiness— it had been for the remarkable. But this job wasn't remarkable. This restaurant wasn't remarkable. Nothing was, except my outfit. So what was I still doing here? Proving idiots I couldn't care less about wrong?

So in a Danish restaurant shrouded by torrential rain beating against the windows, its duck-egg-blue walls closing in on Eve and me, I wondered why I had come all this way just to give myself, my youthful spark, and now most of my livelihood, to someone so full of contempt for me.

I'd plopped myself into that culturally familiar scenario, but I'd ended up with a mediocre job and a mediocre boss, who had possibly the most unearned ego of anyone I'd ever encountered. I was barely even in New York emotionally, on account of my mind's being consumed by longing for what I'd left behind—my friends and my family, Ace—and the chances of my becoming a writer or even a drag queen with any earning potential vanishing into thick Fifth Avenue air. No way was I time- or confidence-rich enough to strike out as a queen with Eve riding my back while I ride her boyfriend's. I was further away from everything I'd moved here to get closer to.

It was as if I'd taken the red pill, realising that all this was worse than worthless; realising that the only times I'd felt at home in New York were when I was on Face-Time with Ace.

So, in a classically ill-thought-out move, I did what

people spend the whole movie willing the goofy lead character to do. I chose to run. This time, to. To Crystal, whom I let brim forth into this restaurant like Boudicca but with better clothes.

I tore up the contract. I tore it up into tiny little bits, at which point Eve nearly choked on a lump of charcoal that had been floating in her glass of water. "Fuck you and your fucking ponchos. I quit."

Yes, Crystal, we surged forth like Cate Blanchett in *Lord of the Rings* when she wants the ring and goes green.

Eve went to reply; I raised my ten-dollar manicured hand.

"I thought you were a golden ticket, a mentor, someone for whom I could shine. But you're a monster. And not even in an iconic, *Devil Wears Prada* kind of way. You're so much less impressive. You'll never be Miranda Priestly!"

She rolled her eyes, and for a second I mentally agreed with her that my analogy was far too gay to be taken seriously. But I had to simply focus on the task at hand.

"I'm done. You don't own me. And while you say I need you, it's painfully clear that you need me. I'm smart. I'm charming. I am good at everything you ask me to do, and I come up with, like, ninety per cent of your ideas all while keeping your sex life afloat—the split should be ninety:ten in my favour . . . of your earnings! And if sapping my talent with no return is your idea of sponsorship, then frankly I'd rather eat my own farts. You'll never see me again."

"Farts? Really, queen? Andy Sachs would never say 'farts,'" Crystal judged.

I hushed Crystal, and as I pulled my scarf-cape* from the back of my chair with the flourish of a matador, I was triumphant, liberated by finally speaking the truth, by finally redistributing a small plash of the abuse she'd flooded my world with for almost five months. As is on brand for me, the wake of my scarf-cape whipped our fish platter off the table—everyone watching while the slate plate clacked along the dark wood floor—but chaos is glamorous so I leaned into it, worked with it, as if it were intentional.

When you first start drag, you think it's all about the look, the transgression, the ability to thrust yourself so far out of normality that you can say and do anything you want. This always manifests either as promiscuousness or bitchiness—two things, when performed as traits of femininity by predominantly gay men, are reductive and misogynist. But a drag queen, or king, or anyone who drags anywhere along, between, or outside the binary, is much more. Being a drag queen is a collection of experiences that gives you insights that others, by way of not seeing the world from elsewhere, simply don't have. I'd left drag behind for a stable career. But here, as I gave my parting shot to Eve, I realised that with her I'd survived on less money, and with more abuse, than I ever got for being a drag queen. This is what I needed, this is

---

* Yes, that sounds like a poncho, but it's just a stunningly big scarf—huge difference.

what I'm running to. "I'm a fucking drag queen, Eve—and that's what I'm gonna be. A drag queen. I'm gonna be a star!"

It all clicked, and Crystal and I converged. "No. I *am* a star!"

I pranced out of the Danish place, stepping out under a pissing sky. Then I realised I'd forgotten my handbag, which had my passport in it, so I had to google the number of the restaurant, then call and ask them to snag the bag and keep it aside. I waited an hour in a nearby doorway for Eve to leave before I went back to collect it, blasting Martha Wash's "Carry On" through my headphones on repeat, getting a little wet from the rain but rejoicing in how glamorous this whole thing was, how drag this whole thing was.

Fuck Carrie. I'm a Samantha.

7th January / le 7 janvier

I awoke to a pretty curt email from Eve studded with a colourful array of compliments such as "I've never met a more ungrateful cunt," "I'll be billing you for all the lunches," "I pity your lack of direction," "You'll never work again," "Ponchos are in!"—all of which reinforced all the reasons I quit, but still, I'm having doubts, terrors, even.

Terrors that I'm going to have to do the worst and admit defeat, call my mum, call my friends and everyone else at home who'd waved me off and shed tears at my big Gone but not Fag-gotten party some months ago.

Terrors that I haven't made it. In fact, what I now have to do is not only admit defeat but also admit that I've been swimming in a pool of delusion for nearly five months: not only have I failed at my "dream" job, but it was never a dream job in the first place. I have failed at New York, at fashion, at money, success, fame, a green card. I never even came close to succeeding in this city. Instead, I've had all the wonder sucked out of me. Such a stupid privileged problem.

I believe in this theory of celebrating things that would usually be deemed a fail. Such as falling over on entering an exceptionally glam party or reading someone's behaviour as flirtation and then spending months and months convincing yourself they're in love with you, unpacking their behaviour behind their back with any sucker who will listen, only to watch them fall happily into a relationship with a girl as they tell you they were never gay anyway. The power you can find by repurposing that failure into humour has been a genuinely life-changing technique for me and loads of queers.

My friends and I call these things "team." Like if your mum catches you wanking, it's team; if you shit on a hot guy's dick, it's team; if you break your leg the day before running a marathon, it can all be made better by teaming it. But this right here—spending all my money, of which I had little in the first place, and lying to all my friends that this is the life I've always dreamed of, while slowly decaying under the savagery of being cashless and emotionally battered by my boss—all this is really, really not team. It's too bleak for team. It might be team in a few months. But right now it's WAB—"weird and bleak." Another term my friends and I coined when we went to Iceland and stayed with this person who had painted literally three hundred self-portraits and hung them all in the guest bedrooms.

It's actually a complete mess. I don't know what to do.

I intend to reply to all my messages, "Sorry can't chat today! Mad day at work xxx."

It's not. But I plan to spend the day working on an escape route, finding the right way to be honest with everyone I'm lucky enough to have care about me, a right way to battle back my shame at failing before revealing it to everyone in my life.

8th January / le 8 janvier

Around this time last year Ace and I were talking about what it means to be "yourself." The queer conundrum is knowing where yourself stops and the conception of what and who you should be starts. Judith Butler says that when you're alone, you don't feel your gender because gender is brought about by the presence of others. Of course, as Judy says, when you're alone, you can remember the presence of others and feel it. But when I'm alone, I don't feel my gender: I feel its absence, as well as the confusion at my body and the things demanded of it, combined with knowledge that none of the (male) things society demands of me fit. Sometimes that makes me feel standout, like a star, sometimes like a leper.

I remember all the years I spent narrowing myself down to a small stereotypical box of what others perceive gay people should be: fab, bitchy, promiscuous, reads *Chat* mag, good at curling hair. But that box is not me. I've learned so much how to "be" through existing in my narrow gay box that I'm not sure what is a result of the gay box, a result of my reacting against the gay box, and what's just me.

I'm grateful for the box, in a way, because it helped me survive, but I'm also always unsure how to escape it. When I reminded Ace of this year-old conversation over FaceTime earlier today, he said he feels that, too. It's taught many of us, I'm sure, to be funny, quick-witted, emotionally intelligent. But one can't help but wonder what we would be like without such narrow conceptions and representations.

"I feel like I'm fully myself when I'm with you," Ace said as we chatted, our faces pixelated by a six-hour and two-thousand-mile time and space difference. Holding his phone to the speaker, he played our favourite song on his laptop: "Love and Affection" by Joan Armatrading. I knew I wanted to run home.

10th January / le 10 janvier

My voice has always been the giveaway. High, precise, my *s* sounds so sibilant it's as though there's a thousand snakes in my mouth. Yes—it's the archetypal gay voice, with a heavy northern drawl, and people would take the piss. Until I sang.

Singing is a skill I learned from women. As I'd practice my drag, I'd sing along with every love song Celine Dion ever released. I never had singing lessons, but from childhood, through puberty, I kept belting, higher and higher. I wasn't aware I was learning to sing because this practice was more about administering the healing power of love songs to myself. I needed love songs.

Every night I would go home and listen to more Celine Dion, watch old VHS tapes of her live in Memphis in which she wore a full gold lamé look, and it helped me to understand both performance and power. There, with one of the only people who had allowed my emotions to flow freely and not put me in the position of fab or fag, I was allowed to escape, to work out who I was for myself. And I learned to sing—to jump my voice between numerous octaves and riff over choruses by extending words and vowels to the moment your breath runs out.

Now people don't take the piss out of my voice. Some people don't care, but others gasp, and sometimes it makes people cry when I hit a top note they've never heard a person with a male body hit. It makes me feel powerful, and it makes my gender feel insignificant. There's nothing like the shock on people's faces when they hear I can sing like a girl, whatever that means—such as last night at Cora's family home, where we were plonking round a piano singing crap songs, and I let out a series of high notes. I feigned an unawareness at my skill, the way any gracious star would, but nothing gives me greater pleasure than to sing and challenge people's notions of gender at the same time.

13th January / le 13 janvier

My friend Ellie always says that a good measure of how life is going can be achieved by taking stock of your friends. I look at my friends and think that I must have done something right because I bagged these living icons as my family.

It's been three days since I wrote anything down because I've spent it with these friends. Friends on Face-Time, friends on the street and met over my final days in New York while eating pumpkin pie at Sugar Cafe, friends over email, friends over Instagram messages, friends dancing with me all night at the Boom Boom Room, friends who skip the queues with me at every difficult door in town, friends who spend sundowns getting glammed up with me while we drink rosé, beating our faces and telling one another we look fierce, friends to whom I send GIFs or with whom I have conversations only in meme form, friends who roll out of taxis with me and get early-morning dollar pizza with me, friends who have sex with me or who kiss me in a rage of utopic queer power on the dance floor, friends who wear my wigs, friends who lend me theirs, friends who stick their fingers down one another's throats when we've all drunk too much while holding back aforementioned wigs, friends who take me to their mom's house in New Jersey, who in turn give me three-inch-long acrylic nails for free, all while reading my tarot cards, friends of all kinds who didn't have a single thing to say about my failure other than a collective "We're proud of you, we love you."

Friends mean family. Friends mean protection and understanding. They mean sharing the problem, the shame, the violence—among fifteen, or twenty, or two.

I've decided to leave New York, and I feel a sense of relief I haven't experienced since I got the results of my last STI test. Worried about cash, though. Don't have enough for the flight. Maybe I'll swim—the first drag queen to do a solo crossing of the Atlantic.

14th January / le 14 janvier

Pak is a Filipino Swiss femme gay man who comes from a rather conservative, wealthy family. I met him at uni, I coached him through his coming out (a regular role in the life of a longtime-out queer person, a baton that you pass on—Pak is now helping his housemate do the same, while kind of getting with him, too). Unrecommended, but gays have a propensity to fuck their friends and then forget about it. Kind of sweet, really. Plus his housemate is hot. Pak and I weren't friends in the beginning—I didn't think much of him at all: rich, judgmental, superficial, and straight just wasn't (and isn't) my scene. But Pak turned out to be a grower, not a show-er. Incredibly generous—both with his time and his belongings— and perhaps because of his pretty vicious family, who all vote Tory, he harnesses a rare ability to be unfazed by most things. With Pak you could slip up and he wouldn't be perturbed. He's not apolitical; he's just more forgiving than a lot of my radical queer friends (me included).

He called today, with major anxiety about his career choice as a music producer. This confession of doubt was uncharacteristic for him, but since I had made a Facebook announcement that I was coming home, and that I'd learned more by hating it here than loving it, people have been more forthcoming with the ways they're feeling worried about stuff, too.

Pak opened the conversation with "I always thought I was going to be discovered."

Same.

"Yeah, well, I had a thought, like, two days ago that actually we probably won't be. Like, while we read about all these people who blew up overnight, I reckon that their narratives have totally skipped out the years of scrimping and saving and waiting days on end for emails back from people whose work you don't even respect."

Thing is, Pak has his own house in South London, so he doesn't know about scrimping and saving. I had to serve him the truth about our economic and class differences, something I've promised myself I'll do more.

Then, we spent an hour planning how we'd "do it," although classically we're not 100 per cent sure what "it" is. But some kind of change. Something both ambitious and driven. Pak's—to make a go at being a producer; me—to, as Alyssa Edwards says, "get a grip, get a life, and get over it." To stop wasting hours worrying about how people might perceive me, my success or my lack thereof, and start trying to demarcate what's good with things that feel good, rather than things that look good. Such as drag. This plan, somewhat ironically, consisted of all that bleak shit about personal brand management and social media followers—and then Pak said that he was going to go to Ibiza to relax (to which I said, "Ibiza is tacky").

"When you're home, we can work on making it together!" he said before he hung up. At this I strangely got an erection—maybe a kind of success erection, about two queens making it in the big city. It's every queen's dream.

Then I wandered around the Lower East Side, and I wondered what it's like to be rich, culturally and financially. I wonder about this all the time. I roamed past all these fancy places totally out of my reach. Some nights, I would get dressed up and go to these fancy places just so I could sit there and watch rich people, miming to the maître d' that my friends were "super late, sorry!" when they weren't in fact coming. I would be desperately waiting for someone to leave a smidgen of a drink so I could minesweep it (something I've mastered after months of not wanting people to discover just how broke I am).

While waiting for the dregs of that sweet, expensive nectar in those sweet, expensive places, I would think about how life would change so immeasurably if I were just gifted a mil by some Dickensian-style benefactor, it turning up in my bank account, no strings attached.

But then there's my working-class pride: my want to have built myself from the ground up; my want to have read the books because I had the time and the money and the inclination to; my want to own property and give handsomely to charity—all because I could and all because of me, not because of some windfall money but because I did it all, I worked myself from the shores of Morecambe Bay to the top office in the One World Trade, where Anna Wintour currently chills, her Clarice Cliff vases neatly lined on the windowsill.

"Am I the next Margaret Thatcher?" The woman who famously only believed in individualism, in pulling your own self up, in working for your own lot. I worry as I obsess over pulling myself up by my own bootstraps, of going from poor to rich, of losing my capitalist critiques as I'm lured by the trappings that come with cash.

These feelings are at odds with my hatred for how capitalism oppresses minorities such as me and mine. Were I to receive a huge sum of money, I wonder if I'd lose that belly fire that drove me here in a mad want for something "big," even though that something big turned out to be something bleak.

Truth is, now I'm ready to leave, I can think of nothing "bigger" than being home, in my own context. I have been transfixed by the idea that *big* means "different" and "financially successful," but perhaps *big* just means "full."

The other truth? I secretly still believe I'll be discovered like Bowie or Iggy or Madonna or Cher Lloyd—that's Crystal, and I love her for it.

But I'm going to stop worrying about my flawed class politics and, instead, look at my shoes and think how amazing they are. A knee-high, lace-up kitten heel, in black suede. Sounds gross but they're fashionable right now. They will be for the next five years, too, because, apparently, we're at the dawn of something called the Half-Decade Trend, according to Jess Cartner-Morley at *The Guardian*. She once won an award for a piece of

journalism entitled "What I Wore This Week: Earrings."
You have to laugh.

17th January / le 17 janvier

Last night had been a final hurrah, a funeral for the par-
tial life I squeezed out of New York.

Save for Cora and Lily, attending were, mostly, drag
friends, whom I'd met in the queues, loos, on the dance
floors, instantly coding each other as gender-skewed siblings who share a cultural DNA; one just as strong as the
biological alternative.

We started at Le Bain, at the rooftop of the Standard
Hotel, in which there's quite a bleak pool.* Next, a swing
through the Cock (a kind of nostalgic nod to seedy sex
clubs of the Meatpacking District pre-AIDS, which is a
weird aesthetic to invoke—not because AIDS is weird
but because associating it with shady sex is a little un-
helpful, if you ask me), ending the night backstage at the
Box, watching a woman whose act is to pull a corkscrew
and a bottle of wine out of her asshole, snort coke off a
hot dog.

We lived, clicking and tongue popping, our form of
worship. We drank, and we lived, and we danced, and
we lived, and some people took pills and we lived, some
people didn't drink a drop and we lived, we loved and

---

* I *never* go in pools in public because I had chlamydia once when I
was seventeen and I was convinced I got it from a pool at Oceana in
Warrington. Ugh, so bleak.

lived and poured our emotions onto one another about being separated and we lived: these queens and queers and trans women and club icons I've come only to know by the flash of their phone lights during the taking of an iconic picture and their varying postures as they all recline on the city's club couches like glistening panthers, raking in cash for simply appearing, living by night, between pay cheques, wearing heels to the gym and eating one meal a day while rhinestoning their next garment.

As I peeled myself away from the back room of the Box, cuddling Lily and the bouncers who always let me skip the queue since my first night in town, knowing I'll see them all again, I hurtled down East Houston and picked up my case from the charmingly dated Remedy Diner. From the corner of there and Norfolk I walked to the subway, weaving my way through the appallingly signed city rail network that, despite cunningly dodging people I'd assumed to be plain-clothes ticket officers for nearly five months, I never quite got the hang of.

I woke up as the J train pulled into Sutphin Boulevard. I must have fallen asleep. My head had pressed against a glass partition, leaving there my final, perhaps most significant, mark upon New York: the waxy, oily print of the left side of my face, the kind that would stay there all day until some unwitting passenger accidentally put their hand on it and then feel incredibly worried about the germs on the subway.

Deep breaths as I entered JFK, where I was about to attempt the biggest heist in my New York history: a free flight home. I've always been oddly good at getting things for free. To the casual outsider, I pretend that each time it happens—be it free coffee, a free haircut, a free shag—that it's a total shock, a first time. But I think it's because northerners, especially in the U.K., have a charm that many from other places don't. We're famed for our warmth, and while it can feel manipulative to use it, sometimes needs simply must. Or perhaps it's the Crystal charm. Or that I look so desperate that people take pity on me. Whichever way, I have seventeen dollars in my bank account and a twenty that Cora slipped into my pocket as I left. Not quite a transatlantic flight.

What ensued was sixteen hours of tactical begging at different flight vendors, all of whom said no with varying degrees of brutality.

On the verge of giving up, I connected to a Wi-Fi network somewhere near the hell that is Michael Kors and checked my emails. Ace had responded that his parents are chill with me staying with them for a bit in Clapham, until I find my own place. At least I'm sure of my destination. With a newfound confidence, a reason to head home, it was time for one final push.

"What fragrance are you wearing?" the wonderful Wizz Air lady queried.

"Ah, I don't know—I've been here sixteen hours, had a strip wash in the loos, and I think, probably, doused myself with something obvious and expensive: Tom Ford, maybe?"

"Ooh, my husband wears Tom Ford, I love a man with good taste," she enthused. "How can we help?"

I didn't dare explain that I wasn't a man, or that I

think Tom Ford has become quite tacky. Instead, I explained my predicament honestly, and she made a phone call to the man at the end of the Wizz desk. "We can get you to Reykjavik . . . any good?"

I squealed so loudly that nearby armed guards tensed their hands around their giant guns like apes clutching their cocks. This makes me feel unsafe, which is the opposite of the point of seeing armed guards everywhere, right? I figure that for those who fit into the normal parts of the spectrum, guns don't feel that scary, but for people who have frequently been the target of violence by men like the ones here with the guns—white, buff, male, manly, cis, het (I'm assuming, probably correctly)—guns do the opposite of inspiring a feeling of safety.

She checks my bag, hands me a ticket, tells me she feels a "connection" with me, and I respond, "Ditto," with a smile of unbrushed teeth.

Now I'm flying. As we bump through the clouds, I catch a final glimpse of Manhattan in all its long, thin, morning glory and think about giving up on a dream life that was 40 per cent within my grasp. I press my head against the window and relax into the thought that in my past giving up on stuff has led me to better things, weirder things.

I scored a place to study veterinary medicine at Cambridge and quit, then I got to finish in philosophy and become a drag queen. I tried to be a heterosexual for a bit in my teens and quit, then I got to have way more salacious sex than the rest of my peers who were in serious relationships throughout high school. I signed up to Duolingo to learn German once and eventually quit, then I got £4.99 more a month to spend on cigarettes. As I leave Eve and my Union Market ban behind, I'm starting to feel excited about what will be born from torching my most recent plan to ashes. Maybe I'll start going to the gym?

18th January / le 18 janvier

Still on the flight. Food gave me diarrhoea. Should've gone for trusty veggie option. Sitting next to a baby who has taken a liking to me, which is unusual, so the mum asked if I would hold it for five minutes. It fell asleep on me, then I fell asleep on it. Cute: a little innocent drag queen and a little innocent baby soaring across the world at thousands of miles per hour, asleep together. For a second after I woke up I thought about stealing the baby, but then I realised it had done a shit and I instantly went off the idea. Probably don't want kids.

I can't get back to sleep, which is distressing in one of those nonspaces where everyone else is asleep and you're the only one awake for miles up, down, left, and right. Thinking about Crystal, about building her. There's no pinpointed moment when she arrived in my life. It's a slow process—becoming a drag queen—one that might start with an accent, or a look, or a persona, or a deeper nuanced understanding of why that persona exists.

Building a drag persona is less contrived than it might appear. You don't make a mood board or cut and stick your idealised drag you into a scrapbook. It's much more natural, a kind of slow unfurling of all of the references you adored as a kid, a teen, an adult; an expansion and performance of all of the things you are desperate to be—be that the lost Romanov girl (which is Crystal, by the way, call off the search), or a multimillionaire murderess serial divorcée. It's like a massive pan of soup that you just keep adding ingredients to, and every time it tastes better and better. Sometimes you might put a little too much of one thing in, but with a bit of time you make up for it by slowly adding another.

For me, Crystal is a mix of all the things I could never be. First of all, she's a woman—something that is definitely inside me but has never created enough concentrated dysphoria to have me be sure that I'm a woman, that I should transition. But here I get to express this feeling, and when I do have zings of dysphoria, Crystal leaps forth and reaches for a wig or a heel, and my heart slows and it'll feel good to be in my body again.

She's American; I think there's nothing more glamorous than being American. Unless you're a Bostonian, which is many things but, sorry, not glam. But I always thought of America as the place where glamour lived. In Lancaster, the idea of even going to London, to the capital, was outrageous, so the idea of going to America—anywhere in America—was something I genuinely believed I would never do in my lifetime. So if I couldn't go to the land of Whitney Houston and Cracker Barrel and *Friends* and Carrie and the Met and the Upper East Side and Hollywood and real McDonald's, then I would bring it to me.

Crystal is a famed dancer, singer, writer, actor. She's a first lady and a prime minister, she's a shoe designer and a dominatrix, she's Velma Kelly in *Chicago* and she's Beyoncé singing "I Was Here" for the UN.

These are all the things I gave her that I could never have, kind of like having a child.

19th January / le 19 janvier

I landed in Reykjavik and couldn't get a flight for love nor a crafty blow job. I fell asleep in an outdoor smoking room, bitter Icelandic air having possibly replaced anything that produces heat in my body. Eventually I made the call I never wanted to make. Bless her heart, Mum wired me two hundred pounds that she certainly doesn't have.

Unfortunately I was unaware that I'd gone over my overdraft limit, so the money was half-swallowed by charges on my account brought on by coffees and morsels of food I'd bought at JFK and in-flight. My card was declined by Norwegian Air for a flight costing seventy-four pounds. I had to make a second call I never wanted to make. I facetimed Pak, who sent me another two hundred pounds.

Got the flight.

On the flight I was lured by a shopping magazine and spent fifty-six pounds on a bottle of Jean Paul Gaultier Fleur du Mâle, as an ingenious yet manipulative "maybe this'll make you love me" gift for Ace when he picked me up at the airport. My guilt at borrowing all that dosh wore off pretty quickly, but love is more important than money.

When I touched down in London, even after I'd spent some time smoking a few ciggies, Ace was nowhere to be seen. Turned out he was somewhere with William, and we made a new plan to meet at Ace's family home, which is also mine for a while. This feels possibly like a bad idea, but rent is free and it's in London. I love Lancaster in many ways, but moving back there after Manhattan, despite my newfound perspective, felt like a tumble too far towards the past.

I took the Piccadilly line from Heathrow to Leicester Square, emerging in Soho to drink in the glorious stench of what once was the best gay village on earth, reminding myself of this place I'm in love with but have never actually lived, although I know it well after countless visits during university holidays. I stopped for a quick coffee and six cigarettes at Bar Italia on Frith Street, watching all the gay men in their multifarious cloaks of masculinity gathered outside Caffè Nero, dishing the dirt on who's fucking whom and who's definitely not fucking whom. "I'm doing it," I thought. "I'm moving to London." For a split second I was impressed with myself, especially after just having been burned by the other big city. This one's different, though: my friends are here, my family is here, and if it all goes awry, I can blag my way onto a train back to Lancaster, surely? I looked around and tears rose to my eyes, and I gave myself a moment to feel proud, proud that I did New York, and proud that I was mature enough to admit that it didn't work out.

I arrived at Ace's house just in time for family dinner,

from which Ace was absent. I regaled his sister, Savannah, and his mum and dad, Lara and David, with tales of Eve, Laurie, the nights out clubbing, the time I met Kristen Stewart at the Box, the time I faceplanted in front of Tom Ford himself because my heels were two sizes too small but too cheap and too statement not to buy, Lily, DPing with the Beaumonts, all of it, as they scrambled with laughter and listened sweetly.

Now I'm red-wine tired and in bed, but unable to sleep. I heard Ace come home. I heard two voices ascending the stairs and approaching my door. Outside I heard Ace and someone else—William, I think— bouncing through the upstairs corridor, smacking into walls and shelves as they kissed their way to bed.

On my first night back!

Should've been me. My heart feels as if it were splintering.

They're having sex. I can hear them having sex.

It's my fault for not making a move. It's his fault for not realising I was too scared to make a move. "I would die for you"—I reminded myself of him saying this, as I paced around my room weeping while listening on my headphones to Celine Dion's masterpiece, "It's All Coming Back to Me Now."

24th January / le 24 janvier

I've been going out most days, pretending I'm busy, sitting alone in cafés having one cup of coffee and staying all day while staff members grimace at me because I'm taking up a table, even though their cafés are always less than half-full anyway.

Most of these free days have been spent looking for jobs, prepping all the paperwork, then chickening out before hitting send because I don't want to get it wrong this time around. I am trying to think of slower approaches, more careful.

I'm also looking for drag gigs.

It can be extremely intimidating, entering a city's scene. In each you'll find stacks of drag kings and queens with specific skills—looks, sewing, lip-syncing, dancing, singing, reading, reading to children, being in pantos, more looks, specific looks, being funny on social media. You'll find queens who are protective of their families, and kings who (rightly) don't want you around because queens, historically and still, get all the attention, all the priority.

But these people, these performers, often dedicate most of themselves to a somewhat unforgiving scene. And drag is time-consuming: the self-promotion, the getting in and out of make-up, building networks, performances, DJ sets, promoting nights and booking acts and making sure that everything you do is safe, and most probably finding and working in another job whereby you are paid well enough to live but aren't committed so much it becomes your main focus and steals all the bright-eyed energy you would once have put into your drag. Thus, it's a natural site of contention if a performer barges into a scene and takes the few meagerly paid bookings and slots other queens and kings and non-binary performers have tirelessly worked to secure. We are protective of our scarce income and of the few spaces we are able to run, to be safe in. We all want to think of it as a big loving scene welcoming everyone like family, but practically speaking a queen has to eat, like anyone else. So territories are preset, and one mustn't assume one can simply barge into them and piss all over them. Gentle and respectful infiltration is key, and sometimes even that isn't an option.

DRAG PERFORMANCE MEMO: Last night I saw ShayShay use an iPad and body paint to lip-sync a Björk song, kind of queen becoming robot, robot becoming queen. Tech and drag. People went wild.

26th January / le 26 janvier

The thing that connects most drag queens is an appreciation of femininity, or an innate femmeness.

I know drag queens who have severed ties with the women in their lives, I know drag queens who are misogynist, I know drag queens who are women, trans, assigned female at birth, I know drag queens who—when they're not in drag—present as hard masc, muscular, save for the small clumps of mascara that no make-up remover ever seems to clear, leaving these little elasticky balls hanging there, accidentally divulging your departure from your manhood. I know heterosexual drag queens. I know one asexual drag queen. I know religious drag queens, atheist drag queens, old drag queens, young drag queens. I know drag queens who have seen more than you can imagine and still get shocked when you try to tell them your pronoun is *they*. I know drag queens who are radical activists, who are bored of politics, who only have sex when they're in drag or who never have.

The thread that links these drag queens is femininity. But that's not a singular, reductive view of femininity—something our detractors might not believe. It's not one that abuses femininity by leaning heavily on male privilege, to be saluted for slut dropping when a woman, who isn't a drag queen, might be shamed for the same. No, the femininity I've encountered on the drag scene is wildly variant, much like the women who aren't drag queens I've encountered in my life.

Camp suffering—which drag is an expression of—and female suffering are similar in many ways. Both sets are punishment for not being "men," and, yes, those experiences are different—but both are violent and both are structural. So femininity, when repossessed from fossilised ideas of what it should be, whether by drag queens or women, becomes a place of play, of beauty, of power and culture and strength and colour and utter brilliance. That's why drag is so glorious, that's why women are, too.

28th January / le 28 janvier

I've always been quite popular.

At school, I had no real sexual value and was the target of many of the frustrations of the men around me who loved to explore their raging masculinity by either bullying me or forcing me to suck their dicks, then bullying me. So I used comedy, outrageousness, gossip, good fashion sense, and an unusually adept knowledge of relationships* to claw my way to the top of female-led social circles. I was easily the funniest, most "fabulous" person on the teenage circuit, because I had to be to gain some sort of respect, and not die of the unrelenting homophobia or, worse, invisibility.

Then at Cambridge I had little intellectual or cultural value due to my bookshelf-less background. But what I could provide, by the bucket-load, was humour and honesty, a knife with which to cut through people's poncey bullshit. And they, too, loved me for it. I became skilled at knowing how to make the right friends and the right enemies in social situations. It sounds manipulative, but as most queer folk will confirm, it's one of the keys to our survival.

To gain such social agility, I've always leaned heavily on the popular mantra "I don't care what anybody thinks of me"—it's funny how you spend so many of your younger years funnelling yourself into singular ideas. You realise over time that you do actually care, deeply, what people think about you, or at least that people think of you. I'm currently having said crashing realisation: that I've moved back to this city—me, a popular homosexual who doesn't care what people think of them—and I'm feeling unusually lonely, and I'm start-

---

* Which I learned from *Sex and the City*, God help us.

ing to wonder if people think terribly of me or, worse perhaps, that they don't think of me at all.

When all your friends move to the big city after university, a scattering occurs—everyone is plonked in any old place, in any old part of zone three and beyond, crammed into tiny houses paying obscene rent, separated by trains that only run every thirty-eight minutes and take a further thirty-eight minutes to reach their destination. All this means is that their ability to socialise the way they did at university—whether ritualistically getting smashed every Monday and Wednesday, or spending the following days together hungover, paranoid, but bathing in one another's reassurance that you did nothing wrong last night—gets crushed on the slick steel wheel of capitalism. But that social process changes swiftly, and you're lucky if you get a text back, let alone a drink, with your hungry friends who are now busy chasing their dreams.

And in watching your friends chase their dreams, it's hard to calculate how you might fit within them. I've spent the week travelling to see some of these friends, who say they feel it, too, when I intercept them for a quick drink postwork before they have to head off to the theatre or date night, or home to meal prep, such as my friend Hannah (definitely cutting her out—meal prep, in my opinion, is a fate equally as bleak as death).

February / février

"Well, this is a joke!" Probably the worst response a prospective employer has ever given me when looking at my CV, the nineteenth I'd handed out today. This one to a guy who runs a wanky brunch place in East London, the kind that I'd tut at when I walked past but definitely end up eating in on a hangover Sunday morning.

"Turkey farm manager? Drag queen? Oh, it's this bit that kills me, under 'social skills': intelligent, canny, a fantastic listener and an even better friend."

I cringed at myself. But then, as the guy put his glasses on and stood up, I had an odd feeling that I'd slept with him, some years ago, a last-minute Grindr meet during a visit to London.

"Is your husband a jewellery designer?"

He lunged towards me.

Yes, I'd definitely slept with him—I remembered the shoes he was wearing being kicked off before he'd pissed on me in the shower. It's hard to find employment in London.

PERFORMANCE MEMO: Travis Alabanza read a spoken-word piece about racism on Grindr. Never thought poetry was for me, but it's actually about sentence rhythm—of course the content and words are amazing—because by the end people were on their feet, screaming, as if a queen had just done a death drop. But instead of falling to the floor, Travis has made so many people in the room feel seen. Flawless.

6th February / le 6 février

It's been a futile series of days searching for jobs and catching up with friends, who are all just telling me how hard it was for them to find a job. Some are working in coffee shops and late-night boozers; one cleans a gay sex bar in King's Cross, where at closing time he has to mop up used condoms and bits of poop; others have full-on salaries at theatre production companies and law firms. I like these lawyer ones the least; they don't offer to pay for dinner even though they are rapidly rocketing towards the 1 per cent with their £95K starting salaries and secondments to Hong Kong.

Something I've noted among my friends after university is that the playing field is no longer equal. We are divided into two stark subgroups: the rich ones, who are stingy with money, and the ones on minimum wage, who earn a pittance and still offer to buy you a drink.

Today I went to Mediterranean Café on Berwick Street with my friends Cecily and Ellie. We spent the day watching the old-school Soho set stumble over the cobbles in all their faux opulence, wigs or tattered coats, guarding an array of filthy secrets. Cecily and Ellie are two of my best friends from university, whom I met one gay night out, during which we invented a cocktail we now call gava: gin and cava! It's only to be consumed if undergoing a break-up/postsurgery/death in the family, or if there's any lying around.

Ellie is taller than average with a small waist and giant boobs that make her look like a vintage burlesque lesbian—despite being a power bisexual—and she's leaned into the queerlesque style. Cecily is cool but doesn't know it. A proud dork, which in the past pushed her far to the bottom of the social ecosystem, but now she reaps the rewards from sticking with her lame tastes because everyone now loves what she loved then. She sends links to viral videos before they're viral and often provides some of the most incisive input at the times you least expect. The two women are both part of the minimum-waged generous set.

Ellie said she can get me a job at this art-space-studio-space-gallery-space-yoga-space-restaurant-space-concept in East London. "It's really niche but my bosses are look-ing for drag queens to sort of 'spice up' the place. I know it's bleak, but you'll get to perform and they'll pay you all right."

I've decided to go for it. Although Ellie warned me the boss will probably be high on coke and he's defi-nitely fucking the girl who's head of marketing. His wife has just had a baby. Can you believe?

"Ugh, sounds perfect! Do it!"

We erupt into cackles knowing we all would prob-ably do the same as him. Cecily adds that if it were us, we would be better because "we'd be honest and, like, probably have an agreement re polyamory or some-thing, right?"

I sometimes wonder if our laughter at those on the more normative end of the spectrum comes from a place of being terrified to admit you want into a system that has only caused you hurt. From an early age we are conditioned to want this stuff—marriage, kids, good job, money, house, car, to vote in the interest of what is good for you and yours and nobody else. When you come out as anything that strays from this norm, you feel as if you've failed those who wished you an easy life. "What about grandchildren?" homophobic family members cry. "It's a phase! Once you find the right girl, you'll forget all this."

But the very nature of being queer means questioning what society wishes on us. Queer is always the horizon, never the shore, as sexy theorist José Esteban Muñoz says. And marriage and kids are absolutely the shore, surely?

But what if we do want in? Around my radical queer friends—the butches who wear thick belts squeezed into the dark denim belt loops of their jeans, the full-time activists who are the first on-site at any and every protest, and the queens who have often given up families, friends, potential careers, safety, to have the chance to blister themselves in a pair of heels—it can sometimes feel as if you lose queer points if you admit to liking the idea of getting married, or that you might one day want children.

But it isn't as cut and dried as social and identity politics winning out over every life decision. Politically I want the system of heteronormativity to burn, but personally a thread runs through me, sewn there by only being shown one option when I was growing up, that makes me want the normal things: the marriage, the kids, the safety. While we can unpick much of that stuff, write it off as being wrongly nurtured, I can't quite shake the feeling off. So what do you do when your personal and your political are at odds?

No idea. But from where I'm sat, I don't understand why I can't have a life full of gender nonconformity, promiscuous sex, political resistance, and cocktails in the morning. I also dream of a big house in the country, kids running around in high heels, and a wedding ring on my finger. Perhaps one can have both models, blended into one: if the content stays queer, then maybe the form doesn't matter?

9th February / le 9 février

Went out yesterday to a big night at the Troxy in East London, run by a collective called Sink the Pink. I was with Glamrou, Aphrodite, Electra, and Shirley. These queens are my sisters in a band called Denim. We were pretty big at uni, although I guess that's not hard when uni was a tiny enclave of repressed students desperate to find an ounce of subversion in their routine of interminable study and excessive normativity.

It's probably a year since any of us performed together, but while drunk last night, Glamrou announced a gig on the horizon. She's in talks with Bethnal Green Working Men's Club—the same place that launched the sequinned ships of a thousand drag careers, including that of Sink the Pink.

We all decided that we were desperate to reunite, like the Spice Girls, so in the middle of the beaming disco we pulled up our diaries on our phones, all of which were alarmingly empty, and scheduled a meeting next week to "lock it down." When we formed, we never aimed to mimic the Spice Girls, but as a five-piece, loud girl band with distinct personalities, it's hard not to make the comparison, even if they are all Tories.

I'm Posh Spice, obviously.

Aphrodite is definitely Sporty. She's sheathed with muscle, incredibly hot, but also deeply weird in a funny way. We lived together at university, where we'd smoke in our room and gossip for three hours at the start of each day, often setting off the fire alarm and being threatened with fines every other week. Aphs is the most pragmatic of us all, but even she's willing to ditch her crap money-earning job tutoring kids English to become a full-time queen. Something that makes me feel better about wanting the same. Aphs loves babies, even though she doesn't know if she wants them. She grew up with six siblings, so her drag is all about being a mother—healing the underappreciation she had towards hers while living out a fantasy of being one herself.

The Geri of the group is Glamrou: outrageous, cheeky. We have phases where we speak every day and where we don't for a while, because when we get onto Big Stuff, we often exhaust each other with how much we hate certain parts of the world and how scary it is. She's like a giraffe—tall, beautiful, soft, clever. Her drag is all about healing the disjunction between queerness and Islam. So she mirrors her mother, wearing beaded bikinis and singing "Bad Romance" by Lady Gaga to Allah.

Shirley is Baby. (Shirley is also Ace.) She has a blond

beehive and performs a kind of maniac-meets-Texan-preacher's-Stepford-Wife in drag. She's a character queen—someone whose drag is totally different from them as a person, who uses it as a tool for critique and exploration. Shirley is all about the terrifying aspects of whiteness, so each performance she brings you in close, gets you on her side, then reveals she's setting up a giant suicide cult and there's no way out.

Electra is Scary. She's naive, dogmatic, and incredibly loyal. Her love for crap pop and deeply sincere musical theatre informs her drag persona, which, for her, is a return to her childhood—allowing her to openly love the things she loved in secret then onstage now. She'll sing a song from *Fiddler on the Roof* with a fake Justin Bieber tattoo on her arm.

It's funny how drag means and mines so many different things for so many people.

For Glamrou and me, drag redresses our trauma and shame, finding a space to feel truly iconic. This comes when I sing. I've been told I have a great voice by a few people ("Millions," Crystal says). For Glamrou, this comes through comedy.

For all of us, drag gives a space to explore wants and desires without having to take full responsibility for them, out of drag. You can kind of test the water with your drag character, and often things that emerge through drag will be absorbed by you when you're out of drag—such as confidence or politics or the way you hold your femininity. Bringing these selves onstage is even more wild, because not only have you started to heal yourself by building this person, now you're onstage being celebrated for being them. Being celebrated for all the things people criticised you for. Being celebrated for being a massive fag.

The rest of the night consisted of being pushed and shoved in a sea of topless muscular torsos, the gays taking this would-be queer space and making it into one big homogenised IRL Grindr meet. I ended up getting with a guy in the loos, which I never do, who whispered sexily, "I don't have a dick." Obviously it wasn't an issue, and one knows not to enquire as to why or how. He was most likely trans.

We left the stalls to get a drink, at which point he offered me a bump of MDMA. I obliged—but as an infrequent drug-taker I've never snorted anything, so I just gummed a tiny bit to be polite.

After I bumped the bump, Sivan (his name) took my hand and shoved it down his pants, guiding me to his clitoris. He took it out again and licked my fingers, asked me if it was okay.

"It's wonderful," I said.

He guided my hand in ovular motions around his junk, new territory for me, and we made out and he quivered as if he was climaxing, him doing all the work, my hand a mere joystick. He took it out of his jeans and we both kissed my fingers. It felt glorious and brand-new for me, as if gender and sexuality could be anything in the world as long as all parties were consenting.

"That's the best orgasm I've had today," Sivan breathed out.

From ecstasy to agony. On the night bus home, Ace was sobbing. William hadn't showed up, and I felt both disastrously smug and like a terrible friend. I comforted him as best I could, but then Ace revealed it was because "William doesn't like it when I'm in drag." At this I lost it.

"Why the fuck would you want to be with him?"

It's so distressing, these stupid masculine gays. I get it's complicated for men like William, who can conceal their gayness at a second's notice, who can pass in a straight world. Femininity scares them; it represents something that has been used as a tool to attack them, us, our whole lives. "But an explanation is not an excuse," I wagered.

"Sure, but I really like him."

I didn't reply. The desire to be a good friend was outweighed by my jealousy of this man who most definitely doesn't deserve Ace. And the hope that Ace might also like me back was sucked out through the loud, open, hydraulic doors of the London bus like so many of my "relationships" past, in which I dreamed up a far more elaborate entwinement than was ever on offer from the other party.

Back home, we made some toast and had a vodka. Ace fell asleep in my bed as we watched the start of *Devious Maids*—a show we'd promised to watch together, so I lied and told him, "I haven't even started," even though I'd watched the whole season since I got back to London to the muffled soundtrack of his fucking someone else so loudly it felt like he was trying to assure me we were never going to happen.

As Ace drifted off, I went to the loo and had a wank about Sivan. Best orgasm of my day. I went to sleep disappointed I never got his number but elated that I got to spend one night sleeping next to Ace. I might have to start getting over him tomorrow.

12th February / le 12 février

Today is my mum's birthday. Been thinking that, more than any man, she's probably the love of my life.

I called her to wish her happy birthday, but of course I didn't tell her the rest of it.

It's also just over a decade since I came out to her. I hear other stories of people's parents saying, "We know, and we love you." But when I stood in my fluffy polka-dot dressing gown holding that mug inscribed I LOVE SHOES!, revealing my homosexuality to my mum, it couldn't have felt further from that ideal. Her exact words were "We'll see," in a stroke negating any agency I had harnessed in deciding to glide out of the closet at age thirteen.

For years thereafter, we undulated between subtle disapproving digs to monumental fights because I'd wanted to wear a decorative Venetian mask to a masquerade party and she'd hated the idea that I might "parade" it around. "It" being my gayness. These things may seem innocuous, but when they're about who you are, the slightest disapproval from someone who should love you unconditionally burns like a hot poker searing into pig's skin, a brand of shame for life.

For all those years I was full of blame towards my mum: bitching behind her back about her disapproval of my sexuality and gender identities. I held things back and built other things up. She in turn misjudged and angered and grew frustrated with this kid of hers who wasn't exactly what she'd expected, especially after she'd dedicated so much energy and all the money she could muster to making me happy, safe, protected, empowered, and intelligent, in the ways she knew how.

One of our biggest arguments ever, brought about by something unmemorable like her not wanting me to wear skinny jeans, erupted in a statement I still believe to be true today: "If you're going to have a child, you'd best love it for who and what it is. Any other shit is on you and your judgments." Enough of these stories of people kicking out and disowning their children because they're gay or trans or queer or something that doesn't fit neatly into a suffocating plan laid out for a child by a parent: the number of friends and LGBTQIA+ siblings I have who still have gaping hang-ups and constant therapy because of their parents' disapproval is galling, and such a waste of their time and their beauty all because of something they didn't do.

The other day I was telling a friend, Jessie, about all of this, explaining the details of those rarely revisited memories. She couldn't believe it because my mum and dad are now exemplary parents, and even better allies. I would, in a heartbeat, call them for anything: an HIV scare, a bad date, a particularly homophobic comment made, a question about work or love or sex or anything else that I wasn't sure of. I would tell them anything, pushing them, sometimes inadvertently and sometimes calculatedly, to understand ever more about what it means to live as queer.

"Sometimes I have group sex with loads of people" gets less than a batted eyelid from a mother once so disapproving. Wild to tell your mum this full stop, but even wilder to the person who used to want nothing more than for you to just be normal.

"How did you get here though?" Jessie asked.

"Hard fucking work, from both of us. An assured knowledge that I was who I was, and my mum's deeply good heart, which we both knew was there." I sipped a cosmopolitan like the wealthy city slicker I am.

The work is different for each person, and it doesn't always pay off. In some instances blame is justified and the effort isn't worth it for an undeserving loved one or relative. But for me it was about being uncompromising about aspects of my life that Mum might have me change: "I am a drag queen, I am wearing these clothes, I am having sex in this way, and if you want to be a part of it, then I will tell you it all. If you don't, then I will tell you nothing; I won't even be in your life." My siblings roll their eyes at my honesty with her, but I can't understand the harm in telling her: she has lived a life longer and in many ways fuller than mine, and her understanding of my experience only seems to yield even more acceptance.

I worked hard throughout my teens to recognise that she owed me nothing, and that a lot of her hurtful actions and words were because of fear and miseducation, and mine were because I was hurting and scared. It's a weird moment when you realise your parents are flawed humans whose knowledge doesn't encompass everything, whose opinions aren't always right.

My mum would say that the difficulties in our relationship came from her wanting to protect me. In the same way I've learned to be patient, she's learned to see my world as something blooming with culture and love and not as something that would bring violence and judgment. She doesn't "feel pride, because that's somewhat patronising"—a quote I always remember her saying as she was getting the shopping in Aldi, looking after my poorly grandma, and doing another hundred things at once. Instead she feels "grateful," grateful my friends and I have opened up a whole culture to her and my dad and welcomed them in. It makes her excited and moved. It makes her feel full.

In Catholicism you pay penance for your sins by action. I fucking hate Catholicism, bar the campy visuals, but if anyone has paid penance, it's my mum. There's no need for forgiveness on either side because we both worked hard. We burned down our relationship and built a new, stronger one on the ground that was cleared. Both of us have learned how to blossom together, with much hard work and mutual education.

She's taught me so much, as any true love does. But mostly she's taught me the power of learning and unlearning, and working hard to do it.

13th February / le 13 février

People think drag queens are stupid.

This is misogyny in action: they think that because we feminise ourselves, because we spend a lot of time on make-up and hair and getting exactly the right look, we are vapid, bitchy, and stupid.

People are wrong to think drag queens are stupid.

We get fluffed off: called "darling," "fabulous," coded as frippery, before "foxy" or "smart." We get underpaid and exploited, but we're aware; we're just too broke to lose the gig. We make a living off laughing at you laughing at us. We know exactly what we're laughing at, what structures we're punching at, what strings to pluck to make you gasp with shock or huff with laughter.

We created a culture that the world marvels at, wishes for, sponges off. We know how to navigate cities and spaces in the smartest of ways, mapping out routes to escape people's stupid, ailing masculinities. We know how to wear heels all night and not feel the burn. We know how to make a mockery not of women but of what you (men) think women should be, whereas you (men) just, simply, mock women.

It's stupid to think drag queens are stupid.

14th February / le 14 février

It's now become the kooky, intelligent position to be anti–Valentine's Day, right? Every year viral tweets, memes, think pieces, go on about how Valentine's Day is for sucky assholes who are obsessed with capitalism and single-shaming.

But this year I've decided to appropriate V Day from the straights and devote it to my genitals.

I don't remember much about being a young child, an astoundingly small amount, but I remember growing my first armpit hair. I remember seeing it and feeling jubilant as, ever since I could remember, I had courted a feeling that my insides were ill matched to my outside. But here was puberty and I was jubilant because I was becoming male. Finally the confusion would stop. I would like girls. I would hate dresses. I would play football. I would be *normal*. Now that word sends shivers down my spine. Then, desperate hope for normality kept me alive.

In pushing out this tiny armpit hair, my body confirmed my maleness, my normality, and herein I would be free of all of these doubts and dysphorias. I willed more to grow—every day I used shampoo and conditioner on my one armpit pube in the hope that such brilliant care would coax more of these sticky little hairs to prick out.

Eventually more grew, and I hated them. More grew on my chest, and I hated them.

More grew on my face, my ass, my legs, my arms, and I hated them. All of a sudden these changes were happening, and instead of my feeling more normal, I felt as if every little hair was an alien growing out of me against my control.

Then the worst happened—not only did my hair grow, the other thing, the other piece of conformation of my maleness grew. And I hated it.

I toyed with changing it; I hid it between my legs and stared in the mirror for hours, pulling sleek fabrics over my body as if I were a wealthy woman with fine taste, who had lots of time for preening herself and saying, "Ooh la la," and, most crucially, who had a stunning vagina.

I did drag in my bedroom accompanied by my CD player, and eventually I brought my drag out onto stages in my late teens. I had sex in the receiving position—for years forcefully ignoring the urge to have my genitals touched, pleasured. I felt they weren't mine, my penis an appendage that got in the way of my role as pleasure giver in the bedroom. But as a young, confused femme I'd imbibed the messages of a society that erases female and femme pleasure, so I lay back and made pornographic noises, pretending that all I cared about was the pleasure of the big, bad, deserving man inside me.

Last summer I gained a lot of weight. This isn't unusual for me; what usually follows is a winding spiral of self-loathing, crash dieting, and pleasure-destroying punishment on this body that has always seemed to fail me.

Last summer I also came out as non-binary. For the first time I said what I felt about my body—and it wasn't how much I hated it, how much I wanted to change it, how much I wanted to hide it—no, for the first time I was offering it the care it had always deserved. For the first time I had seen it.

Through starting to accept a gender I'd always been, looking back on those forgotten years as a child, I finally gave my mind the tools to reframe the way I thought about my body. A body that had previously felt like a lost cause, like a wreckage built of cigarettes, blisters from heels, years of violent homophobia; one constructed of all the ways I'd failed being male, and all the ways society had punished me for that failure.

But being non-binary offered a place to step away from the pains of maleness and masculinity and look at my body—penis included—and see it first as mine, not as society's.

I don't see my hair as man, my fatty boobs as woman, I don't see my small feet as female and my cock and bollocks as a big lumbering justification for structural dominance. My body is just mine. It belongs to me. My penis is femme; my penis is masc; my penis is an alien; it's soft, a flower; it's hard; it's anything I wish it to be. It is a site for pleasure. Pleasure that I deserve, that I am learning to receive. I don't have to make my pleasure smaller for someone else's to be bigger.

So, this year, Valentine's Day is dedicated to my penis, my flower, my junk, my thing that doesn't make me male or female because it's mine and I am neither. And thus ends my queering of Valentine's Day. I'll take a table for two at Carluccio's—one for me and one for Brenda, my penis.

17th February / le 17 février

Last night I had dinner with Ace; Lara, who was in iconic form; and his godmother, who is a living icon. She's perhaps the most cutting person I've ever met and routinely throws boulders midconversation. Such things as "Aren't you a little fat for that top?" or "This story's offensively dull." It sounds vicious, but once you immerse yourself in those acidic waters, it's remarkably refreshing.

As is often the way at these drunk dinners when a drag queen is present, the conversation progressed to talk of drag. "It's misogynist," Ace's godmother rattled. "You're allowed to do so many things that women aren't allowed to do because you're 'brave' enough to sacrifice your maleness and put on a dress."

It's a difficult question—the one about drag being anti-feminist. Sure, a lot of cis male drag queens do exploit femininity and femaleness in ways women wouldn't be celebrated for doing. The most common portrayal of drag in mainstream culture is by and for cis men only— look at *RuPaul's Drag Race*.

But labelling all drag misogynist—and don't get me wrong, a lot of it is—reduces gender and identity down to a deeply boring and limiting binary in which men are men and women are women and any transgression from these oppressive posts is misogynist. It leaves no room for exploration.

"I disagree," Ace responded to his godmother. "I'm not a woman so I can't know what it feels like, but do you not think drag, when done cleverly, smartly, can actually undermine the way femininity is loaded with so many expectations from society?"

We all swilled back our red wine. It was all frightfully middle-class, the kind of dinner I shamefully revel in.

"For me, all I know is that drag saved my life," I

piped up. "When I put on drag, I'm never thinking about becoming a woman, I'm always thinking about disentangling myself from the concept of maleness that has always brought me pain—both from the outside and inside—because I was too feminine for it."

Ace agreed.

"My drag definitely started as misogynist—empowering me to act slutty while women around me were shamed for it. But I think a lot of us, whatever gender, are having these conversations now," I said.

We're all learning. Well, everyone except the powerful, stuffy men who go on and on about Political Correctness Gone Mad (such a nineties debate, literally get over it). But while they drone on, we're here spending time learning how to get it right, do it better, fight for inclusion and as broad a range of nuanced viewpoints and opinions as possible. We are, simply, progressing beyond the tiny minds of the tiny men who, for centuries, made us feel tiny. The picture is shifting, slowly.

We talked all of this through, our conversation lubricated by, like, three more bottles of wine; I lost count. "I think I was wrong actually, perhaps drag isn't always misogynist, just most of the time," Ace's godmother retracted. She was a little shocked at herself. Then we had Viennetta and talked about whether football was homophobic.

It defo is.

21st February / le 21 février

This morning I woke up to find this guy from high school had gone through every Facebook profile picture of mine and commented "fagget [*sic*]," which I found weirdly funny.* This random guy, one I literally forgot existed, took the time to misspell *faggot* under 267 of my profile pictures, one of which he's actually in! It's truly comical to imagine someone sitting in their bedroom obsessively copy-pasting such a non-insult beneath every image. It should be noted I'm not laughing at him for misspelling—that's just classist.

I am a faggot; I got the memo way back when I watched Christina Aguilera's "Beautiful" video and saw those two men being stared at for kissing, realising to my terror (and eventual joy, like ten years later) that they were me. Being a faggot is not a problem for me.

I find these comments oddly validating for two reasons, and both of them make me laugh somewhat smugly. One—if you've got this much time on your hands, your life is certainly not as exciting as mine. Two—if you think this is something that will offend me, because you obviously think it will, I'm glad I don't fit inside your worldview. It's way better where I'm standing.

Of course, the Crystal part of me wants to drag his

---

* I reckon this rogue commenter is probably gay. (Although not all homophobes are secretly gay, and I think when people say this, it removes accountability from the person dishing out the abuse. We wouldn't say all arachnophobes are spiders.)

ass all over the internet and send my friend Beth's rock-hard boyfriend round to his house to deck this loser. But, no. I take the high road, dragging Crystal up it with me, kicking and screaming.

Anyway, off to the dry cleaner's to pick up three sequinned gowns that had started to stink.

I love being a faggot.

22nd February / le 22 février

Today was all about Denim. We had our first meeting in ages.

We've all taken time to try different things, subsequently failed, and are committing to the original girl band. So, there we were, pulled back together and in need of the nourishment that is our drag family. I like to think of drag and queer families like quilts: all patched together from different places, offering different things. We all play roles of mothers and children, make-up artists and cash machines: each stepping up when another might be in need. It's reciprocity in the most beautiful way. It's fighting, and forgiving, the way you do with siblings.

We spent the day excited, talking about the things we want to say and do and portray, and who Denim are now (now we're in London and not at university, where it all began). We agreed that the way forward was to launch a full-scale attack of delusion: "From now on we are the biggest band in the world," Glamrou explained.

Fake it till you make it.

We spent a while budgeting and came to the realisation that it's no good budgeting if the money doesn't exist. Glamrou decided they could afford a grand on their credit card—an offer we all softly protested but eventually took because we all knew it was the only option. Bless her.

As for the show, we've decided it will be about gentrification and Soho losing its queer spaces because of a strange life cycle it seems that only queer places undergo, a life cycle that seems particularly accelerated right now, which looks something like this:

1. It opens.
2. Queers have it for about a month, in which time it becomes a little pop-up utopia.
3. A subculture magazine writes an article about how amazing it is.
4. Straights get a whiff, stampede the place, queers stop going: paradise lost.
5. It's no longer cool in the way aforementioned subculture magazine decided it was.
6. Custom declines.
7. Rent goes up (6 and 7 are interchangeable/ simultaneous).
8. It closes.

It's been pretty buzzed over as an idea, but people have kind of stopped talking about it—except the amazing activist group Friends of the Joiners Arms. The fight for the future of the LGBTQIA+ spaces in London and the world over has felt like a losing battle. These community spaces are more important than just being venues for a drink, a dance, and a hookup. They're emergency rooms for people who can't express their sexuality, their desire, their gender, and their dance moves anywhere else for fear of violence.

It's our job, as the biggest band in the world, to make a literal song and dance about this.

25th February / le 25 février

Today was my first day on the drag job Ellie promised me would be "on my own terms."

"Oh my God, what was it like?" Ellie laughed down the phone to me.

"Well, I thought it was going to be like street performing, which I found pretty bleak as an idea anyway. But turns out I'm selling spiced cider and putting on an 'old cockney fishwife accent'—how your boss described it—and saying things like 'Yar come for mama's awwwd spiced cider, the best in awl the land!' I even blackened out a tooth."

Ellie was literally howling.

Given the number of guys I've shagged in East London, all of whom I've told I am a successful journalist—something I've decided I might try to have a go at, proper, now I'm back in London—meant that every time some bearded bear who looked as if I might have sat on his dick went past, I had to put my face to the wall.

As I peeled off an eyelash on the overground home, recounting my day over the phone to a hysterical Ellie,

five queer femmes looked over at me in full solidarity—
they, too, understanding what it feels like to be a shiny
queer token.

At least it paid in cash—forty-five quid. Although I
spent six pounds of it on a spiced cider. Which I would've
stolen but the boss was watching me with his bastard
cokey hawk eye.

Welcome to the worst part of drag: the money jobs.

27th February / le 27 février

The tradition of the nightly family dinner is fairly new
to me. My family, because of my mum's and dad's work
schedules, usually scooped dinner (made by one of my
parents) off the breakfast bar (which was cluttered with
piles and piles of ironing, from which we'd excavate a
single garment and iron it in a rush if it was needed),
and then we'd crowd around the TV. All four siblings
squished on one sofa, punching one another so hard we
bruised to win control of the remote. The worst nights
were when my dad got it and would make us watch the
fucking news, which was, back then, unimaginably boring and insignificant to a group of teens who just wanted
to watch *Will & Grace* (my sister and me) or *The Simpsons*
(my brothers).

But at Ace's house the family dinner is an important part of their bonding ritual. Every night, around
8:00 p.m., we set the table, the plates, the rock salt in a
beautifully decorated pot, and sit on plastic school chairs
painted by Ace's mum in different motifs that all mis-

match in that perfect unified way I could never pull off. One a landscape, one a person, one a still life of a pink flower. She's cool.

A bottle or two of red wine is shared as a starter, and we'll graze olives and talk about our days. And then Lara will present the table with something made in one pot and delicious—perhaps her famous bolognese, or a hunter's stew or something chicken. We all tuck in, salivating. It feels too trite to tell the family how much this inclusion means to me.

Most nights there's a guest—a friend of Ace's mum's from art school back in the day, or a friend from his sister Savannah's group, which is merging into Ace's and my group—all of us hitting the gay clubs in a gaggle every Saturday, sharing tinnies of Red Stripe and cheap bottles of wine. Sometimes a tequila shot if someone's been paid.

Anyway, tonight William came for dinner.

I tried to make other plans but it seemed as if everyone else in the world were busy at a theatre opening or a gallery opening or opening their legs. Annoying. Why do all my friends have to be so sex positive?

"Have you guys met?" Savannah asked, unaware how many times we had indeed met, and how many times Crystal and I have plotted William's "tragic," "accidental," "whoopsie" death, me ending up as the shoulder for Ace to build a relationship on.

"I don't think so?" William replied, knowing full fucking well how patronising that is, because we met about seven times back when he and Ace first started dating three years ago. Having my name forgotten is something that infuriates me hugely. I always say that if I don't have my memorability I've got squat.

Anyway back to dinner: there's William pretending he doesn't know me, which has tipped me over the edge. So Crystal, unable to hold back, said, "I've completely forgotten your name! Remind me?"

It obviously infuriated him, too.

One point to me.

"I thought Ace would've mentioned me? We've been spending so much time together recently," he said, smirking, dimples deepening in his cheeks (which would make a gorgeous punchbag).

One point to him.

> *Round one—Crystal the Queen versus William the*
> *Posey Douchebag. Ding ding ding.*

"Nope, Ace hasn't mentioned it at all," Crystal zings.

It was tense in the ring. Everyone else watched as if we were uppercutting each other in slow-mo. (Obviously, I was Hilary Swank in *Million Dollar Baby*.)

"We don't really talk about this kind of stuff though, right, do we?" Ace offered meekly, trying to defuse the fight between his best friend and his boyfriend(ish?).

"Oh, so you're not as close as I thought then?" William said, feigning innocence.

Damn, he's good. Point to him.

"We're closer than you can understand, probably. I think romantic love at such a young age is doomed, it's a dead cert, there's statistics and everything. Platonic friendships, especially among queers, that's true love."

I honestly can't believe I said that in front of Ace's family. I felt deeply childish, like I was back in my thirteen-year-old bedroom with my friend Leyah fighting with boys from other schools over MSN. I feel bad for Ace. I'm aware I'm being fully shit here, not considering his feelings at all.

Two points to me though, a good burn. If a little pathetic.

"Dinner! Chicken! Just for you, William!" Lara shrieked as she plonked a shredded roast bird in our shared eyeline, William's and my gaze fixed like a savage lioness's on its prey, both of us unsure who will be the victor.

Round two—Crystal the Great versus William "I'm so cool I grew up in London blah blah I love literature blah blah blah." Ding ding ding.

"Ace told me you're unemployed at the moment?" The bastard. One to William.

"I thought you didn't know who I was, William?" Nice one, Crystal.

He fumbles.

"Anyway," we cut him off, "I've actually just got an amazing new job! Someone heard about what a good singer I am and they've hired me to sing at the weekends in this brilliant, really niche, but well-respected jazz bar in East London. I'd say come but you need a membership."

Wow. Lies. More points to me though.

"We'd love to, but I'm taking Ace away this weekend!"

William grabbed Ace's hand and stroked it while he said it, and Ace, in his shock, could do nothing but squeal like a ferret being stepped on.

I felt a weird quiver down my spine, like the one you feel when you're wanking and your parents pop into your head.

"Barcelona." William looked around the table as the family's eyes lit up.

A barrage of questions: "Where are you staying?" "What's planned?" "That's so romantic!" "Oh my God! You guys are so cute."

So many points to him. So many points my nose is broken, I'm on the floor, and I'm about to be tapped out.

One final try: "I'm not a fan of Barcelona."

A swing and a miss; everyone ignored me, and I fell to the floor, Crystal towering over me shaking her head in disgust. The family crowded William and gawked at his wonderful generosity, his amazing romance skills.

It's a KO for Crystal.

28th February / le 28 février

Tonight I have no plans, and Ace is on another date with William. They have just moved into the phase of posting mysterious pics of each other on Instagram—the silhouette of one of them with a backdrop of the raging club they danced in all night, atop the caption "London nights with this one . . ."

I've decided to leave the house, put on my headphones, a floor-length leather coat, and Christina Aguilera's saddest song,* full blast, coaxing the inevitable tears to fall. Blockbuster-romcom-style. I'm Katherine Heigl. This is my twenty-eighth dress.

29th February / le 29 février

After I left the house last night, I wandered around Wandsworth Common, tears spluttering from ducts, as I soundtracked my heartbreak to a Spotify playlist called "lonely ass bitch," which is followed by one other person. For a moment I felt somewhat slimy about swimming inside someone else's loneliness playlist, imagining them weeping while making this Demi Lovato–heavy selection. Spotify is strange like that: it makes you feel kind of small and insignificant by reminding you that other people have felt so bleak they made a whole playlist about it. Although that also makes me feel less alone, I guess.

After two hours, I found myself alone in the park, distraught and with one of those awful headaches that can only be induced from running out of tears.

I decided to wallpaper over my emotions via Grindr: the home of muscular-torso pics, the graveyard of emotional intimacy.† Frantically, I messaged the first twenty

---

* "Hurt," from the album *Back to Basics*.
† Disclaimer: I know a bunch of people who wound up in happy relationships from Grindr, not that it's always the end goal.

men on my home screen* the same "You up, fancy some fun?" message, one after the other after the other, literally copy-pasting.

I often think about how no-strings sex has always been a feature in the gay community. We were outlawed and classified as mentally ill, and so sexual promiscuity was a political act. Promiscuity is still political, in that it rails against normative regulation, but it's not illegal in the U.K. so it's a different kind of statement. Beyond politics, casual sex actually built much of this community—it's our way of finding touch and connection when there was little elsewhere.

So I started listening to Rihanna's sexiest song,† waiting for my knights in shining Grindr to message back, feeling 50 per cent turned on, 40 per cent aware of the gaping lacuna left by Ace's Instagram happiness, 5 per cent aware that a Grindr meet would in no way fill this gap, and 5 per cent terrified I was going to meet a murderer‡ who would stab me to death as I entered his house, lured by his promise of penetration.

I paced furiously across the common. I was quivering—the way elderly people in movies do when they have an orgasm—the tension between my extreme sadness and extreme sexual desire proffering an incredi-

---

* Who can afford Grindr XTRA at £3.99 a month?
† "Skin," obviously, from the album *Loud*.
‡ It's an awful stereotype, but every hookup or dating app user has been scared by unavoidable *Daily Mail* headlines that tell shocking tales of murder and catfishing. It's also our primal instinct to expect danger. All part and parcel of the thrill.

bly vulnerable brand of arousal where I either wanted to cuddle someone all night or get pounded at knifepoint.

"Obviously pounded at knifepoint."

I had two replies (from twenty messages, what a blow) and I instantly replied to them both. They asked for a dick pic, so I went behind a bush and took one with the flash on my phone so bright that the image looked like a Juergen Teller original. They both loved it.

I scheduled a shag with one, down the road, for an hour's time, and one with the other for which I instantly jumped into an Uber.

I arrived at location number one, pacing patiently, my muscles spasming uncontrollably—the Pre-Grind Shakes, as they're affectionately termed. His name on Grindr was Top4Bottom—radically imaginative. I walked up five flights of stairs to the fourth floor, irrationally irritated that there were more stairs than floors. Out of breath, I knocked on Top4Bottom's door, which swung open eerily fast—as if he'd been waiting for me right behind it. In these moments a slight terror always washes over you, filling your head with the standard questions like "Will he like me?" and "Do I like him?" and "Am I going to be murdered?" This guy looked as if he could be a murderer, but in a hot way. Problematic? Yes. But I don't know if fantasies and sexual desires are policeable in the same way as what you say and how you act. That said, having a type that falls on the lines of race or level of mascness, for example, can be bleak. This guy—who didn't offer his actual name—must've been sixtysomething, although the orange buzz of the lighting from inside his flat was made hazy by what smelled like weed smoke, so it was hard to tell exactly. He was tubby at the middle with slim legs, a bulldog tattooed on his right arm, with a bald head. He was wearing only slippers and white underwear, a rolled-up fag hanging out of his mouth. The gaps between his teeth were almost black, but I get off on certain types of dirtiness, and when he kissed me, I found my tongue sweeping across his front teeth trying to encounter some of that grime, which made my ass clench and my penis rock-hard.

I entered. He pulled me into the lounge and ripped down my pants, shoving his dick in, no condom, even though my party line on bareback is that I don't do it. But sometimes I let it happen. I often feel guilty afterwards, but in the moment my lack of responsibility makes me feel present and in control. He fucked me on the sofa, over a computer desk, and eventually he put me on my back in a kind of beige orthopedic chair, as he pile-drived/drove(?)* me, eventually withdrawing and coming all over my face from above.

Before I could clean up, he threw my stuff at me and told me to leave. For some fucked-up reason I found this incredibly hot and did as he said, leaving his house covered in his cum.

---

* A pile-driver is when the receiver lies on their neck, hips up, while the giver stands up, squats, and thrusts. According to Urban Dictionary, most porn stars can't do the pile-driver for long because they pass out when too much blood rushes to their heads. Top4Bottom and I managed just fine.

En route to Fuck Number Two's house, I kept think-ing about something Top4Bottom had said when he was in me: "Cover your nails, they're so faggy." I found a pub bathroom to clean up in and spent a minute looking at my nails in the mirror.

I did as he instructed and hated that I did. I love my three-inch neon-green-and-gold acrylics. I'm used to this kind of femme-phobia from self-hating gay men who can't stand to be associated with anything but mas-culinity, but in the street I never listen to it, and, sure, I don't want to have sex with it. But in this scenario it's easy to move the goal posts of who you are just to feel wanted.

> *"They* are *pretty faggy,"* Crystal slides in. *"But that's the intention, baby. They're fucking iconic."*

Fuck Number Two went much the same as Fuck Num-ber One, if a little less throw-down, and he wore a condom upon my asking. He also didn't have a problem with my nails and we chatted afterwards. He's a forty-four-year-old plumber and nobody at work knows he's gay.

I told him I was a drag queen and that everybody at work knows I'm gay.

He was absolutely stunned, unsure how to take this quite basic information. "But your pictures were so masc?"

I was naked, butt hole slightly agape after a double pounding, gagged, readying myself for Act 50 in the life story of any Grindr user: "Latent Homophobia from Gays Who've Just Bummed You." I've been in this exact situa-tion too many times—gay men, who have just been deep in your ass, spouting their issues with "drag queens" and "gays who rub it in your face" and "femmes." I went into his bathroom, cleaned up, and dressed. Crystal is much more nosy than I am, so at her will I spent a good three minutes snooping around his bathroom cabinets: meds for hair loss and acid reflux, intense medical-grade mouthwash, and a small picture of a small dog blu-tacked to the back of his toiletries cabinet. I thought this was sweet; Crystal thinks it's tragic: "Pets are so pedestrian." Upon my leaving, he didn't protest or apologise for being a femme-hating shit, even though I'd just let him piss in my mouth so I thought I deserved some small bean of respect. As I was saying bye, I saw the orange glow from Grindr reflected on his face; he was looking for his next (fingers crossed, more masculine!) hookup before I'd even left the house.

I'm over it. Am I over it?

"I'm *over it.*" ⧘

This is why I keep falling in love with my fucking friends. They don't have a problem with my nails; they love me because of them! I go to Grindr in times of sadness, hoping desperately to find someone who is looking for the thrill of an alternative approach to having sex, too. And too often I leave with a feeling of disappointment, rejected for some facet of my personality, and with a more deeply ingrained sense of disassociation from the gay male community. I'm sure my partners feel the same.

Grindr—built to make it easy to meet other gay

men*—has made our sexual appetites incredibly specific. On the app you can select your preferred height,
weight, age, race—your profile a faceless body beholden
to none of the social etiquette it would be in physical
space. The app is rife with blatant, seemingly accepted
homo-, femme-, and transphobia and tons of racism.
"No fats, no femmes, no Asians" is the usual profile tag-
line. So this radical site for sexual potential has, for
the most part, become a hunting ground for the classic
masc-on-masc shag and nothing else.

As evidenced by Grindr, we have more freedoms
than ever.† Now that we have the chance to be "normal"
and get married, it feels like a huge swathe of gay men no
longer want to engage with aspects of our culture that
gave us our "freedoms"—one of which is most definitely
drag, another is gender nonconformity, and another,
damn it, is these acrylic nails.

I feel numb with boredom as my brain whirs constantly over Ace. I feel numb about the blisters on the
ends of my little toes because of my new trainer heels
(imagine a stunning fitness shoe with a built-in four-
inch rubber heel) I'm wearing at the moment. The only
solution is to get undressed, get into bed, and furiously
masturbate.‡ So the cycle continues.

---

* Much like Tinder is for straights. The gays did it first because
straights can't seem to have a single original idea.
† Although it mustn't be forgotten that in some places such as Egypt
the state has used Grindr to hunt down gays.
‡ Neither Grindr meet finished me off, I should add. The usual,
frankly. Fuckers.

March / mars

I couldn't decide on what to wear today. My go-to look is over-accessorised with crap, but some days, such as today, I want to prevent people from staring at me, so I opt to tuck the more garish side of myself away for safe-keeping.

In moments like these, Crystal commandeers my psyche like a glamorous pirate invading an unstable ship, urging disappointedly to pick the most garish thing in my closet—"Fuck it: do sequins in the day, be your inner dinner lady, you pissing wimp!" I agree with her in principle, but in reality—a reality in which she certainly doesn't live—sequins in the day are the kind of thing that inspires the chucking of an insult or a can of Coke from an abusive, fragile passerby. So I bat her away and opt for safety.

Yet, when I left the house and walked down towards Clapham Junction station, my first encounter with another person was with a guy who kerb-crawled me for about three minutes, calling me a "faggot." Such effort!

"Probably wants to fuck you," Crystal reasons.

All my life people have stared at me and I've never known why—even when I'm me and not her. It's incomprehensible. To you you're just you and you don't stare at yourself. Unless you have a spot you need to squeeze.

These stares vary in their intent: sometimes it's like

"Whoa, there's a freak on the loose" and, on the other end of the spectrum, it's like "I see you, oh, beautiful gender non-binary body, and I accept you." I prefer the latter, but even those come with complications—a pinch of the patronising when I wasn't asking for anyone's approval in the first place. It's an issue that we congratulate people for not being homophobic, for not being transphobic, for not being misogynist. We say things like "God, your boyfriend is amazing" because he does the washing up and believes in equal pay; or "Wow! Your parents are so supportive" because they didn't kick you out when you revealed your homosexuality. But you don't applaud a fish for swimming, so why applaud someone for being a decent, nonviolent human being?

With expressions of gender, we're so often punished for how we transgress out of a prescribed role—because we're excessive, over-the-top, attention-seeking, we're regarded as the rightful recipients of abuse because "you brought it on yourself."

When I dress up, it's always for me, even though I've amassed so many stares because my presence makes people angry as it challenges other people's beliefs about what bodies should look like. But if those beliefs can't withstand questioning, then they aren't sound. When I dress up, I feel authentic, as if I've questioned what's around me and this is the result. I take ownership of the could-be wreckage of my body, after it's dodged the insults of countless people, and cover it in things that tell people who I am in the way I want to say it.

On days when I get kerb-crawled, when the energy in the air is febrile, I remember that it is I—we—who are lucky. We have been lucky enough to peek behind the curtain of life's binaries—something you'll see in abundance at any good drag show, where a whole world that exists behind that curtain is pulled into view.

DRAG PERFORMANCE MEMO: At a show tonight my friend Dinah Lux used the imagery of wealth to celebrate and mock it—like pretending to be exceptionally rich, living her own fantasy. I think it's enthralling, and Glamrou said, "If we're gonna live under capitalism for this moment, then queers deserve palaces."

2nd March / le 2 mars

Today I'm obsessing about four things:

1. The fact I can't get into my larger dress for the spiced-cider-stall gig tomorrow, and I have trawled every internet shopping site and there are literally zero options for a "plus-size drag queen." My dresses are all the largest size on the standard U.K. market, and I've finally tipped over the edge into the barely catered for "plus-size" category—especially if you want glamour. The only thing seemingly on offer is wrap tops that have been attacked by gaudy prints and jeggings. One site is for larger queens, but I kid you not the dresses are all called "sacks"—like "The Georgy Girl Sack Dress" or "The Miley Sack Dress." Nothing makes

you feel sexier than being relegated to the sack section.

2. The fact that last night I had an intense sex dream about Ace, and the whole thing was like a stop-motion movie of his six-pack tensing and relaxing. In the dream he was consenting to the sex. In reality he's in a relationship with William, officially, ever since their seemingly stunning trip to Barcelona, and I'm working on getting over it.

3. The fact that my desire for a man with a six-pack is weird, because my type was never toned. I'm finding this specifically confusing because for much of my life I was into sleeping with big, fat, older men, ones we gays and Lana Del Ray–aspiring girls might term Daddy or even Grandpa, in return for their calling me Son. Weird, I always thought, because I have a glorious nonsexual relationship with my wonderful father and both of my male siblings, so it confuses me that I spent almost all of my free time from the ages of fourteen to twenty-four—a decade—seeking out the oldest, fattest men I could find, saving them as "Daddy 1" or "Daddy 2" in my phone and then riding them like a donkey on the Blackpool seafront: tired, low stamina, but so much fun.

Back when it all started I was also very fat. I'm still fat, but my body has grown so the fat looks more "big," less "puppy." In Lancaster, there was little opportunity and no gay scene. I only ever had one friend who was gay and had never knowingly met a gay person before I came out at the

age of thirteen. Catholic school was full of homophobes (many of whom later turned out to
be gay).

My parents weren't sure what to do with a gay
kid, let alone a non-binary drag queen, and no
amount of booze will let me forget the look on my
mum's face when she found me at thirteen, in a
sequinned dress, singing along to Celine Dion on
the chaise longue in the dining room.

My best friends both adored me and fetishised
me, and the internet barely dialled up in those
days, let alone allowed a space for me to find like-
minded people. The only thing in my life, for a
long time, that was constant, supportive, and provided me with an escape from a fairly fear-filled
existence was food.

Greasy food, cheesy food, sloppy food, doughy
food, heavy food, rich food, unhealthy food, fizzy
food—any food that would make me feel full to
bursting, on the brink of being sick, so that in
that moment I was simply alone feeling my body,
filling the space that was usually occupied by
the gut-wrenching terror of life as a preteen drag
queen, exhausting myself by putting up a ferociously fab façade. A child who grew into a teen,
who grew bigger and bigger, who took up more
space, and who was eventually only bullied from
afar because, even though I was incredibly effem-
inate, I was bigger than everyone else.

My extreme eating and my obsession with being fucked by old men are linked. I refute the idea

that my sex with old men can find its entire basis in shame. However, over my years of proudly gobbing about these experiences, and as my circle became more emotionally intelligent, conversations eventually moved from "Yassss, queen, get that granddaddy dick!" to "Why do you think you have a desire for older, fat men? Of course that's fine, wonderful, if you do. But where does that specific need come from?"—they, especially the thin ones, being cautious not to come across as ageist or fattist, even though they are, just a little.

I used to say that older men are good in bed; they've done it all. In part reductive, but in part true.* But also I was fat. I had built my body to be invisible to normative desire and big enough to crush a bully; undesirable—scary, even—to my peers, but suitable for older men, who society thinks deserve less, especially in a world where youth allows you to overstep beauty standards a little. I always thought of myself as the worst possible option—I was fat, gay, femme, and pimply. So, as I was the embodiment of undesirability, my only option was desperate old men. An abuse of my position as a young person, but I had to get it somewhere.

But these fat, often unshowered older men genuinely turned me on. They still do. While I believed them to be my only option, I still wanted

---

* Especially with Stan, who has unfortunately passed away :(.

them to fuck me, and I wanted it so bad. It's your collective experiences that inform your desires, that's like Sex 101, and my collective experiences told me I was undesirable, so I found sexual solace in those more undesirable than me.

But these men taught me what it feels like to be desired, and in bed with them—or in the toilets of a florist or the freezer section of a food-delivery truck—I was free from all the disappointments I'd imbibed about my body.

But just in bed with them. Everywhere else was, and often still is, filled with self-loathing.

I can never seem to pin down exactly why, though. Yes, I'm intellectually aware it's all society's fault: my body is desexualised as a fat person, and it's also fetishised. Thin bodies equal attractive, and fat ones are taboo. Society is working overtime to force us all to consume in excess but then tells us never to show any external markings of said consumption. But whatever, I'm smart enough to know that this is just society's problem, not mine. But being aware of the societal structures around us—fashion, advertising, lads' mags, men's health mags, the body-fascist gay community—is not the same as ridding yourself of the feelings of self-loathing and learning that someone might want you in all your fat, femme, gay, spotty glory.

Capitalism hates everyone, but it really hates fat people: we remind others of the effects of all this consumption, and we take up space in a world that is obsessed with keeping people small and invisible. So the journey to accepting your fat body as something wonderful and powerful and sexual is more than just bandying about the terms *self-love* or *body poz*. It's about constantly pushing hard against set ups that desperately want you to fail. It's about upending everything you see, everywhere you go, by proving to yourself that the entire world is wrong about your body and you are not. It's about making outfits look good even though you saw them modelled on a tiny body. It's about remembering how much your body does for you even though you've never seen yourself in a fitness ad. It's about looking in the mirror and remembering that what's there is you. You're the only you, so how can you not be perfect?

I'm not yet at the place where I feel empowered enough to show my body publicly in a tight top, though. As a drag queen, that's tricky because people expect a certain level of b-o-d-y—and my looks have come under criticism, which is fucking annoying when the person saying, "You really need to step it up, you look like Adele on a Monday morning," is some random from uni's straight boyfriend who works in a hedge fund and is definitely wearing a mark-down suit from Debenhams. But those words hit. Right now a tab is open on my computer that says "wikiHow: Burn away stretch marks."

I forgive myself for these moments. We are all learning to love ourselves all the time—and

there's no end to it because every time you man-
age to chip away at the internalised hatred, you
clock another ad or read a statistic, and you internalise yet again. It's not about the five-step guide
to loving your bod whatever its shape. No. Instead, it's about learning to just be in your body.
Not to fill it up with food, or granddaddy dick,
or compliments from a loving partner. It's about
learning to let go of feeling full of, and hence dis-
tracted by, something external; it's about dropping comparisons between yourself and other
bodies; it's about having the courage to sit with
your body in its reality, for a moment, as a body
that exists. I have never done that, but I'm trying.

4. The fact that I had KFC for lunch and dinner yesterday, and I want it again today.

3rd March / le 3 mars

"It's called Wally. Annoying word in itself, but basically
a radiator fell off the wall the day after I moved in and it
had *Wally* scrawled on the back of it in blue permanent
marker, so I just thought it was a sign. Like, 'Whoa, this
is a sign,' I thought. And then, that night, I had to sleep
under a table under a bunch of cardboard boxes because
the lock on the door wasn't working and I couldn't afford a bed and so I used the radiator to prop the door shut
like in a crap action movie or something and then I felt
invincible and that's the power of Wally. So we named it
Wally. Do you think it feels like it's called Wally? I want

to respect the space by getting its name right, you know. I mean, to me it feels like Wally."

This is Hatty. She's tiny framed, flat-chested, with a head that she describes as "a pea," and hair that is accidentally bigger than any drag queen's I know because she cuts it herself and rarely washes it so tufts stand up. Like a budget mullet that's way more visionary than your standard East London one.

Hatty can pull off a budget mullet better than you or I can pull off a crew cut, black jeans, and a T-shirt. I've never met anyone else like Hatty. I don't know her well yet, but I also feel as if I've known her for hundreds of years, in past lives, which I don't believe in but Hatty tells me are definitely real. She's an oversharer, like me, and talks faster than anyone might believe is physically possible. From what I can glean, all of her clothes are various items of nightwear layered over one another in absurdly random patterns that look absolutely genius in combination. She has two pairs of shoes—one awful pair of brown boots, which she once pissed in when she was trying to break into Glastonbury and felt bad about urinating on farmland, and another huge pair of iridescent creeper boots, which are way cooler than they sound.

Everything about her is bathed in queerness. She's artistic and considers things in ways I genuinely would or could never. Like, if you ask a question about her shoes, Hatty, instead of answering, will spend the next four minutes pontificating about shoes and gendered labour. She's right, when I think about it, and I'm obsessed with her, with all of this.

But she's not patronising; she's just unbridled her brain from normative modes of thinking that all of us still get caught up in. Hatty feels like the future. As if she's seen beyond today and has arrived into a new place where everything and anything can be radical and queer. When you're with her, it's like having synesthesia—all words becoming colours and moments becoming images and sounds becoming emotions.

Wally is her home. I use the term *home* lightly because it's a total mess and the walls are filled with asbestos and they might bulldoze the place at a moment's notice. We met because we've been rehearsing Denim here for the past few weeks. Wally is this giant warehouse on the Commercial Road, "the most polluted road in Europe," Hatty told me proudly, enshrining her narrative in the artfulness of being poor—which she is, very.

This old office building has had all its fittings gutted out. The brown-carpeted, yellow-stained-walled, asbestos-laden skeleton was what remained. Until Hatty redecorated the place. It's now bestrewn with chiffon and artwork she found on the street that has deep gouges she scratched into it while doing her "wanking art: which is where I wank with one hand and then scratch paintings with another because I want to see what a visually realised wank looks like. It always looks really bleak and cloying, and kind of painful—never pleasurable, even though I can have up to twenty orgasms a day, it still hasn't translated onto the painting. Sometimes I wank and scratch about things that aren't even sexual: like playing the Pyramid stage or being a notable musician and then writing a book called *Just Queens*, à la Patti Smith but more real. I always get really bored the moment they start to 'make it' in that book. Maybe that's my problem. I don't know."

I think Hatty is the most unpretentiously artistic person I've ever met. I feel like a baby queer in her presence—my flawed politics kowtowing as she sets me straight (not in the het way) about things I find confusing, such as how sexuality can be so rigid when gender is so fluid. "I think it's about masc and femme and words we don't have for everything in between, them all swirling into a big spiral when you're attracted to someone. We're all everything, or we can be, so genitalia is as much of a lie as the Tory government working hard for everyone, or the fact that you told me that blond is your natural colour. There's no need to lie—hair dye is my favourite invention."

In this house, this Wally, she's created a utopia: since we've been rehearsing here, I've seen queer photographers come to take queer photos, queer barbers chop people's hair into queer hairstyles, a group of trans women rehearsing a dance they're hoping to perform for International Transgender Day of Awareness. I've seen Hatty naked about thirty times in x number of days/hours/visits.

Hatty asked me to move in, one night after rehearsal when I stayed for dinner.

"Rent's thirteen a week, ridiculous I know, and there's loads of spare rooms on account of everyone moving out because they all wanted real jobs and real stability. How boring. We'll have to pack away the beds every morning in case there's a random inspection—the property-guardianship people assume it's just me living here, which is why the rent is such a steal. All three toilets are broken so you have to pee in the sink. But there's a loo in the café over the road, which they let you use if you need to poo."

I need to tell Ace that I'm splitting us up. Not that he's been home for five days. Perhaps this'll be for the best. Or perhaps it'll be the perfect way to ensnare him, by getting him to miss me, yearn for me, then turn up on bended knee.

5th March / le 5 mars

> What you up to tonight?

A text from Ace.

> Am supposed to be seeing Ethan. You?

I replied.

> Oh, Ethan. I thought he was in Berlin. Was supposed to be seeing William, but he cancelled, says he needs some time apart. Would love to catch up with you . . . feels like it's been ages x

So frustrating. A month ago I would have, and did, drop everything to spend any time I could with Ace.

In New York we'd speak most nights, and I'd cancel dinner plans with friends just so I could account for Ace's schedule, so I could see his face, so I could firmly keep half of myself in London. He never asked me to, but I did it nonetheless. And that shut out the potential of a fuller picture in New York. They say love is blind: I say it's antisocial.

But here, in London, even though I've been living under his parents' roof, we're more distant than we've ever been. Still hyperaware of where the other is in a room or what they're doing most nights—fully entangled in each other in microscopic ways that take more than a series of Grindr dads doing increasingly sketchy piss things to you to obliterate.

In matters of the heart it's a waste of time trying to diagnose the other person, where they're at, what they're feeling. But if I were to diagnose, hypothetically, I would say that the potential promise versus potential risk of what seemed like a budding romantic relationship between Ace and me all became quite overwhelming for us both. Then, when William reappeared, he provided Ace with an easy out—a way to escape complex emotions and, instead, tread old, safe, risk-free ground.

My hypothetical diagnosis isn't getting me anywhere since I'm essentially rendered speechless whenever Ace asks me the most basic questions, like "Do you want a cup of tea?" or "How are you?," because I don't want

to accidentally blurt out my inner monologue in which
we're pregnant with each other's child. But the result-
ing silence hardly makes me an enthralling prospect.
Crystal knocks about my head whenever he's around
and screams at me to pull myself together. If she had
her way, I'd just fuck the consequences and get on the
floor, open my mouth, and flick my tongue about, miming anilingus, at Ace's knees.

But instead I retain shreds of hope here, hold on to
the subtle wording of texts there, read every smile or cup
of coffee as a secret code that actually means "It's you,
Carrie, it's always been you," without his actually saying
it. I'm bored of myself and how pathetic my devotion is.

So I replied:

> Yeah, he's back! And he just broke up with
> his boyfriend so we're going out-out! Sorry,
> we must catch up soon though. When are
> you next free? xxx

> Sure thing, have fun then! Maybe tomorrow
> night? We could go to that Italian in
> Peckham everyone's said is really good?
> Or to Zeret Kitchen—your fave! x

I'm supposed to be having dinner with friends from
my new, awful job, but I see them all the time and I find
their enthusiasm for this pitiful job deeply jarring. And
Zeret Kitchen *is* my favourite.

I would love that. Zeret Kitchen, 8pm?
Should I book?

Crystal is trembling with excitement. *"Just fuck*
him already, this is humiliating. When I was trying to
bag my third husband, the Sultan of Brunei—awful
guy, but he has a yacht named Tits *with two lifeboats*
named Nipple 1 *and* Nipple 2, *after mine—I fucked*
him within seven seconds of meeting him. I just dropped
to my hands and knees and he put it right in. Same
with James Franco, but he used his whole arm. Which
got stuck, sadly, and he had to self-amputate. There's
a movie about it."

6th March / le 6 mars

Dinner at Zeret Kitchen was lovely and featured a many-
layered conversation I didn't think I'd be having, plus
Crystal shouting curse words at me as it became clear
the night wasn't going to end with a bang.

So, Ethan is this guy I was once very much in love
with. He was my best friend at university (there's that
pattern of destructive behaviour), where (for the first
two years until he moved to Berlin and swiftly shacked
up with a thinner, cooler, smarter, more masculine version of me) we spent every waking minute together. We
used to get grotesquely smashed on the cheapest red wine
known to man—Sainsbury's Basics, which came in a
plastic bottle—then dance for each other in his bedroom.

He would perform full lip-syncs to the oddest songs he'd heard at his favourite club night in London, Horse Meat Disco, and every time term started he'd arrive with a whole new arsenal of bangers, for which he'd spend the night showing me his choreographed dances—my favourite routine being for Raquel Welch's "This Girl's Back in Town." I would lip-sync diva ballads to him—Celine, Shania, Mariah, Bassey, Tina, Cher, the lot—and we would move closer and closer and closer, stripping to our underwear and dancing more and drinking more, but never actually kissing. I used to walk home from his house at 4:00 a.m. in the pouring rain and listen to "Beautiful" by Christina Aguilera and imagine us being together, reading books, with lots of houseplants and an ailing dog. Funny how hindsight makes you feel so normative.

Over dinner I told Ace about a conversation I'd had with Ethan the night before in the dingy smoking area of G-A-Y—a place I'd vowed never to end up in again on account of the owner being a racist, but quickly realised there wasn't anywhere else to end up in that wasn't mostly composed of pushy bears—a category into which Ethan and I both fit, but refuse to fully descend into. Yes, I'm a bear, but only physically. It's wild that these weird categorisations of gays based on body type and body hair and body fat percentage seem to dictate the sexual behaviour of most in the scene. It's another bunch of binaries we can too easily dissolve into. Anyway, in the smoking area Ethan and I were, for the first time, completely honest about the feelings we'd once had for each other: we'd once loved each other but we weren't in love anymore.

As I told this to Ace, I worried he might think I was dropping hints. But I wasn't. I realised that I needed to get to that place with Ace, too. To decimate these feelings and end up as simply a best friend, which is clearly what he wants on account of his, I dunno, having a boyfriend who is the opposite of me.

Then Ace opened up to me about William and told me about the worries he was having—

> *"Once a cheater, always a cheater,"* Crystal interjected, even though William's not a cheater, but it's Crystal's motto on most men because all of her husbands (eight in total) have left her for their secretaries, except the one who died in a mysterious yacht fire.

But I didn't say that to Ace, and I managed to remove myself from my position of "in love" and offered him advice as a best friend. Frankly, I was proud of myself. In that moment, I did want their relationship to work out because it hurts me more to see him sad than to see him with someone else.

As we left the restaurant to get the night bus home, I told him about Wally and moving out. I think we both sensed it was the end of a (relatively short, disappointing) era, one that was originally imbued with so much potential, potential never explored. But I also felt emotionally closer to him than I had in months.

Maybe it's better, in the end, to be close to him than to be with him.

Of course if he knocked on my door right now and said he wanted to be with me, I would jump at the chance.

I just waited for three minutes to see if he would. He didn't.

So for now we are back to being best friends who would die for each other. The best feeling I've had since I fell in love with him.

12th March / le 12 mars

Today, I dragged my one broken suitcase from the doors of my first home in London to the asbestos utopia in the east.

Ace helped me to pack up my room: he folded bits of fabric and hole-filled T-shirts, collected all the cigarette filters I'd scattered across the floor and put them in a little leather smoking pouch he was donating to me as he had decided to give up smoking. All my friends are doing that. Such sheep.

I went downstairs to make us both a coffee, and when I came back, he'd set up his parents' record player on the chest of drawers in my room and dropped the needle on a vinyl of my favourite album, Celine Dion's *Let's Talk About Love*. I used to feel so ashamed about how uncool it was to love Celine Dion. But then, after some schooling from Crystal, I worked out that you're only cool if you're not pretentious, so I wrote a Facebook status update* coming out to the world as an obsessive Celine Dion fan. I never felt more cool.

This move from Ace was significant because he loathes Celine Dion and he's never been good at organising surprises. He often forgets birthdays or Christmas presents, but makes up for it by delivering all of his wondrous charm when in your company, or getting you a present when you actually need it. People let him off because when you're with him, you're with him. Ace is present, and in today's distracting, virtually obsessed world that's a rarity. We listened through the tracks that had made me. This was the album I played so much when I was twelve years old and terrified of who I was that it melted under the heat of the CD player. It was the album I bought four different times.

The limits of language don't stretch far enough to express my gratitude to Celine Dion for all she's done.

Ace and I spent the first few tracks stifled, cricking around each other, not looking at each other, me with the odd dramatic single tear running from my eyes, brought out by this moment soundtracked by Celine. Ace seemed similarly moved, aware this was the end of something, but he tried hard not to show it, blinking furiously to spread the beginnings of tears across his rainy eyes.

---

* I found it: "Dear Friends, I have been meaning to get this out in the open for a while. I am a die-hard Celine Dion fan. There, I have said it. I am out of the closet. And it feels so good. Thanks for your support in this difficult time xxxx."

When track six came on ("Tell Him," a duet with Barbra Streisand), I blushed at the number of times I'd listened to it, playing out the different ways I might "tell him"—Ace—how we could be together.

But instead of telling him I asked him to dance with me.

He led, even though he's smaller than me, and for a micro-moment we were together. There was no world outside the four-minute-and-fifty-one-second song. As it reached its climax, Ace bleated, "I could, you know."

"I know."

"It just feels too risky. I don't want to limit what we could be. Or the future. Or something like that."

"I know. Let's just listen to the song. Let's just see how it all goes."

Then he kissed me—both of our lips covered in tacky shades of pinkish lip gloss we'd been messing around with while packing. It wasn't a kiss full of promise or sex, or a kiss testing our potential. It was a kiss full of respect. A kiss that made me feel my value.

15th March / le 15 mars

Since I moved to Wally, I've been awash in new feelings, phases, spaces. Last night, some members of the trans dance group Hatty hosts came and hung out and we talked about passing and being trans—opinions differing, with some of us wanting to absorb into the category of passing, and others wanting to be known and seen as trans or visibly non-binary.

"Am I trans?" I had addressed the table.

They all laughed. "We can't answer that."

"Probably not," one of them added. "Plus there's no laser that will remove all of that chest hair."

Then we erupted into a conversation about surgery and how it does not define the trans experience.

I love my new home.

Hatty's boss also came over, after the dancers had dissolved into the sunset. He's a big, surprisingly camp, gay bear who works in a coffee shop and wears the signifiers of his leather-and-fisting fetish all over his body—ring tattoos on his arms, a handkerchief in his back pocket as a hieroglyph of the old gay hanky code, high-shine polished leather boots with thick soles that he evidently takes pride in and polishes "every Sunday" after they've probably been covered in piss, shit, cum, and lube after a night down the hole of some fisting-bottom twink.*

We drank tequila. When Hatty left to get some more from E2 Local, the leather bear bent me onto the table with the forcefulness of a stern maths teacher and started fingering and rimming my hole, consent agreed upon the moment he'd walked in the door earlier that night after exchanging one of those exhilarating "Oh . . . this is on!" looks. He fingered it for near twenty minutes—one finger, two fingers, four fingers, and loads of lube (which he keeps in his backpack). He teased my hole with his

---

* *Twink:* gay slang for "thin, white, into no kinks." Like if Harry Potter were gay he'd be a twink, or Abraham Lincoln, or the Backstreet Boys.

erect penis, but we both knew he was more into hands in the ass.

Hatty walked in on us and didn't bat an eyelid.

Ten minutes later, he pulled my head back and asked if I wanted him to fist me. "Well, it doesn't hurt right now, and that's four fingers, how bad can it be?" I asked naively.

Turns out it was bad, real bad. The moment he got knuckle deep, I yelped at him, "Get out of my hole." Crystal loved it, but I couldn't take the pain. We both lost interest and said our goodbyes with air kisses; he washed his hands and left.

Today, I spent the day at Shoreditch House,* my arse red-hot all day. I've gone from trans to fisting pig to yuppie in the space of a day. East London, while somewhat manic, feels like everything I've always dreamed of.†

DRAG PERFORMANCE MEMO: At Bethnal Green Working Men's Club, Chiyo used the voice recordings of famous politicians telling lies, and during each one they fell to the ground—throwing their whole body across the stage. Was v powerful and effective, painful, but politically invigorating. And they didn't have to say a word. Find me anyone else who could do that?

---

* A deeply insecure-making place upon which membership depends upon having a good body and swimming in the roof pool on a Monday and pretending you're successful and hot enough to not have a job.
† Bar the yuppie bit: turns out that category is full of men who think craft beer is a revolution and go to gym classes where they get called "rebels." People who pay to be called rebels should be buried alive.

16th March / le 16 mars

You know what I fucking hate? I hate the terms used for people with large social media followings. *Disrupters. Influencers.* The worst: *zeitgeist shapers.*

Off to work on the pissing spiced-cider stall this afternoon and I'm pissed off. Why can't I be an influencer? How stunning would it be to just post a pic and get cash in the old account? I once heard that Kendall Jenner charges one hundred thousand dollars to post a picture of her wearing a brand, and she doesn't even have to tag it.

I don't know how inspiring an influencer I would be, I guess, which is maybe why I still haven't hit three thousand followers. Like, "Here's a pic of me hungover at my spiced-cider stall dressed as a fishwife" or "Here's a pic of me asleep on the loo"—don't know how much Kurt Geiger would be into sponsoring that post. Although now I read it back, that's the kind of prime content I'm desperate for.

Got to run—need to black out my front tooth before work.

18th March / le 18 mars

Last night was Denim's first London gig ever, and more gays were in attendance than on Ticketmaster when Gaga drops tickets.

Our vocals were a bit wobbly, but the joyful thing about being a drag queen is that you can get away with a shit ton of mistakes. You're already offering a service of empowerment—you're showing people an alternative way of being powerful, happy, joyful, smart, and that you don't have to be an oppressive douchebag to achieve this—and in that powerful space you're also showing people that perfection is not the ideal.

It's become our tradition to end our sets singing "Spectrum" by Florence + the Machine because it's a fucking good song.* When we started verse one, the room erupted into screams as Florence Welch herself walked onstage, grabbed a mic, and sang it with us. We promptly all died; none of us had spotted her in the crowd, and we teetered on the edge of hard-core fan-girling but also wanting desperately to impress her.

After the show we asked everyone to clear their chairs for a dance floor, then our beautiful soft butch friend DJ Soft Butch played back-to-back Emma Bunton and that song "Sweet Like Chocolate" by Shanks & Bigfoot. Then we did a party set—and we invited some amazing drag kings and queers to perform.

As we filed out, 3:00 a.m., I probably heard about fifty people saying it was the best night of their lives. For me, it was the second best. The best was the time I saw Celine Dion at the O2 Arena.

---

* And because gender and sexuality are both a spectrum.

24th March / le 24 mars

"We'll try really hard, but we might get it wrong," my parents say over breakfast. They're in London visiting.

Now, I've come out to them a bunch of times—as gay, as a drag queen, as a failed vet.* They are, at this point, regular, perhaps even eager, spectators of my fumbling my way out of the latest closet into something new. I had entered yet another one about seven months ago, when I decided to change my pronoun to they/them/their and couldn't find the words to tell Mum and Dad.

I was oddly nervous about this. Once they'd got over my being a drag queen, they quickly settled on calling me "she" when I was dressed up, onstage, trying to present as a her. But this non-binary business is less grounded in traditional signifiers and is more of a head-scratcher for them: nothing has changed about my day-to-day appearance, not outside of the ways it usually changes with how I'm feeling. This is more steeped in intellectual concept, and I can see them both trying hard and failing to get their heads around the idea that there's more than male and female. They've seen me jump between the two genders, and they totally get that, but I can see their faces warping with confusion at my telling them I'm not either one. My dad asks if this is the first step on the journey to transition. I think it's not, but I also didn't think about being non-binary until a few years ago—perhaps because it wasn't an option or

---

* Although the worst was the time I came home, and thus out, with blue hair for the first time. God, my mum freaked.

a well-known concept, or because I couldn't be bothered to come out yet again. But the internet got better and I got more lonely and spent more time working out my gender in relation to my desires and my body, rather than performing it for the adoring fans and homophobes on the streets of Cambridge or Lancaster.

I've known for a few years that using *they* fit me as perfectly as cheese fits on toast, but I didn't act on it because I worried about asking those around me for even more consideration. But as I met more and more people who used *they* comfortably, being non-binary slowly unbarbed itself in my mind. I spent a long while secretly anxious about being a burden, confusing people too much, worrying whether it would put me in the line of more violence. When I told my friends, it was like telling them I'd topped up the milk in the fridge or bought more detergent—welcomed, necessary, not a big deal.

With my parents, however, I felt twelve again—as if I had a secret that would be blown wide-open and cause my family dismay. How could I ask any more of these two people who have been through the big queer wringer in learning to understand me? I felt selfish. But after a week of their being in London and misgendering me—through no fault of their own—I launched into it with them over a casual breakfast on the last day of their visit.

"We'll try really hard, but we might get it wrong." They asked very few questions and we ordered breakfast and the Band-Aid was ripped off. I'm sure there will be more work to be done, the kind of rewiring my own brain took to replace *he* with *they*. But this coming out is different from other comings out with them because we all know it will be okay.

Sometimes people hear *they* as a rejection of gender, or as being "gender neutral." That is very much not the case for me, though for other people this is true. For me, a commonly used pronoun doesn't exist for what my gender is. I definitely have a gender, but it's defined by its fluidity between thousands, no, millions of factors—so how can there be one name for it? Glamrou complained over a drink last week how they feel about being misgendered, and it resonated with me: "It annoys me when people assume my gender, because my external body doesn't always match with what I feel inside—I mean, we're drag queens, and I often feel more myself in drag than I do out of drag."

What does drag say about gender? Well, loads of stuff. What's striking in the context of pronouns and drag is that some people are super quick to match pronouns to their external reading of you. Even though I have a beard, most people are au fait with gendering me "she" when I'm in drag. Sometimes we get men who can't cope with the mix of signifiers, don't know where to look, so they'll call me "lad" or "pal" or "dude" vigorously, as I'm standing there in a floor-length red-sequinned dress. They'll say, "You're so big you should try weight lifting," because they are trying to push me into their narrow conception of gender. I would wilt a little at this—and stay quiet for safety's sake—but Crystal is always ready to bite back with a good old straight bashing: "You won't be calling me 'lad' when you're begging me to swallow your babies after you've huffed a gram of coke." When she's up and out and fully dressed, she calls it like she sees it. I'm so intensely grateful that we're the same person.

But surely the very ability to flip and flit between categories because you, I dunno, dragged some make-up over your chops testifies to just how flimsy the whole binary structure is. It can be hard to communicate this flimsiness, or to survive within the system. But a *they* pronoun is like a starter pack, an easy in, a simple way for people to let you know they respect you.

Pronouns matter. They're about respect; about people deeming you worthy enough to try to understand you. When you're misgendered, or somebody purposefully disregards your preferred pronoun, it hurts; it jars with your notion of yourself—a self that is harder to preserve when people won't even call you something you asked to be called. When somebody does try, however, it feels as if they see you. And that feeling makes all of this thinking and fighting and coming out and pushing back and tears and abuse worth it. It's the little things.

25th March / le 25 mars

It's better to regret the things you've done than the things you never did.

I once read that in a book and memorised it. Or maybe Lily Allen posted it on Instagram. Or maybe Crystal made it up. I don't know.

Anyway, it can apply to so many things. Today, for example, I ate seven slices of Daim cake. Then, as I finished the eighth and final slice, after agonising over it for an hour, I regretted it but quickly agreed with myself that it was better to have eaten it, because I don't want to look back on my life and think, "I should have eaten that," you know?

Off to work again. Last night my parents came to see me on the stall—cute—but then my mum nearly choked on a piece of dried star anise that was floating in her cider. It was all a deep blow—both the near choking and the absurdity of this job and my parents seeing me in it. "This is lovely," my mum said, managing a wisp of smile, bless her. They must be so proud of their little fishwife all grown-up and making it in the big city.

26th March / le 26 mars

From my diary, a few years ago. Most of those old diaries are filled with the warbling of someone trying hard to be overtly pretentious. Perhaps it's age, or just being more comfortable with being a bit of a trash bag, that makes me confused as to whom the hell I was writing them for. At the time I wrote this diary I'm looking at, I was having class dysphoria, so it's all me trying to be middle-class. Lol. Some of it's good, though, reminds me why things are the way they are, reminds me why I love Ace.

> *Ace and I were lying in a wheat field, or something like wheat—long, brown, with sheaths and ears and a rustling sound when the wind blew, which it did, quite*

excessively. We would smoke about fifteen cigarettes before we left the field to go back to the cottage our friends had rented as a pre-finals getaway.

He asked, "What's the perfect relationship?"

"Emptiness?"

"Well, that's an annoying answer. Emptiness. Come on, this isn't a philosophy exam. Emptiness?"

"No, seriously, emptiness. That's what I think a perfect relationship is."

He was confused and obviously thought I was being slippery.

"Right, so I'm lying here—with you—in the middle of a field and I'm not feeling anything, but in a good way," I said—I'm paraphrasing after the fact here, but it was something like this. "I have no worry, no excess, no anxiety, and I don't feel as if I'm performing for you, which I do a lot, for other people. I feel, in the best possible way, nothing. Comfortable, empty, baseness.

"Just like I could say anything, at all, that comes into my mind. That's what the goal of a perfect relationship is. Right? Emptiness. Or maybe I mean fullness. Maybe real fullness feels like emptiness because nothing's wrong?"

"I think you're right."

We lay there for seven more minutes, emptiness abounding, but my heart brimming with hope as to how Ace's and my relationship is so perfectly full of emptiness.

Anyway, some years on, our relationship has taken on a different kind of emptiness. One in which we have stopped communicating, for about ten days. I'm all for a little distance, that's just the natural cycle of intense relationships, but this cold-turkey quitting each other feels like the wrong thing. I wonder whether I miss the anguish of it all, or whether I just miss my best friend.

31st March / le 31 mars

I promised myself not to write one more word in this diary about that heinous job on the spiced-cider stall in all of its fucking bleak hipster glory. And frankly, there's been nothing to report bar a bunch of dicks taking Insta pics of themselves with a real East London fishwife drag queen. If I'm ever famous, I can't wait for that moment in the biopic.

> *"When you're famous, darling. When you finally catch up with me."*

Yes, it's all been pretty non. Until last night. At the end of my shift, an intimidatingly handsome brunette bear plus big beard (so my type)* came over to enquire what I was doing. Both furious and ashamed, I handed him a spiced cider and asked for six pounds, which he paid as he explained he didn't actually ask for it. Still he paid. What a charmer.

We got to talking, then we got to kissing, indescribably fast. He was smart, with one big snaggletooth that

---

* The only thing that's more my type is a KFC.

was soon covered in my lipstick, and we laughed as I licked it off, my padded ass pressed against the creaking trestle table that supported the machinery for my spiced-cider side hustle, there on the bank of a canal just by Camden Market.

Kissing turned to canoodling, and as I cleared the cider equipment into the café my stall is attached to and closed the shop, he fingered me up the ass, grabbing olive oil from one of the inside tables as a kind of lube. Sometimes, when things like this happen, all I can hear is Crystal yelling in ecstasy at just how iconic we are.

"Get it, girl!" she screams as this guy enters me with his digits at my place of work. *"This is the perfect opener for my next large-print Mills and Boon epic."*

Fingering turned to his buying me a slice of artichoke pizza at Voodoo Ray's, turned to us hopping on a bus back to his flat in Dalston and having full-on sex three times in one night, watching reruns of *America's Next Top Model* in the interim, and bits of *Basic Instinct*, naked and wrapped in each other, each of us trying to do the Sharon Stone interrogation moment, opening our legs, our big bellies and flaccid willies hanging between them, and closing them swiftly, like coy murderesses.

I stayed the night, which is unusual, and in the morning we fucked again, this time really, really hard. So hard the condom broke and he came inside me. He'd been relaxed all night, but suddenly the easy-breezy-beautiful charm slid from his face.

"I'm HIV-positive," he gulped, obviously worried at how I'd take this. "I'm undetectable, but I'm still positive."

I collected my thoughts.

HIV casts a shadow on a lot of sex between queer folk. It's the first thing among many that we will be given misinformation about when we come out—to be careful not to "catch it." It's a mixture of both a very real potential that at any moment you might contract the virus—this virus responsible for the death of thirty-five million people worldwide, an incomprehensible figure, since it pierced the world in roughly 1983—combined with the stigma. Now there's PrEP* and undetectability, but you've got to learn about this on the job. In the most extreme cases people not in the know seem to think HIV is the same as AIDS (it's not) and seem to think it's a death sentence (it's also not). But that's where the stigma comes from—mass cultural misunderstanding, which continues deep into the queer community.

So, what's to know?

He's undetectable. This means the viral load in his bloodstream is so low it's practically impossible to contract HIV from him.

---

* PrEP is a little blue pill that has unbelievable success rates in reducing the number of new HIV transmissions between people living with HIV and those who are negative. There's also a big Tory wanker fight over who should fund it. Obviously they don't want to. What absolute douchebags.

"You're undetectable? How up-to-date are you with your bloods and meds?"

"Very. I'm at about seven copies per millileter. I'm so sorry about this." He was in bits, jittery, with his shoulders rising higher and higher. I sensed that his disclosing his status had in the past been met with some real clangers that had left unhealed scars. That's the impact of the stigma.

"It's okay. I'm not on PrEP because I don't have so much bareback sex. But if you're undetectable"—I touched his hand—"then that's fine. Would you like me to get a test?"

Truthfully, I was a little worried. I didn't know this man, although he did inspire trust. But I had a niggling feeling, as with any lay, that he could also simply be lying about his undetectable status. That's the work of the stigma, too: something inside me mistrusting this man only now I've learned of his positive HIV status. One has no obligation to disclose one's status, but naturally that first thing you heard when you came out is the first thing that comes to mind in a scenario such as this. I didn't tell him this—if he was the good guy he seemed to be, then the last thing he needed was to be made to feel like a morally bankrupt trickster. Society does that to people living with HIV quite enough without me replicating it.

"I mean, sure, you should go to the clinic. Explain what happened. There's no need to worry, I don't think, but this has never happened before. I can come with you? I'll just call work and—"

"No, no, honestly it's okay. You go to work, this'll be totally fine—probably nothing; at worst I'll be on PrEP for the month. Give me your number, though, I'll let you know what happens?"

"I was planning to, anyway."

As we left, he asked if he could kiss me. I obliged, more than happily, not remembering the last time a one-night stand had asked to kiss me after the deed was done. And on the street, too, which always, no matter what anyone says about gay progress, feels like an act of bravery. He jumped on a bus, blew me a kiss goodbye—another bold, gay move—and wished me luck at the clinic. I phoned it immediately.

Later, I checked my email on my phone. One, surprisingly, from him.

> Hey, I found your email through Twitter and thought it was classier to communicate this way.
>
> I just want to thank you for being so generous with your response to my disclosure this morning. It is something which remains a site of difficulty, and being undetectable means I can avoid that at all costs. But I thought you deserved to know, since the latex failed us.
>
> Anyway, this wasn't as risk-free as I thought because I actually enjoyed last night more than I usually let myself, especially since intimacy has been a strange world for me to navigate since my HIV status changed.
>
> Whatever's next, it was, really, my pleasure. I've never done it with a drag queen before. Am I a chaser?
>
> Warmest wishes, and let me know how the clinic goes xxxxx

And there, in his signature, the game-changer: an editor and journalist. An important person in online media. I didn't hesitate, forgot about the HIV stuff, and watched as my dead journalism career blossomed into a stunning garden right before my eyes.

"Go for it," Crystal urged, pressing me to Lean In— an idea she originally gave her good friend Sheryl. Crystal is a business mogul, that's simply a fact, and as we drew on a fag and walked through the middle of Soho, cum leaking from my ass, I agreed that I must send an email asking for a commission. I'd count this kind of move somewhat gauche usually, but Crystal doesn't believe in awkward. Plus I've been complaining to all my friends for years that a working-class queer writer could never make it in a world of journalism that only hears the voices of those who claim to have built themselves from the bottom up but have Daddy, trustee at the *Times*, getting them all their bylines.

I waited to reply. I ran through Soho and spent a while on the loo in Balans trying to poo out his cum* while thinking about what I might say.

My potential HIV worry was then quelled by a lovely, but direct, sexual-health nurse,† and the day rolled into sunset.

---

* Iconic!

† She said I could have PEP if I wanted it, but it didn't sound high risk. PEP is a pill you can take after being exposed to HIV that can stop seroconversion and thus infection. It's pretty cool, as is PrEP, which is the same but you can take it all the time. Gorj!

I've now written my reply:

Hey, how are you?

Sorry for my delay—been busy swabbing myself all day. Lol. All good at the clinic, nothing to worry about. Thank you for your candour, though; I felt very reassured by you. I hope you're okay, too.

Now, this is rather forward, but there are two things I'd like to ask:

(1) Would you be interested in a second date? Perhaps we can watch *Fatal Attraction* this time and spend the night flicking lamps on and off à la Alex Forrest?

(2) I notice your email signature—so fancy. I know I didn't mention it last night, but I'm a writer. Would you be open to helping me get a few journalistic commissions? I have been trying to write for various people forever, but I'm about as unconnected as it gets. Of course, mixing business and pleasure is quite tricky but my advisers say that if you don't ask, you don't get. Plus you've been inside me, and we had an intimate HIV scare together, so I figure we're definitely line-crossers.

Hope this finds you well. Now that I've mixed our pleasure with business I'm unsure how to sign off. How about "Best love," xxx

Now I'm hovering over the send icon wondering if my joviality about HIV is the most professional tone in which to jumpstart my career.

But this is step one on the road to becoming a bollock-busting journalist, reporting from the front lines of anal sex, gallery launches, and other queer protests.

April / avril

A text to Ace—

> Hey, it's been ages. Sorry we've both been so AWOL. Have loads to tell you! Let me know when you're free, and we can meet in the middle. Love you, miss you always xx

I've been trying to escape him, busying myself with my new career as a Pulitzer-winning journo-type (no reply from the media bear, by the way) and a new life in East London. After university we were like each other's safety floats, watching as the cushty cruise liner of being a student floated away. We delayed the onset of postuniversity dread for each other by creating a teeny tiny (and indeed privileged) bubble, where we spent all the money we had left from our student loans roaming around different American states talking about anything but getting a job and a real life. We quite swiftly created a shared worldview: talking about how we'd never sell out, we'd only pursue our dreams, and we'd absolutely always be best, inseparable friends. But when change is the central factor binding you to someone else, it's only natural that the nature of that bind also changes.

It's been two weeks since the Denim gig and it feels

---

* Lavigne xxxx.

as if my life has a gaping hole where he would fit. I'm
sad that it feels like this world, here in East London with
Hatty and all the wank art and the fishwifery, and that
world, with the family slant and the drunken walks on
Wandsworth Common and a deep understanding of
each other, are disparate things.

A reply:

> So odd. I dreamt of you last night! We were in a
> butterfly garden, drunk together? Missing you
> always, too. William and I are kind of over. Will
> explain when I see you. We have the Denim meeting
> on Friday, want to get dinner before? Xx

I say yes to dinner and send my condolences, secretly
jubilant about William.

2nd April / le 2 avril

I awoke to a response from the media guy: both a text
and an email. One, the text, explained that while he'd
had a great time with me, he isn't in the "place" to date.
I don't buy it and feel utterly baited by his whole "what a
special evening, I finally let my guard down" shit. Also, I
asked him on a second date, not to date. Big distinction.

"But of course it's in his interest to shut us down, before
we can shut him down because we're so indescribably
stunning; he was obviously just scared of our sacred

> *lightning power and pulled out before he was left*
> *rejected by the love of his life."*

Yeah, that's it. The brutal tennis match that is gayting. Or he just wasn't that into me.

No, definitely the former. My friend Pak confirmed over text that it's the former.

Then the email, in reply to the work bit of mine, which, according to the time stamp, was sent three minutes after the text:

> hey, sure i can help. will intro you to my colleague jen who will take care of you. see you x

The real brushoff. Handing me to a colleague. One kiss. He didn't even capitalise. "See you"?? It's like taking a bullet.

I remind myself there are wars and poverty and this is a way in and pull myself together. An intro to Jen, polite but equally divested. I reply—

> Hey, thanks so much for this!
>
> And hey Jen, nice to e-meet you. Will send over some pitches today or tomorrow.

I've just checked Jen's Twitter—it says she's an editor at a big online news site, and three years ago she tweeted that the phrase *nice to e-meet you* was among her most hated. Texted Pak again to see if he wants to go to Golden Dragon in Chinatown for dim sum. I'm shirking responsibility* and choosing dumplings and a day overspending and talking with Pak about our brutal rejections.

Diary update: I was on the money. I'm home from lunch (which ran into dinner and then drinks) with Pak. Like me, like every *Sex and the City* fan who's been taught to be somewhat irrational in matters of the heart, he's having boy trouble, too: living with his kind-of ex, who just came out and kind of dumped Pak on the same day. They're also best friends. Classic.

I'm white-wine wasted and can already feel my hangover but am too lazy to walk to the sink to get a glass of water even while knowing this will only worsen my hangover. It's time to fuck shit up, and I've decided to email Jen with a list of fifteen pitches. The best, in my opinion, are:

Piss perfect: meet the people who drink their own urine.

If my gender is fluid, why is my sexuality not?

Are these the foolish ramblings of drunk drag queen (yes) or are these the theories of a nu-age prophet (also yes)? Only time, and Jen, will tell.

3rd April / le 3 avril

On the back of advice last night from Pak—who, as he paid for another of my meals, told me I have to learn how to budget—I've decided it's time to use this diary for a purpose beyond my emotional outpouring. For a

---

* Not sure what responsibility, but I'm shirking it.

week, only a week, I'm going to track my spendings, something it has never occurred to me to do. The aim here is to shock myself so intensely at how much cash I waste that I push myself into pits of turmoil and never spend anything ever again.

Drag queen and *savings* aren't words that usually find themselves in the same sentence. This applies, heavily, to me. I spend my life skirting over what I spend, never making any money and constantly dodging stuff I need while paying out extortionate amounts for deeply unnecessary things, like the sequinned eyebrows I just ordered, bespoke at seventeen pounds a pair (x 3). Yes, like most interesting people I have a terrible history with saving money but a colourful history with spending it. One time I got a Raf Simons hoodie on final sale (£550), and it took me seven months to pay it off. I have lots of incredibly loose theories about spending cash that don't stand the test of reality, but I live by them nonetheless, a lot of them bolstered by the idea that Crystal is excessively wealthy.

"Treat yourself, baby."

Some of these theories are:

1. Why move to London—the epicentre of amazing food—to eat packed lunches?
2. What am I saving for anyway? A house? As if.
3. You can't take it with you. And I'll be damned if my kids get it.
4. Extravagance is next to godliness (I just made that one up).

I went online to find out the right way to do this, so the first thing I have to do is list my monthly incomings and outgoings, something I was, until now, totally unaware of. My cavalier attitude to money, and my lack of education about it, comes from never having had it growing up, I reckon. You see, when you don't have it—and I mean don't, not like "Yeah, so broke I had to ask Mum to buy me a flat, oops!" don't—money or the lack of it isn't something you focus on because you can't focus on something that doesn't exist. You spend because you know you'll never have enough to save. When it runs out, you get a speedy job, you don't eat well, or you go to the university finance man and cry and then he somehow finds you two hundred pounds and then you have to go to a dinner with an elderly, wealthy, Conservative heterosexual couple three times a year and sing for your sponsorship.

Anyway, turns out you ought to write all your ins and outs each month.

Job: (in my head) drag performer, freelance journalist; (in reality) spiced-cider seller/fishwife (I'm just so done with this job).

I'm a twenty-four-year-old living in London, and I've just projected that I'll be bringing in anywhere between six thousand and nine thousand pounds this year. Thank my drag stars that I only pay fifty-two pounds a month in rent and often skip the barriers at the tube.* I'm finding this quite distressing. Now this

---

* A fabulous thread on Twitter lists all the barrier-free stations around London. Yes, squeezing through the barriers makes me feel

online budget generator is asking me whether I have savings.

I called Hatty in to ask if she has savings. What ensued was a twenty-five-minute conversation in which we flipped from intense laugher, as Hatty revealed that she was flirting with a bailiff who keeps calling to demand she pay off her second overdrawn account "and he loves it, he basically calls for a daily flirt," followed by intense dread that money will probably hold us back from most of the great things we can do in life. "Don't worry," she said. Hatty always calms me. "We'll be famous soon enough. We have to be."

Later: I've recorded, in a notepad with an eyeliner as I couldn't find a pen once I'd left the house, what I spent throughout the day, and now I'm transcribing it here. Okay. Here goes. My shame diaries.

10:35 a.m.: For breakfast, I always get the same coffee and croissant from the same place because I'm disorganised with my personal food habits so I never have breakfast at home. Even if I do, nobody would undergo such carbohydrate sacrilege as to have, let's face it, a bagel every morning, so I usually just skip that, get hungry, and buy breakfast out. Obviously if Hatty has bought bagels, I'll steal two and have both, which she doesn't mind as long as you don't eat her last one. Once I did and she called me a misogynist, and she was right. But

---

bad since people far more worse off than me probably pay, but it also makes me feel thin, so . . . you do the math!

having two bagels at home doesn't stop me from getting the croissant. Anyway. £4.80.

12:15 p.m.: My friend Cecily is having a tough time, so I took her out for a cup of Earl Grey. She's never tried it before and I ask her why she's a peasant. Then we enjoyed the tea . . . and spilled the tea. £2.52.

1:00 p.m.: As mentioned, I don't ever pack lunches. I decided a few years ago that I'd rather be broke than be someone who packs lunches because it's the ultimate sign of adulthood and that's a category I hope to never reach. It's so normal to be an adult. Plus, I'm a drag queen, so why should I not be glamorous? There is genuinely not one possible glimmer of glamour to be found in and around the world of Tupperware and Ziplocs. If you take a packed lunch to work with you, I admire you but we can probably never be lovers, sorry. Anyway, a classic Pret—which, don't come for me, is glamour because there's so much choice and we don't have them in the regions so it's fancy London stuff— was the lunch du jour today: halloumi-and-falafel wrap, sweet-and-salty popcorn, honey-and-yoghurt granola pot. £6.93.

2:09 p.m.: Another coffee. I sat down to check my email (singular) in a bougie café in Angel. There was no fucking plug socket and my laptop was out of charge, so I had to move. £2.80 (wasted).

2:35 p.m.: Finally find a Starbucks, even though chains are the devil. Bought an orange juice so I'd be allowed to work in there. On day one of budgeting I decided to quit the spiced-cider job via email. Then I went to the loo and had a sit-down dance to M People's

"Movin' on Up" through my headphones as I took a poo. £2.80.

7:39 p.m.: We had a Denim rehearsal/meeting tonight, and nearly every night this week, because we have a gig in a niche gallery and queer wrestling centre (obsessed) later this month. Ace has cancelled the dinner we were supposed to have beforehand. A blow. Scanned the streets of Angel, where we scammed a free rehearsal room from a dancer Glamrou's sleeping with, for anything decent to dine on. Swiftly settled on a glorious, girthy burrito. Obviously I would also never dream of packing dinner. That would be impossible to return from in my eyes. £7.70.

Total: £27.55.*

4th April / le 4 avril

9:10 a.m.: I had a work meeting with a make-up brand who reached out two days ago on Instagram. Wasn't into them because I think influencers are the scourge of the earth and they're all about that, but then they gave me loads of free make-up! And they paid for breakfast as they're a multinational company and I'm a struggling queen. Had an organic muffin, which was dry as hell. And an iced black Americano. £0.00

12:25 p.m.: Had lunch alone, job hunting at magazines and newspapers to zero avail. I decided to do what

---

* Realised I have a calculator on my laptop but don't dare go back to work out monthly budget—at this point that just feels cruel.

I always do and stupidly not check the prices on the menu. I ordered a coffee, a sausage sandwich, and a side salad (that's a lie, it was a brownie) at an expensive place in Soho. £16.10 (oh, God, what have I done?).

5:15 p.m.: Saw my friend for a quick coffee because they'd just hooked up with a supergreat girl they've had a crush on forever, and we wanted to debrief. We talked, also, about bi erasure a lot, and I am checked on sometimes erasing the experience of bi people, or assuming it's not as hard for them as it is for me, which is an easy pattern to slip into and I promise to do better. I paid because, despite my harsh judgments on those who use Tupperware, I'm really a kind-hearted queen. £5.20.

8:00 p.m.: Dinner out again, before Denim rehearsal. It was either another burrito or a Pret. So a Pret it was. Same again: halloumi-and-falafel wrap, sweet-and-salty popcorn, granola pot. So uncreative. Also realising now I haven't had one vegetable today. Omg or yesterday . . . unless pinto beans count? Anyway. £6.93.

Total: £28.23.

5th April / le 5 avril

9:00 a.m.: Coffee, no croissant, as I was in a rush and the croissants looked particularly dry today anyway. £3.20 (for a fucking coffee, I know . . . London).

11:30 a.m.: Coffees for me and my friend Amelia, a journalist, because we wanted to catch up and smoke loads—nothing is better than a cigarette and a coffee. I paid—even though she's employed by *Vice* and has just scored another long read in *The Guardian*—because part of me likes to pretend I'm as rich as my successful friends. £6.08.

12:23 p.m.: Bacon sandwich. With a fried egg. Oh my God, I'm gonna get scurvy. £4.95.

1:24 p.m.: Ran out of rollie tobacco and now it's so pricey because of new laws that are supposed to stop us all buying it. But we're still buying it, Theresa, we're buying it for sure. £13.99.

2:20 p.m.: I totally forgot I'd agreed to meet with a friend for lunch, and I'd already had lunch with that bacon sandwich. But we went to Wagamama, and I love Wagamama even though I hate their corporate pinkwashing around Pride. Got a chicken-and-prawn yakisoba and a ginger beer. I decided to eat again on account of there being some (very few, but some) vegetables in the noodle dish. £12.25.

8:00 p.m.: One of the Denims bought me dinner because the spiced-cider stall has delayed its payment. Probably because I quit. But I had to, as Marx would say, lose them chains. Anyway, we left rehearsal and had another burrito. At this stage I'm questioning who I am and whether I will soon just be a burrito . . . with scurvy . . . and no money. £0.00.

Total: £40.47.

6th April / le 6 avril

8:58 a.m.: Today I'm dead broke. Of course, I refused to pack a lunch or eat breakfast at home. Grocery stores are deeply unglam, and while not shopping in them feels like the right ideological position, sometimes it is distressing to never have any food at all in the house because sometimes you just want a fucking piece of toast. Anyway, I bought my morning coffee as ever. Wincing, waiting for a "Declined," I tapped my contactless card over a reader that said £3.20 . . . for a coffee . . . again. £3.20.

1:35 p.m.: Lol, McDonald's for lunch. I truly mean it when I say that I never, ever have McDonald's for lunch. Except the one week where I'm writing this bloody budgeting shite. It was a double cheeseburger, three Chicken Selects with sour cream dip, fries, and a DIET (!!!!!) Coke. Not gonna lie, it was a pretty special lunch. Paid in floor change prised from the sticky beige-carpeted floor of Wally. £6.00.

7:07 p.m.: Received a text message notification from my bank telling me I'd breached my overdraft limit and am now spiralling into debts on my debts, upon which Santander, the nichest* of the banks, are applying charges. Spent about sixteen minutes seething, wondering how poor people are supposed to get out of poor situations when they're charged for being poor while fucking posh moneyed douchebags get tax breaks and rewards on their rewards. Make a note that the problem with capitalism, or one of, is that people think that the only limit to their personal income is how much or little effort and labour one's willing to put in, which arms all rich people with this fucking irresponsible

---

* *Niche-est*, the "most niche." Made-up word, but surprisingly useful.

moralising power that they are harder working than people on minimum wage. If work and labour equalled money, then my parents would be trillionaires, and all the mothers in the world would be, too—given they're both the breadwinners and the child carers at once. Fuck capitalism. Decide to get an artisanal coffee to take the edge off capitalism with £3.00 I found in my backpack xxxx. £3.00.

8:18 p.m.: My invoice from the spiced-cider stall has been paid! I'm rich! As a celebration I had, of course, another burrito. I would like to talk candidly here for a sec: I urge you not to rehearse for any shows in Angel, dear friends, because—unless you're willing to trek to Upper Street—there is only a Pret and two burrito shops. It's a joke. Anyway. £8.60.

Total: £20.80.

7th April / le 7 avril

11:33 a.m.: Another friend is having a difficult time at the moment. We met for a late breakfast at that place in Soho I went to the other day that cost me too much, but I was feeling flush from being paid. I had granola and apricots and loved feeling fleetingly middle-class. She had a green tea; I had one coffee. I paid. £20.81.

3:25 p.m.: Pret lunch. But, shocker (!), this time I had a banana and a ham-and-cheese sandwich. Feeling proud of myself for eating fruit! £3.80.

4:00 p.m.: I've been wheeled out for a drag gig tonight somewhere in Soho, but it pays forty pounds so obviously I said yes. I was bored of my look and made a snap decision, with a hard push from Crystal—who is conspicuously absent from this budgeting process, perhaps because she finds budgeting triggering since her first husband was done for fraud—to go to the most iconic shop full of sequins and glitter, Taurus, and buy a headdress and some elbow-length Lycra gloves. Spent the fee and then some before I'd made it, although spending money on her always feels totally justified because she's my job, but she's also a wealthy woman and mustn't lose face in front of her adoring fans. £55.00.

7:00 p.m.: I sat on an unpaid (fuckers) panel at the Tate Modern about queerness and mental health, which my friend Amelia asked me to join after someone else dropped out, then I had to rush back to Soho for the show. I grabbed a duck banh mi from a street vendor and ran to the tube. Then I dropped the banh mi on my right foot. I screamed a curse word and carried on running like the trouper queen I am. £7.00.

7:30 p.m.: Needed more cigarettes if I was ever going to be able to sing properly for the show. Bought a big bottle of water, too, and a newspaper as a prop. £19.00.

12:30 a.m.: Three beers. Four beers. Five beers. More beers. So. Many. Beers. All free for performers. I live my life on drinks tickets. Sucked a tall, thin guy's cock in an alleyway on the way to the tube because he'd watched the show and told me he thought I had a beautiful singing voice and offered to help me with my bags as I was struggling and we were going the same way. I knew it was a come-on because he was nervous but in a cheeky way. But then cheeky turned rapidly to choky as he grunted like "Gag on my meat" and, the best, "Let me ruin those vocal cords" as his dick was fully triggering my gag reflex. Funny that he wanted to ruin the thing that he'd complimented me on—my voice—but that's men for you. I was halfway between personas—face, but no wig—something he was obviously into as he came all over my perfectly contoured cheeks and smacked his seed across my face with his oddly heavy dick. Crystal was so, so pleased. £0.00.

Total: £105.61.

8th April / le 8 avril

1:44 p.m.: Slept till 11:00 a.m., then rushed to Hackney to sing in a DIY gig in Hatty's and my new band, which we aren't sure what to call. Maybe Fantasy Ice? It was pouring down and we were playing in an alleyway. Anyway, we had to wait around for four hours. So Hatty and I bought beer, bagels, and the saltiest prosciutto and it was joyful. We sat in a leaky warehouse in Hackney Wick, where we watched some straight dudes play instruments on loop (with the aim to do so for ten hours). Visionary . . . £12.00.

Afternoon: We ended up getting quite drunk, and time went somewhat hazy. But we found an in at the café near where we were playing and got loads of free beers. It was great. We played the gig and headed home, soaking wet. £0.00.

9:00 p.m.: We are having a party tonight in the warehouse, and so before it all kicks off, I cooked a fresh carbonara for a few friends—Hatty, Ace, Ellie, Cecily, Glamrou—with delicious salad. I also bought beers for the night. £22.25.

Total: £34.25.

9th April / le 9 avril

1:00 p.m.: I was heinously hungover, and also on deadline for a piece for Jen! She responded and I'm writing the article about being non-binary but having a sexuality affixed to a gender. This is it. I'm a journalist now. I had coffee and a bagel at home. I felt remarkably proud of myself. £0.00.

6:00 p.m.: Pak and I went for ritual hangover KFC. It's the best thing in the world. I felt alive again, until a man in the park near our house started screaming homophobic slurs at me. Happens all the time. £6.80.

9:00 p.m.: Hatty cooked a roast, which took ages but was amazing when done. We had chicken, potatoes, broccoli, asparagus, and honey-and-mustard carrots. We drank wine and watched reruns of *Friends* and the *Spice World* movie. It was the best hangover cure ever. Although I missed my deadline; will send tomorrow. A great start to my budding journalism career. £4.00.

Total: £10.80.

10th April / le 10 avril

I spent £267.71 in the week. That adds up to £1,000 a month(ish) and I haven't even accounted for rent, and if my maths A level serves me well, I'm spending way more than I'm bringing in. In fairness, I didn't count the cash, which I keep in a ball in my bag, I bring in from drag gigs or this one kid I now tutor in biology.* It must be what keeps me afloat.

So ends the money diary. I'm never doing a budget again. I'm sick of everyone moralising at us millennials (although I wish to categorically reject that label because it's become tragic since brands got on board) that we need to save and be better with money. If we hadn't been so utterly fucked by the people telling us this, we'd be fucking rolling in it. Socialism, not budgeting. That's what I say. Expunge the baby boomers, that's what I say. Universal wage, that's what I say.

I think you just have to choose to worry about some things and not others. For me, money is at the edge of all my worries. Not because it's free flowing but because I watched my parents support four children on low-paying jobs, spending to the very penny what they brought in each month. The worry was always there for them, and it will probably always be there for me. Sure, with a (bad) Cambridge degree I could still probably be lucky enough to get a well-paying job and expunge money worries altogether, but a different person from me would make

---

* Unsure whether I have to declare tax on this?

that choice, and money isn't worth becoming another person for. It might please my parents, but they didn't pay for any of my tuition because they couldn't afford it, so my career is luckily not owned by them. And that's a choice I have that my parents didn't—to self-actualise on the back of their labour, and I'm intensely lucky to even try to follow my desires of writing and dragging and queering. People like me, from where I'm from, don't get to do that.

But growing up never having money means I'm comfortable worrying about it, with spending it, with the knowledge that I'll never own a house or take a year out to travel or afford to do a master's degree, so I think it's best to spend it. Because the pleasure I get from living the way I live outweighs the worry not having much money at all brings. I worry that if I saved, I would feel guilty about having money and not giving it to people who need it. Pak thinks this is ridiculous, but he has never known not having money. It is hard, but the Crystal part of me thinks it's thrilling. So I'll spend and I'll live.

Anyway, there's a lot to catch up on in the world outside of money.

A week of Denim rehearsals has been somewhat transformative for Ace's and my relationship. A specific brand of brutal honesty mounts as a show nears, as the tension rises: one in which you can say things you wouldn't usually, if time weren't so pressed.

At a quick dinner, four nights ago, eating a chicken burrito, a conversation:

I said I was sorry about him and William breaking

up; Ace said I obviously wasn't as I hadn't mentioned it all week, even though we'd seen each other every night. We were eating said burrito, and my hands, covered in a mulch of sour cream and rice and sauce, smelt for the rest of the night.

I reminded him that he hadn't asked a thing about me either. I told him I'd had an HIV scare (kind of), I quit my crappy fishwife job, got my first paid writing one. He was both concerned and happy for me, so we talked all that out, then I asked him about William, properly.

"Well . . . he fucking slept with Steve. Remember, that builder-fetish guy we once met on the common? Turns out, he slept with him, repeatedly. And I found a video! A fucking video! I can't . . ."

"Fuck. A video." I feared, for a moment, that I'd also slept with Steve on a Grindr rager. "Is Steve that builder who isn't actually a builder but dresses like one, really convincingly, for gay nights? A kind of ginger, brown, grey, tricolour beard?"

Ace confirmed it was indeed the same Steve I'd slept with who had torn Ace and William apart. I was planning not to mention this to Ace, and then, burrito in hand, it frothed from my mouth like an exploding can of Diet Coke because I'm always drawn in by my next shocking story, while sometimes bulldozing the feelings of those I care for.

"Are you fucking kidding me? Now two of the men I love have slept with Ste—" Ace stopped himself.

"Two of the men you love?"

Clock ticked, break over, back to rehearsal we went. But he loves me, apparently. Which I think I knew. He also gendered me as male, but I just wanted to savour this moment of validation instead of hitting him hard with a "get my pronouns right" retort. He usually gets it right; he calls me "his person." Then we didn't talk about it again. This moment or the dynamic had no awkward air; we've just become good at completely ignoring our feelings. Like the time he staged a full dance and lip-sync in a car park in Nashville with some friends we'd met there, to Taylor Swift's masterpiece "State of Grace," which he said reminded him so much of me. We both cried, overwhelmed and in love. Then we drove for seven hours and didn't mention it once. It's usual; it's unresolved.

"It's fucking boring."

My first piece of journalism was published and I shared it on Facebook, proudly. Three people commented on it, on the news site, calling me some form of freak or pervert. That was gorgeous.

Emailed Jen more pitches, and now she wants me to write one about dominance and submissiveness in homosexual relationships and whether that pertains to gendered stereotypes that uphold normativity. I think that a lot of gays are now synonymous with normativity, but I didn't tell Jen, obviously. I invoiced £120 for my first article and calculated that to survive I must write three to four of these articles a week. Maybe the money diary has helped. The problem is, I only have, like, six things to say, and I've already said one of them.

Time for some new experiences.

17th April / le 17 avril

I finished my dom-sub piece and was deeply proud of myself for finally being able to quote Cheryl Cole in something the public might read.*

I've been working on my next piece, about exploring masculinities in the gay community. I think, after only two published articles, I've worked out my beat (as they cringingly call it in journalism), which is "homopolitico."† To me, it seems unremarkable: every fucking person I know is a hard-core homopolitico, with radical sexual, social, and party politics. But the world of traditional journalism has a dearth of any such inclusivity or diversity, and that's just among the gays, let alone any other, less represented voices.

A godforsaken theory also has it that only women and other oppressed people can, and should, engage in personal journalism because the reporting, the fact dishing, should be left to straight white dudes. It's infuriating, but it makes writing way more exciting for us. I'm here to take up space and tell you what it's like to live these experiences, rather than report on them like some armchair anthropologist. The ways stories are told and accepted as "good" and "proper" and "to a standard" are dictated by the most privileged and, thus, dull. Selling your trauma to pay your rent is a complicated question, but since I can't afford therapy, perhaps that'll be

---

* It was a lyric from her masterwork "Parachute," a stunning moment in the pop canon.

† Made the word up, but sounds gorj, right?

helpful anyway. The whole point of writing about personal experience is that some people, somewhere, might connect with it.

For this piece about masculinity I've spent five days anthropologically exploring the gay male community. The premise is that this is a sort of survey, an ethnographic study, of gays in London right now. Here, I present my findings:

1. Grindr/Scruff/Recon/the apps: The apps have arguably killed serendipity in the gay community. Now, you can switch on, click click, boom, and you've got three bears spraying their loads all over your back while you think about what takeaway to get on the way home. Indian. Our sex has become a virtual transaction, often no more than a transfer of data, and Grindr's users have developed a secret currency based on muscular-torso pics, racism, and femme-phobia.

   A usual Grindr chat goes:

   Top or bott?

   Bott, but sometimes vers

   Wanna fuck? U accom?

   Sure, sure, any pics?

   TORSO PIC: sometimes hot, mostly boring
   FACE PIC: often them on holiday
   somewhere, cropped tight, a bit burnt
   DICK PIC ONE: taken from above while sat on
   the toilet. Imagine them pooing
   DICK PIC TWO: flash: too high; pubes:

oddly shiny; boxers: undesirable, stiff
cotton

DICK PIC THREE: good pic, hot pic.
Sometimes this one will be with weird
precum visible, which is never a turn-on;
sometimes it will be them bareback in
some twink, which makes me both worry
about STIs and also makes me jealous:
"Who the fuck is she?"

RARE, ODDLY ANGLED, HOLE PIC: so rarely got
right, often taken in a smeared mirror that
makes their butt hole look the colour of
raw meat that's been left out overnight.
Sometimes, however, a dirty hole pic is the
hottest thing in the world.

> Come over. So hot. Play safe only.
> *Send location*

Three hours later, after mediocre sex:
Block

2. XXL: Interestingly, this is a specifically bear
sex club, built entirely on deifying the hyper-
male form—muscular bears or big-bellied rugby
men only. On entry, on a Friday night, I wear
my sneakers with a heel and a fringed dress
and, naturally, I'm standing out from the crowd.
Some of these burly men love it, looking me up
and down in the way only gays and the women
of *Dynasty* do just before a physical fight; others
are visibly disgusted by my feminising presence
at this should-be masc mecca. A bouncer, front

of the queue: "You can't come in here wearing that, boss; it's menswear only." I'm deeply shocked. Luckily Glamrou, my assistant ethnographer for the night, quickly steps in: "Oh, please. Gender is literally a lie. XXL, more like XX-transmisogyny. I'm gonna tweet about this!" The bouncer's eyes shift side to side: "Right. Fine. I love it, but if my boss sees, I'll get in trouble." He lets us in and grabs both our arms as we enter: "By the way, I get off at one a.m. and would love to see both of you from a bird's-eye view, if you get me?" Glamrou and I giggle like little school-theys, which causes more polarised looks from those around us. Inside, the place is alight with testosterone, and toplessness, which we despise—half because we're failing to achieve it, half because we've seen what toxic and misogynist and femme-phobic behaviour this kind of masculine mix can engender. I also dislike the fact that there are no women or femmes here, except Glam and me.

Perhaps my anger is misdirected and I should just leave the bears alone to have their man-fun. But when queers have so few spaces they can go, even in a city such as London, because they're all closing down, it feels as if those who are unified in some kind of experience of otherness should be welcoming to others with similar experiences. Perhaps I'm deriving this from a feeling more than a reality, but XXL has rejected femme-presenting queers quite openly, yet we come here because there aren't many other heres to come to. A few years back there was a big spate of gay men chatting about hen dos and women being allowed into gay clubs, calling for this practice to be ended. But the gay community has relied on femininity and women in so many ways—the women in my upbringing taught me everything I know—so I feel this territoriality should be reserved for cis het men. Sure some behavioural practices could be observed such as, I dunno, no homophobia allowed, but these spaces to me are a Noah's Ark for those of us oppressed by male dominance. And I want women and femmes on that Ark, too.

Glamrou and I dance, sweat, drink tinnies of sweet, gross Red Stripe. I talk to three huge, burly men with their bendy dicks hanging out, and I'm heartened at how undeniably camp they are even if they are wearing a costume of excessive muscle. Eventually, I take two of them into a dark room, and I suck their dicks till both of them cum all over my face, my neck. I lose Glamrou and find them later in a chicken shop. Have a chicken burger with cool mayo and feel stunning.

3. Chariots sauna/general saunas: There's a strange code that everyone in gay sex saunas seems to understand, though there's certainly no rule book. If you like someone, you don't look at them, you definitely don't speak to them, you simply walk past them and prod them with your finger as if checking the ripeness of a tomato. If they like you back, they'll likely follow you to a corridor/Jacuzzi/

sex booth. I enter Chariots in Vauxhall, on Saturday night, alone. Heart pumps hard as I walk through the café-bar, where they serve tuna melt paninis twenty-four hours a day—delicious, but perhaps the only thing less arousing than estate agents on a Christmas pub crawl. I take a moment to appreciate the myriad ways gays have found to have sex and smile at the reclining, naked older men who use this as a literal community centre, many of whom have probably got wives at home. Head through corridors and shower, eyeing up guys. Some have evidently taken excessive amounts of drugs, as they stare at red lights, their eyes flashing like rabbits bouncing around this gay sex rabbit warren, and I feel momentarily worried for them, then I chastise myself for being judgmental. Next, walk down a corridor edged by sex booths. Catch glimpses of assorted men inside: bottom twinks moaning for men to come and fill them up like parodies of busty blond women they've seen on porn; five people in one in a kind of Renaissance-style tableau. Feel very fat as I realise all five have twitching abs and tight little buns. Accidentally walk into pitch-black orgy room, step on a used, spermy condom, and within ten seconds feel someone try to finger my butt hole. Unsure, not feeling it, bum clamming up, leave orgy room in search of a Jacuzzi. There, get talking to an incredibly sweet old man called Patrick who ends up holding his nose as he goes underwater to give me head. He takes me to the smoking area, lights my cigarette, and stands over me—dick at eye level, precum glistening (hot? I can't tell). We head down to a sex room, where he lubes me up and puts on a condom and shoves it in me, his whole weight bearing down on me, and it's very, very hot and I love his camp whispers. As we go for it, another guy comes in, equally old and chubby, and asks if he can put his dick in my mouth. I oblige, excitedly, and then they switch around. We all cum. I shower and leave. I walk out into London, my hair wet, the sun bulging through the clouds, forcing dawn, and as I ride the tube, I feel thankful for these sensitive men who made me feel sexually attractive in a scene full of muscle and masculinity.

4. Heaven/Soho: We used to frequent these places all the time—shots, shots, shots, dancing, surrounded less by sex and more by camp queens getting their kicks to the likes of Kylie and a mass balloon drop at the climax of the night. Here, we used to go to dance and never to score. Under the roofs of these various G-A-Y franchises my friends and I all found our gateway drug into:

5. The East London gay scene: Much cooler, far more politically engaged if you search for the right kind of night. Denim sits on this scene, in its own little way. It encompasses everything from queer femme-girl-only nights to parties like Batty Mama, BBZ, and Pxssy Palace, which, rightly, lift up and celebrate queer bodies of colour. Those nights are beautiful and offer a varied conception of

gender to the point where, for one night, people can freely move without worry and violence.

Other nights, we all know, are designed to make money off straight people gawping at drag queens and pushing queer women out of the way, but I don't want to be too shady because I have a lot of friends who partake in those spaces to make cash—even I do sometimes. Those nights, no matter where they are, reek of farts: straight men coked off their faces, farting their way through queer space as if it were theirs. The only people who should be able to fart in those spaces are the queers and the little twinky bums who have to get it out of their system before Daddy checks the pipes at the end of the night.

6. Other: The moneyed and cultural-capital-obsessed homos of middle-class London. Think galleries, think "soft launches," think fashion gays, think bookstores that serve craft coffees, think panel talks about "gay mental health."* These are the worst kind of gays, after the misogynist, muscle-obsessed ones. These gays find my loud, queer mouth displeasing and inappropriate, and my class background unsightly.

Unlike the muscle gays, who are obsessed with the aesthetics of masculinity, the cultural-capital-obsessed gays are cosy in their campness or queer sensibilities but are loathe to seek out and fight

---

* Yes, I'm aware I did one a few days ago, but I needed the money.

for rights for queers who differ from them. They
handwring about gentrification while funding a
new gallery space, they think marriage was the
be-all and end-all for the gay rights movement,
and they don't follow a single trans person on
Twitter. Regarding masculinity, they aren't comfortable losing out on all its privileges just because
they take it up the poo pipe. Not my scene.

So what of gayness and masculinity? What's the con-
clusion? Masculinity is a dangerous trap, and if society
shows us anything, failing at it can be even worse. Failure is abused and mocked, and while the gay male scene
might offer the most diverse portrayal of masculinity in
the West, it's still full of men who've internalised this
violence against them because of said failure and then
replicate this violence against men who've failed more
than them: the mascs hate anyone more femme than
them, the femmes hate anyone more fat than them, the
fats hate anyone more disabled than them, the whites
hate anyone with browner skin than them. All of them
hate women. And so we are divided and conquered.
Of course, gay men can be some of the most beautiful,
wonderful, caring creatures bouncing around the atmosphere, but they can also be just as violent as the men
who took their power. You know if this is you, and you
know if this is not. We've all done it. We all do it. I'm
doing it now.

18th April / le 18 avril

Being a drag queen is like having a split personality. It's like having a filing system for parts of yourself—the bits you retain for day you, and the bits you put aside for drag you. It's like having a constant fairy godmother, or like a morally bankrupt, drunk auntie sitting on your shoulder, goading you to do the thing you want to do but society tells you not to.

At least that's what it's like for me.

I spent years nursing the feminine me, concurrently escaping the masculine me, although I'm not sure which of these two acts incited my want to become a drag queen. Before Denim, I'd only ever done drag on my own—tending to my femininity in my bedroom, as I would be stunned by my beauty, inspired by my violence, moved by my tenderness, invigorated by my sexuality—and the beginnings of Crystal were found at this confluence. I studied women—divas, mothers, sisters, friends—and found nothing more alluring or comfortable than a soft femininity with a hard bite, a generous femininity with a narcissistic edge. I grew into a seasoned performer, a global superstar who had come from humble beginnings and arrived at international fame.

When I first started drag performance, there was a disconnect between myself out of drag and myself in drag. Bringing her out for the first time incurred some changes. I had a strong grip on how to carry, to conceal and reveal my femininity, when alone, but I'd only ever known how to shroud it when in public. I'd had years to get this right, yet the first incarnation of Crystal—a name stolen from a wonderful friend with whom I no longer speak, but absolutely love—some seven years ago, was rushed. She was quiet, timid, sexual, a bitch; she was narcissistic, she spoke over the women who had given her everything she was, she used words I'll no longer even write in my diary to describe herself and her womanliness, and she was selfish.

This was never me out of drag, but for the first years— perhaps two or so—it was as if a dam had been broken, and torrents of rage and dysphoria and repression flooded everywhere Crystal went. People loved it—they tongue popped, and twentysomething university students cared little about identity politics and more about pills and getting off with that guy from their sociology seminar. We were all muddling through.

But as time passed, as we all moved through university and became pretentious, idiotic bachelors of philosophy and critical thought (lol, how gorj), we picked things apart and pieced them back together. We spent more time in drag bars in London, watching videos online, aligning ourselves with what would be our chosen tribe once we left this absolute bubble of privilege, and we were decidedly queer. And to be queer meant to be on point, inclusive, awake.

So I listened. Crystal listened. Hard. We read about drag and misogyny. We listened when friends from dorms or nights out would tell us how our behaviour upheld misogyny, even if we were in wigs and heels. We watched dynamics in rooms and worked out where our privilege sat in each one, and how that affected the way we were taking up space. You should take up space, you just have to be cognisant of how much you're taking up, when you're taking it up, where you're taking it up, and from whom you're taking it.

There's less of a disconnect between Crystal and myself now. We're essentially the same, bar the fact she's a multitrillionaire, the lost Romanov daughter, and currently splitting her time between her penthouse in San Fran, her alpaca farm in the Romanian hills, and her chain of restaurants in the popular seaside resort Blackpool.

Now, people tell me I carry my femininity beautifully, something of which I couldn't be more proud. She informs me. I inform her. Our politics are the same—although sometimes she might slip in a problematic joke, but she's always punching up.

DRAG PERFORMANCE MEMO: Watching Shirley sing odes to killing men is very different from watching Ace rehearse the same song. It's wild what you can get away with when you put a wig and a face on.

19th April / le 19 avril

Tonight we have a Denim gig at that queer wrestling place.

I'm late getting ready because I spent the day trying to make a dress out of some old fabric I found in a cupboard full of shit that was left in Wally before I got here—a kind of wipe-clean plastic tablecloth printed with dark brown and red fruits on a white background.

I'm a crap seamstress, but I've got no money, so needs must. In the dress, I looked the spitting image of a used tampon, which could be a cool look, but it won't work with my neon-pink thigh-high boots, and I'd sewn it so hastily that my silhouette was like a badly stuffed boxing glove. I also spent half an hour making out with Hatty because it's fun and we love telling each other that the other is a good kisser.

I'm feeling oddly nervous about tonight's gig. Not the gig bit—once I'm in geish* I always feel ready for anything stage-wise—more the dancing after, when the club bit turns dirtier, and everyone starts finding their Saturday squeeze. I detest these spaces; I always feel like the last one picked in PE class. I especially dislike being picked last at PE when I'm in the line-up with Ace.

Of late we've been in much more contact. He slept over at Wally last night, in my bed, which is just a series of old sofa cushions placed side by side, after we went out for Turkish food on Watney Market and drank so much bring-your-own-beer that he couldn't face the journey home. At Wally we returned so quickly to old us: laughing, smoking (he's started again, thank God, since he binned William), him not checking his phone every twenty minutes to see if William's got back to him, engaging each other in deep conversations. I'm less cutting, more considerate, less "cold for no reason." He and Hatty also found each other ferociously funny,

---

* Drag colloquialism for make-up. Just googled spelling and realised it comes from the word *geisha*. Now I'm thinking that probably the word isn't mine to use.

and by the early hours we'd polished off a full bottle of cheap tequila and had dressed in the most iconic clothes we could find, blasting out Lady Gaga's best song ever—"Fashion!"—while filling saucepans full of freezing-cold water and pouring them on each other, à la Jennifer Beals in *Flashdance*, soaking the carpet. Something about fucking up your surroundings is so freeing. In this sensational, borderless night we all moved over each other fluidly, with the ease of three sisters who maybe also wanted to have sex?

After we had collapsed in bed, still soaking wet, Ace looked at me and told me he loved me but didn't know how that translated into reality. I welled up and asked if that meant he was too embarrassed to think of us together in public.

To which he stayed silent. To which I got the message. To which I turned over. To which he kissed the back of my head. Tonight the indefinable will become the acidulous. I, the less visually desirable of the pair, will be celebrated for my drag look, my voice. But after the show, I'll be chatted to, but never up. If I had a sequin for every time someone's come over in the past to me to ask about my hot friend (Ace), I would have about 338 sequins. Tonight will be no different.

There's no feeling in the world like it. To be looked over by someone who knows you and by someone who doesn't at the same time, then to watch him kiss another all night as if it were the most glorious kiss both had ever had, as you wait, hoping that he will actually see you tonight. You put yourself into the new guy's position and imagine the feeling of the mouth and stomach fireworks they're both experiencing as they drink their cocktail of kissing, booze, and a dab of something serotonin-freeing. The human experience is so obscenely lonely when you think that every single person is never feeling the exact same thing as another.

But there's them, the Saturday-night squeeze who had the courage to make a move on Ace, and then there will be me, later this evening: twiddling my thumbs, dancing with strangers who look over my shoulder for anyone hotter than me to end the night with, while Ace and his man are against a wall, unstoppable, eating each other. No other feeling in the world is like that in which you're kept interested by meagre suggestions of love here and love there, then cast aside the moment someone with pulsating abs steps in front of you in the club. It's that song by Robyn, "Dancing on My Own,"* multiplied by the confirmation that you are, in every way you'd suspected as a teenager, undesirable.

Anyway, must get into make-up and have a bottle of wine to take the edge off. Glad that she's coming out tonight—because in those moments she's my saving grace. Painted, pinched, a face and a body I feel so comfortable and powerful in. Black eyeliner, glittering beard, sharp contour, button nose. She takes my feelings of unworthiness and makes others seem unworthy of me. Not by being mean but by being powerful.

The transformation is slow. It starts with about forty

---

* I know this is a reference from *Girls*, but it's ubiquitous. Plus I have a tattoo of Robyn's logo on my leg because I thought it was arty (I miss being nineteen).

minutes of messing around: unpacking make-up, doing a poo, making a coffee, sharpening my pencils, and complaining about not wanting to get into face. The galling process is especially boring if you have to do it three times a week. But slowly, as her presence builds with each pat of powder or dusting of highlight, no matter how tired or sad or lonely I am, my mood swells and suddenly everything I tuck away is let loose and I become the most I can be. There's no aha moment. It's more like a dragon slowly awakening: its wings are my femininity, its fire is the belief she gives me that I can do anything, its thick scales are my ability to draw immense strength from my glorious transgression.

"Dracarys, bitch!"

22nd April / le 22 avril

When I was a teenager, I used to write down all my experiences with homophobic abuse—at school, with friends, at home—in a little notebook and keep it inside my pillowcase. I used to think that if I wrote them down, I could stop the words or the stones or the saliva turgid with hocked-up phlegm from bedding down inside me, instead leaving all those encounters there, in a closed book, nearby but out of sight.*

When I left home for university, I toyed with taking

---

* I also had a book for pictures of men's torsos I'd torn from magazines, but I kept that under my bed.

the notebook but decided against it. The night before I left, I took it into the shower with me, opening and soaking each page, watching the ink run down the drain, choosing to finally excoriate these endless tales of pain from my possession, knowing that by leaving Lancaster and going to Cambridge I would finally be among people who understood and accepted me in ways I'd never before known. A classist assumption, I soon realised, phobia of all kinds penetrating class boundaries and chasing me wherever I've ever been like a recurring dream.

I have a lot of friends who say they have never experienced such violent homophobia. I don't understand why; we are equally as queer and as camp. I wonder if it's my bigness that intimidates men, and how at odds that is with how unmissably feminine I am. Their masculinity unable to compute the contrast.

But I stopped keeping a diary of homophobic abuse as I learned to understand the world more, to recognise the systems of oppression that lead other oppressed people to take their rage out on someone like me, like us. Instead I built a better circuit board to compute these varied, but fairly constant, incidents.

However, this computer is malfunctioning, and I can't understand what happened to me three nights ago. I am unsure how to write this down. But I feel that I need to, to write it here, as an account, so I can deploy these feelings of shame and purge the violent energy from my body before it manifests into more bouts of unsafe sex or torrid self-hatred or getting a credit card and maxing it out at Balenciaga.

After the Denim show ended, I waited for Ace to

finish snogging someone. Together we took an Uber back to Wally as the streets never feel safe after dark when one is in full drag. As we stepped, heels first, out of our car and opposite our front door, some exceptionally generic-looking men appeared, vodka bottles in hand, yelling vicious homophobic slurs. Naturally, as we learned at high school, Ace and I stuck a middle finger up at them, and we shouted simple retorts of "Fuck off" and other reactionary, unintelligent defences. As we crossed to the middle of the busy road, a lone wolf from the group peeled off, smashed his vodka bottle on the street, and ran quickly across the shard-covered tarmac, heading for Ace. At that moment, a bus came, and as I was in the middle of the road, while Ace was already by my front door, I reached out my arms and instinctively held the lone wolf back from being hit by the bus, which would have led to his body being smeared like a thin red stripe across the road.

We were now stuck together on a concrete island in the middle of the road, the mania of night-time Commercial Road closing around us like a vise. He was half my weight with eyes beaming back the light of late-night East London, panting like a hot dog (not the food), seemingly switching from full hatred to full gratitude. My shoulders dropped, and for a second we were two people who had life. My saving his had been our equaliser.

There, on a concrete island in the centre of the dual carriageway, he stared me square in the eyes and said, "Thank you," in absolute earnest. Relieved, heart still shaking a little into my oesophagus, I went to respond, and he, still looking me square in the eye, retracted a

fist and punched me so hard in the face I heard my nose
crack and my brain bounce around my skull like a jar
of pickles being shaken. My sight disappeared and I was
floored, my mouth filled by blood coursing from some
unknown location on my face.

> *"Get up!* Get up!" Crystal urged as she stood over
> me, watching my blood pool onto the pavement.
> She's never been rendered witless, but all she
> could say was *"Get up!"* with increasing vigour,
> tears streaming down her face.

I had been many things and had many things done
to me, but never had I been punched square in the face.
Imagine a scenario in which someone despises your
existence so vehemently, so fervently, that, even when
you have genuinely saved their life, they feel you still
deserve physical punishment for being. I can only envis-
age being on the receiving end of that exchange. I don't
even think he deserves physical punishment for inflict-
ing this on me. A full-on physical hate crime.

I haven't left the house since Ace brought me back
from the hospital. My door, the corridors, the pavements,
are covered with aubergine circles of dropped, dried
blood. A full bloody handprint has dried, cracked, and
is peeling off the light switch in the corridor. I can't connect any of that to me. I can't seem to locate Crystal. I
feel different now. Sadder now. More disappointed now.

I feel exhausted now. I'm going to sleep.

24th April / le 24 avril

I don't think it's possible to instantly tell how something such as a violent attack will affect you as time goes on. I've been attacked so many times, in so many ways, and it feels self-indulgent to talk about it. I used to come home from homophobic school, off the homophobic bus, into the house where I would act miserably so my parents would assume it was my hormones, not people's hate, that was making me silent. I would lock myself in my bedroom. The back of the door was covered with hundreds of images of Madonna and Celine Dion, framing a small mirror I'd bought from the market in Lancaster. I used to take off my clothes and wrap myself in a cheap faux-fur blanket I'd bought from Matalan, like a dress, put in my crackly headphones, and press play on songs that would make me feel like a superstar.

I used to look into my own eyes and promise myself, "You're a superstar. You are going to have an extraordinary life." And it worked. It lifted me to a place where I was not just healed, but where I felt formidable. That's where Crystal was born.

That thirteen-year-old is stronger than me, over a decade on.

Since I was attacked five nights ago, I can't go outside, especially at night. I feel as if me and my friends, my wonderful friends who have come to visit in all their queer, joyous droves, have been burdened with the rage of this man who slinked away into the night to enjoy his freedom, while we toil and angst over the constant threats to our safety.

I've been jumpy and spatially aware: a car door slamming feels like an attacker, a loud voice or the hydraulics of a bus make me flinch like a terrified animal. I've worn only black clothes: giant black swathes of fabric, hoping I'll be less visible, wanting to be nothing more than a shadow. I even considered, for about thirty minutes, trying to change my walk, which has always drawn attention. But I felt as if that was the definition of internalising their violence, and then they win, so I've kept mincing, my tiny protest requiring mammoth amounts of bravery.

Emotionally I've felt an equal, uncomfortable mix of defeat and fury. Fury that no structure is in place no matter where I look telling me that my identity is acceptable. Fury that the only thing any policeman or authority figure could offer me was that "this happens all the time."

> *"Well, fucking do something about it, then,"* **Crystal would say, as she clenches a fist ready to bash a cop, but violence doesn't get us anywhere.**

But I feel furious. Furious that people seem to take pleasure in reminding me that I'm "a piece-of-shit faggot" (Northern line, 2015), that I should "die of AIDS" (Tooting, 2014), that I'm a "fucking fag" (high school, every day), or that I am worthless enough as a human to use as a punchbag, while these abusers get to walk away and relish in the safety afforded them as straight and white and male while I am left having to put in hours of emotional labour to remind myself that my gayness and my non-binaryness* aren't a curse or a moral wrong. I am left in pain and unable to complete my daily tasks because my head throbs and my nose crunches and my personality crumbles at the hint of anything that could even signal attack. I was strong and intent on taking up space, and now I don't know where that part of me is; it is knocked out of me, somewhere on the dual carriageway. Me, my radical friends, and my family have to spend their time and energy helping me overcome the actions of a selfish man, absorbing his rage and transforming it to our anxiety.

I feel fury that sometimes, when I'm alone and everyone is sleeping, I lie recounting all of the instances of homo-, femme-, and queerphobia I have encountered, then I multiply that by every LGBTQIA+ person in the world, then all of my critical and emotional faculties bulge into a space in my brain that I hate, a space where for a moment I wonder if I've been wrong this whole time. That everything I've so proudly represented these years was a mistake. That I was never a superstar. That if this many people around the world think that what we are is so heinous, so vile, so grotesque, that it inspires beatings and killings and imprisonments and disproportionate levels of homelessness, suicide, incarceration, and sexual and domestic violence, maybe I am wrong and they are right, and everything about me is heinous, vile, grotesque. I cry into my pillow, which has a pic-

---

* A made-up word, but all words are made up, so STFU.

ture of Celine Dion on it, and don't know how to stop and feel so selfish and so disgusted at myself for even momentarily abandoning my queer siblings. Then I fall asleep and forget I ever felt that until I feel it again, another night when these memories come back to life.

I feel selfish when I imagine others who experience far more suffering than this. I feel embarrassed that I was punched in the face and can't go outside. I feel desolate that all the years I have spent building myself up against constant homophobia have been undermined by one fist in the face. A hard fist. I feel a growing fear of men. I feel so loved by the women and queers in my life, and my wonderful, heartbreakingly kind brothers, James and Harry, and my sister, Danielle. I feel determined both to bury this, to wash it away like the words in my teenage notebook, and to address it head-on, unlike so many of my other feelings, which I push off the emotion cliff. I feel as if I'll never again be formidable. I feel as if my heart has been broken and I don't have the energy to fix it.

27th April / le 27 avril

Three days have passed and I've descended into an adolescent state, unable to cope with basic tasks and small demands. Crystal has reemerged, probably because she can see I'm in need of resuscitation. Here she is, dragging me through the days, encouraging me to get up and go, to stop wasting time, reminding me of all the things we've survived together.

"I fled Russia, I survived the Great Fire of London and the Black Plague. We survived high school."

I was standing at the door, and it felt like I was breathing water as I realised I had to step outside this morning for the first time since the attack if I was going to eat. Plus we'd run out of loo roll from all the crying and the pooing, and we needed to do some more crying and pooing. There, on the threshold to the outside world, I was immobilised.

"Here, take a step."

Crystal came back, pushing my legs over the door, into the street. To the shop and back.

"Head down, queen. It's like when I started the Cold War and had to get through security at JFK to make it to my home in the north of Cyprus, one of my three properties from which I, thankfully, can't be extradited."

So, some promises I've made to myself:

I'm not going to wear black; I'm not going to be scared to take up space; I'm not going to avoid make-up or drag anymore; I'm not making sure no nail polish is on my fingers anymore, checking for tiny specks and frantically scratching them off when found; and I'm not going to put earrings on in the morning and then decide against it.

I'm going to work to find my femme energy, which I know is somewhere among all these brittle parts of myself, which feel as if they've been stretched and peeled apart from one another and injected with fearfulness.

Yesterday, I thought of my mum, who used to tell me that she loved me but worried about my being attacked for looking a certain way or acting explicitly "gay." For a moment, I had a feeling that she was right and that I should have listened to her and given in, even though I knew the only way for me to survive was to set myself alight, make a spectacle of myself. I called her and told her what I was thinking. She told me that she was wrong, and that if I'd listened to her, I wouldn't be the person I am now and she would feel eternally heartbroken for that.

"People like you are a beacon of beauty; you show so many of us just how beautiful the world can be. You have changed so many people's universes, don't ever forget it."

We were both sobbing.

"Don't you dare change the way you are. You've worked so hard. Take them all down. Do it the way you always wanted to. Be loud. Do it for all of us who can't be or don't dare to be."

I'm going to go out to get some food again as Hatty is at work. I know I'm about to break all my promises and decide on an all-black health-goth look, desperately camouflaging myself into the dusty streets of East London, but it's only been a week since I was boxed on my doorstep, so failing at my promises is absolutely fine.

May / mai

3rd May / le 3 mai

A note from my diary, this day last year:

> Last night I wore an actual nun's cassock and a dip-dyed
> wig to the gay club. Safe to say people weren't into me in
> all my full-length black-sack glory, but I was feeling like
> the future of fashion, which is better than any validation
> any man in a club could give me. Halfway through the
> night, all of us rejoining into a circle after various split-
> offs and rampages through the different rooms of the club,
> Glamrou dared us all to play kiss-chicken—where you go in
> for the kiss and see who can hold for the longest.
>
> Glamrou was crap at it. Every time you got close
> enough, they would flick their head away and laugh
> hysterically. Sometimes it's so liberating to behave like a
> teenager. Not one pair made the kiss, all succumbing to
> be chicken, except Ace and me.
>
> After we'd come up for air, we looked in each other's
> eyes, inhaled deeply, and both, at the same time, exhaled
> a breathy "Whoa!," the world slowing around us, the
> sound of Loreen's "Euphoria" muffling.
>
> This kiss felt like the kind that turned us both into
> each other's princess.

It's funny how some moments in our history dwindle into insignificance, while some elongate and become
long-stretched memories that exist in full technicolour,
taking up far more time than the seconds it took to do
the deed.

Since I was attacked, Ace has all but moved into Wally, there by my side most days and nights when he's not teaching kids who've been kicked out of their schools to read and write. A literal saint. He's unquestioningly sacrificed his time to sit and watch shit videos with me, or to read while I apply to various internships and jobs, or to go to the shops to get me Nurofen or a tub of Häagen-Dazs Pralines & Cream. That's actually his favourite flavour, not mine—it makes me feel sick—but I don't tell him that and let him enjoy both the ice cream and the thought that he's doing the sweetest thing for me. Which he is.

Last night he was awake, reading, and I'd closed my eyes, nearing sleep. He brushed my hair from my brow and kissed my forehead and whispered, "I really do love you."* In written form it sounds painfully saccharine, but in the moment I decided to keep pretending I was asleep so as not to disturb his secret confession. So filmic. I'm Bridget, he's Darcy.

6th May / le 6 mai

The one good thing about my temporary agoraphobia is that I've had loads of time, when not consumed by dread, to apply for a ton of jobs in fashion and journal-

---

* I got what I call a commitment erection, which is when you get an erection about emotional commitment. Just me?

ism. From internships* to social media positions (which I'd be dreadful at since I hate social media, although I do want the free stuff), from the PA to editors, to fashion cupboard assistants—I've been hurling my CV out left, right, and centre. I even applied for a junior position at Hello Fashion. Obsessed.

I've developed, also, a new skill: anxiously stalking editors and writers on Twitter and Instagram and submerging myself in their worlds in quite an unhealthy way. Fine for now, but tricky were I ever to meet them— me knowing everything about their front-facing selves, them knowing nothing about me.

7th May / le 7 mai

When you're attacked, you learn and relearn many things about the world, about its inequalities, its violences, its unfairnesses. You learn a new kind of empathy with others who walk around with their keys between their fingers, heart beating your treacle-thick blood round your body, it only slowing when you lock your door behind you. You learn to view the world through the lens of violence: what's given and what's received. But the most prophetic thing you learn, perhaps, is that, whether you like it or not, the world goes on.

I got a job!

---

* Note that internships in fashion are the devil, (a) exploiting free labour and (b) allowing only privileged folk who can afford to work for free to do so.

Chic is the magazine my grandma used to buy for me every month, and into the pages of which I'd fall deep and fast: pages of Viktor & Rolf couture or Van Cleef & Arpels diamonds or Alaïa silhouettes or McQueen show reports or endless fantasies that took me far from where I was. *Chic* was one of the first things I ever saw that taught me that the world could be bigger than Lancaster. And every month, as it plopped through my letterbox, I caught a glimpse of what true luxury could be. For someone who didn't realise they already had it in abundance back then—home, love, friends, smarts—the magazine represented everything I would spend the next ten years of my life aiming for.

Funny how life can be so disparate: I still morph into a trembling little deer at the thought of leaving the warehouse; but I've just been welcomed onto the first rung of a career I've wept over thousands of times. This is every fashion gay's dream.

Now what to wear?

10th May / le 10 mai

Hey, I ran into your mum at Morrisons and she told me you're now the deputy editor of *Chic*!? Honestly amazing! Always knew at school that you'd go far! If you ever have any openings I've always dreamed of working in fashion. And I'm so good at make-up now! xxx

Oh my God! Deputy editor at *Chic*? Are you kidding! So proud of you, queen; next time I'm in London you have to take me on a tour of the fashion rooms!! Maybe I could send you some ideas and stuff? Obviously no worries if not, just thought I'd offer! <3

Hi there, it's Linda—I used to teach you at Rock Solid Sunday School! How are you doing? I added you because I heard that you're now the deputy editor of *Chic* magazine? Amazing news! Everyone here in Lancaster always knew you'd go so far; you were born to be famous!! Anyway, my daughter, you remember Lara, is looking for work experience at the moment. She's in Year 11 and I know she would just love to work at *Chic*. How can she apply? Sorry if this is out of the blue—but God gives to those who ask, I always say. Let me know, L xx

Today I awoke to these three incredibly random messages, from three incredibly random people. I called my mum, wondering what on earth's gone on.

"Oh, shit, yeah, it sort of got out of hand . . . I ran into Debbie—you know, that awful woman with alopecia—"

"Mum, you don't need to mention her alopecia—"

"Anyway, she was being really boastful and awful about her son, who just got accepted onto an acting course in London, and it just came out."

"What did?"

"That you're now deputy editor of *Chic*. I didn't think anyone would care, I was just trying to one-up Debbie."

So Mum's the source of my unhealthily competitive side. I never thought it was like her to lie.

"Well, was it not enough to one-up her with the fact I got a beauty internship at *Chic*? I mean, that's still a pretty big deal."

"Oh, I know, I know, and I don't want to diminish your achievement. But I just wanted to really stick the knife in, you know?"

"Well, what should I do now? Should I set them straight?"

"If you could just take one for my team this time, just tell them you're deputy editor, go on, for me? How embarrassing if everyone finds out I've been lying—"

"Mother, this is utterly terrible parenting. But, yes, I'll do it for you."

I've responded to all messages, explaining that I am indeed deputy editor of *Chic* and that when I start my new role, I'll do what I can about Lara's internship or Sunita's make-up skills. Here I am, a mere intern, but at home I'm the deputy editor.

13th May / le 13 mai

I can usually conceptualise most things, work my way through them and around them, but some questions are frankly too big, too monumental, to even consider tackling. The question of what to wear to your first day at a job at *Chic* is one of those few unanswerable questions. I would pray to God, but fashion's never been her strong suit. The whole point of *Chic* is that it's culturally definitive in fashion: it sets the trend,* doesn't follow, and while trends are reserved for the tiny, tiny few in the world who have bucket-loads of money and time and taste (wealth and taste are so infrequently bedfellows), that is not me. It's also not the job of someone at *Chic* to

---

* For rich skinny white ladies.

be on trend; they must be ahead of it, surely? And, let's face it, while much of the produce of this British institution is somewhat staid, whitewashed, and anorexia-inspiring, within its walls it still houses some of the most influential people in the fashion world.

Over the week I'd laid out various options of various outfits, ranging from a giant leather bomber jacket embroidered with an eighties paisley pattern to a jewel-toned fashion turban. I quickly scrapped the turban because of cultural appropriation and gave it back to my friend Violet, who is stylish, and we both agreed that, while it's Prada, the turban should be left to gather dust in the back of the wardrobe.

I'd settled on a long black dress with a fringe at the bottom, Prada heels also donated to the cause by Violet, a trashy ruby necklace, and an oversize maroon bomber jacket. I wanted something that said both "I'm new here, but cool" and "Give me five years and I'll be editor in chief," which is why I added the rich-white-woman jewels.

This morning, outfit ready, I stepped outside, in near full face—it's the beauty department, after all—clutching a Miu Miu patchwork tote that Violet also lent me, and teetering in the Prada heels. I stopped, lit a fag, and felt momentarily terrified by my visibility.

I was basically in full drag on the morning commute, save for a wig and lashes. I took a moment and a deep breath, reminding myself that at the end of the terrifying journey was my first step into my future—and when I get to that future, I can get cars everywhere, anyway. I galvanised myself: the outfit was more important than my safety. I've always been good at ordering my priorities.

As we buzzed through the tunnel towards Bank on the DLR, I saw two men laughing at me, one of whom was taking my picture. It felt like my arse was going to fall out the bottom of my dress, and I kept letting out little farts of fear.* I tried to remind myself that this happens all the time but couldn't quite hear it. "Seriously, fuck off," I shot my rage down the train, direct like a laser beam, Crystal pressing the trigger, giving me the energy I needed for this incoming face-off at seventy miles per hour.

"You talking to us, mate?" They were laughing. "Why don't you fuck off, you fucking faggot?"

Then I did something I'd never had the courage to do before. Addressing the sardine-like commuters on this packed train, I harnessed the potential power of the people: "Hello, my fellow train riders. Sorry to disturb your journeys this morning, but I'd just like a show of hands as to who, in this scenario where these two men were taking pictures and laughing at me, thinks I should fuck off? Show of hands."

At this only the two men, out of about ninety, raised their hands.

"And who, of those who haven't voted yet, thinks indeed that these two men should, in fact, fuck off?"

The entire carriage, bar the two men, raised their hands straight to the sky, engaged fully in my voting system and saying things like "How dare you?" and "If you don't like it, get off our fucking train."

Democracy works. Well, sometimes, as in this in-

---

* Made worse by the kind of clenching high heels force upon you.

stance. But I've been in many homophobic situations where people stayed silent in public, yet here it was reassuring that the majority of people voted to defend the weak. If only that were the case in politics. Anyway, the guys got off under a cloud at the next station and I felt as if I'd properly won.

Revolving doors. Reception. I was greeted by Gillian—"not *Jillian* with a *J* sound, for God's sake, but *Gillian*, like the gill of a fish"—an Alexander McQueen scarf clinging to her incredibly posh long neck. "Quick, it's morning briefing. Don't you speak, just listen."

Everyone collected around a white table, every single decision-maker in the room as white as the table, and as posh as the calla lilies set at the centre.

"Bobbles: it's honestly all about bobbles. The *nuovo* hair tie, the must-have luxe pony-puller, the bobble!"

The women around the table scribbled in their customised Smythson notebooks with the zeal of the twelve disciples listening to Jesus preaching the Sermon on the Mount.

I fought the urge to laugh, hard, at these, the best brains in fashion, foaming at the mouth about bobbles. Literally bobbles.

"Do you mean like hair ties? Would you not say that something as ubiquitous as a hair tie can't be either in or out of fashion?" Crystal piped up on my behalf.

All of the long-necked women craned toward me, eyes darting as if I'd just killed their children.

"And who are you?" the actual deputy editor queried.

"I'm the new beauty intern . . ." My genitals disappeared inside me like a snail into its shell.

"Well, girls, I think the new beauty intern should take the bobble story, don't you?" They all nodded in support, as if they'd won at a game I didn't even know I was playing.

Joke's on them, as it turns out. It was a first-day byline—even if it was about bobbles.

17th May / le 17 mai

Okay, been thinking a lot about *Chic* and wondering how I might see past my infantile fantasy of what it meant to me as a teen queen. How do I now, a much more politically advanced me, tackle the racism and the sexism and the fattism that the magazine has upheld for near a century?

"Change it from the inside," Hatty advised me.

In the room it is utter madness. Even after five days, I've noticed how people are blind to the inequalities that plague the industry, and the wider world. That's not everyone, but so many of the older, white people who run the magazine are so cemented in their upper-middle-classness that the utterance of words such as *queer* or *black* or *equality* are met with a furrowed botoxed brow, which creates a kind of waxy fold in the forehead and for a second it looks as if you could slice the skin like cheese. I wish I could bring them all to Wally to meet Hatty and the Denims, and my other rad anarcho-queer friends, to show them real inappropriate conversation.

For instance, today, someone on the beauty desk told me that she thinks women of a certain age should have surgery, that it's a woman's "responsibility" to age gracefully, "and if that requires a knife, then so be it." Despite Hatty's words ringing in my ears, I didn't dare speak back, and I definitely didn't want to raise the subject of misogyny or classism or ageism. I'm sure that, from someone half her age who can't necessarily empathise, would infuriate her. Yes, surgery is great, but by no means is it anyone's responsibility. It's not her fault; her name is, and I'm not kidding, Theodora—she had no chance.

There's one girl, Amnah, a fashion cupboard intern who is equally tearing her hair out. We're each other's only office allies—meeting up by the loos to have a moment of "What in the fucking hell did she just say?" before going back to our menial tasks. Today those tasks were to swipe different make-up samples across different smooth surfaces to see how they would smear, ready to be photographed like those beautiful glistening smudges of make-up or cut-up lipsticks you see on the glossy white pages of the magazine. It was pretty fucking satisfying, I shan't lie, decimating these expensive products into smudges and smears—the same impulse that makes you want to eat certain soaps or lip balms.

The fashion industry needs to ask itself, especially within the corridors of *Chic*: To work in this industry, why must we compromise both morals and intellect?

Fashion and dress, at least for the communities I move in, have proven to be incredibly, irreversibly powerful tools of protest, of coding, of communication—the hanky code, leather and latex wear, drag, gender nonconformity, that jacket worn by a member of ACT UP in the eighties that read IF I DIE OF AIDS—FORGET BURIAL—JUST DROP MY BODY ON THE STEPS OF THE FDA. But here we flutter around with an air of superiority, as if we're solving world hunger when the chance of an engaging conversation in this place is as likely as a woman of colour appearing on the magazine's cover. The central feature in this month's issue is on types of butter.

Types. Of. Butter.

And this is what is important to women and basic baby-gays? I think absolutely not. I should've known that I was going to feel this conflicted because I'd basically stopped reading the magazine towards the end of university—when I realised that everything was a construct, that the world is full of hard things, that the things in these pages had been my escape route, a kind of class opiate that made me want to leave where I was from and live inside the centrefold. It informed who Crystal is, too—her attitude, her endless riches, her five *Chic* covers—but even she has become more awake to other things in the world. But I was lured back by the name, the status of the job.

While I like the idea of changing things from the inside, the likelihood of that feels as if it were disappearing more quickly than my social life.

21st May / le 21 mai

Here it is, my magnum opus, my *Riverside Chaucer*, my *Complete Works of Shakespeare*, my Bible, my Beyoncé *Lemonade*. My indisputable peak.

At 5:00 a.m. at the club last night I first clocked the time and regretfully tore myself away from friends to make the long walk home, alone. About an hour and twenty minutes later I woke up, the bright May sun forcing the day upon me. I'd slept through my alarm and had thirty-six minutes to make it to morning briefing. My commute, if all goes well, is exactly twenty-four minutes door to door because the warehouse is in expensive, homogenised Zone 1, something I still can't quite believe.

I must become army-general-like in my decision-making, even though I'm a pacifist. A decision had to be made:

1. A much-needed shower and time to pick the right outfit.
2. A much-needed hangover poo, a much-needed shower, and no time to pick the right outfit.

As any good fashion queer knows, aesthetic is everything, so I, with absolute resolve, chose to bypass the poo.

How bad could it be?

I made it to work on time, the outfit was good—a trainer heel and red leather jacket—but while I sipped a coffee, I felt the hangover poo edging toward the outside world, fuelled like a rocket by that first hit of caffeine.

The problem here, the pressing problem, is that you simply can't poo at *Chic*. Perhaps you can pop out a tiny pellet off the back of a discreet fart, while doing a sit-down wee, but the kind of mammoth, toxin-filled hangover poo I had brewing? Not a chance.

I'm in an open-plan office. On this busy, hot day, in

the intense space between my needing a constant IV feed of caffeine and there being no time to take a lunch break to find a place to poop, I was stumped. The poo was growing inside me, the pain from holding in my prairie dog worse than holding a big dick up there.

But I kept on holding, tensing my pelvic floor muscles, an act I thought would eventually pay off beautifully in the favour of any future top lucky enough to score this queen.

At one point in the afternoon, I had genuinely reached a state of poo-induced euphoria. I was James Franco in *127 Hours*. I was Linford Christie running the hundred metres. I was Jessica Ennis bringing it home for Great Britain. I was Jesus, a prophet. I was a mother lifting a car under which her child was stuck, finding strength not in her physicality but deep within her soul.

For a moment, I was God.

Then, around 4:00 p.m., I hit a low. A severe low. I slumped, my brow sweating, my fingertips oily, my ass muscles so exhausted from lactic acid overproduction that I no longer had agency over them.

I was about to go down in fashion legend as "that queen who shat her dress at *Chic*."

Then a light appeared, my editor:

"You look so unwell you're making me feel unwell. You can go early if you want; I think we're done for the day."

I nearly broke down, but kept my composure. Now I had to run to my other job in East London. Instead of doing the rational thing, I raced to the tube in some poo-fuelled mania.

Tube. Heat. Poo. Pain. So much pain. A vow never to drink again. Tube. Heat. Poo. Pain.

I arrived at Liverpool Street and broke into a run. A Wasabi—no loo.

A Santander—obviously no loo, that's a bank. A KFC—a loo! Halle-loo!

I'd found the Holy Grail, and it was a single empty loo. I was finally free from the shackles of my poo oppression, and tears squeaked from my eyes.

Flush.

The water started to rise, rise, rise, and slowly, to my horror, it started to brim over the bowl and onto the floor of the tiny cubicle that opens right onto the restaurant. With it, to my utter chagrin, my hangover log dislodged from its position and was lifted out of the bowl and onto the water-flooded floor, still fully intact. One hardy poo.

The only course of action was to leave this poo there, on the floor of the loo. Me: a terrible person—I did not think for a second about the poor person who would have to clean up the contents of my night out.

I had to escape.

I opened the door, ready to make a dash for the stairs, but before I could, the water flooded out ahead of me, through the doorway, carrying with it my giant poo, right into the packed restaurant. It travelled surprisingly far on the back of the water, like those stones in curling (the nichest sport) as they slow toward their destination.

Screams; cries; one man is so disgusted that he throws down the remnants of his chicken leg and walks out, stepping over my poo, leaving the beautifully crisp yet greasy secret-recipe skin on the table. I think for a second that nothing would make me put down a piece of KFC chicken without eating all the skin, poo in the room or no poo in the room.

This was it. I could either run from my problem or face it head-on. So I went into autopilot mode, cleared my throat: "My apologies! We've had a little accident, but it'll be sorted any second."

I dived back into the loo and wrapped my hands in the paper from a whole toilet roll. I paced back gingerly, careful not trip on the flood, approached the poo, stared at it, desperate not to let it get the better of me. I bent down, knees clicking, the whole restaurant silent and aghast, watching as I took my poo into my own hands. Watching as I took control of my destiny.

I lifted the poo, still intact (!!), and carried it with me back to the loo, broke it in half, dropped it, and flushed it, along with my trauma.

I washed my hands, apologised to the good patrons of KFC Liverpool Street, and left the restaurant into the world, nobody on the street aware that a life-changing event had just occurred not a hundred feet away.

This isn't new territory for me, which is why my composure was such a triumph.

I have more embarrassing poo stories than anyone I know. One time I shat myself during a kiss with a boy I fancied, and he never spoke to me again. Another time I shat my pants, a huge intact log, while giving a speech at a friend's birthday party in front of her dad, who was a judge on *Dragons' Den*. Thank God I wasn't asking for funding. Once I got so drunk I shat my pants in the cinema in front of all my judgmental high school friends. Also, I got sick on a guy's dick after I'd had not one, not two, but three croissants for breakfast. Not an actual shit story, but a shitty story nonetheless. There was the time I borrowed an American Apparel leotard from a friend of mine and gave it back with, unbeknownst to me, some pretty violent skid marks decorating the inside. We did speak again, but she made me buy her a new one. Good friend.

I roll these stories out more regularly than my favourite leopard-print sequin pantsuit because I spent a lot of my life in the violent, painful clutches of shame, which manifested itself in various modes of self-harm, self-destruction, and other untenable behaviours.

But the antidote to shame is honesty. Stark, crass, funny, powerful honesty. Honesty that smashes through notions of taboos. So I tell my poo stories because it's the only way I know how to free myself from the shackles of shame that would see us all bound for life. It's the only way I know how to survive.

23rd May / le 23 mai

I think about my funeral all the time. Literally all the time. My friends know, if I'm zoned out and looking a little on the emotional side, I'm probably deep in thought, Crystal planning every detail of our send-off.

I don't want any of this "Let's celebrate their life, let's all wear yellow and have a shot in their memory" shit. No, I want emotional devastation. I want "Change" by the Sugababes, performed by every Sugababe ever. All seven/six(?) of them.

Today we were sat in a read-through of the next issue—which my line manager oddly invited me to, even though I think she likes me less than her husband, with whom she argues over the phone on the hour every hour. He sounds like an uncompromising wanker who passes all his fragile masculinity on to her, which she then channels on to her team.

Anyway, I was in the read-through—flicking through page after page of young, white, upper-class playwrights and models and thinking about my funeral because it's far more interesting than anything in the pages—and at that moment the art director zoomed in on me: "You, beauty boy, any thoughts?"

Utterly gobsmacked, and misgendered. I hadn't been asked to speak since day one, when Office Manager Gillian—who was now glaring violently my way—banned me from using my voice. "I think it's really pretty. But I think, if I'm not mistaken, almost every single person in the pages is white? Is that not a little irresponsible of us?"

There in that boardroom, I no longer needed to plan my funeral, for every editor just buried me alive in their heads. No memorial service. Not a Sugababe in sight. There was no real dismissal, just a mutual understanding that this wasn't the place for me.

So I cleared my desk. No one looked my way or tried to stop me. We all understood it was time. I swiped a lovely Tom Ford lipstick and a La Mer lip balm so at least I got something. I have been gently dismissed from an internship at *Chic*. I have been relieved of my moral compromise. I'm aware of the privilege in being able to pick and choose the work you will and will not do, and there at *Chic* I'd definitely breached various political parameters I thought were set in stone for me when I entered the all-white white office on day one. I'm lucky to have the CV points for ten days' work, but I'm luckier to have been let go.

26th May / le 26 mai

Since *RuPaul's Drag Race* got all the basics hyped about drag, the earning potential for queens has somewhat exponentially risen, thank God. The number of brands and companies desperate to align themselves with the LGBTQIA+ cause is staggering, and *Chic* just missed the memo. As our presence and our market influence grows, each awful pinkwashing, patronising campaign becomes more transparent, brands happy to feature rainbows and glitter and anything that signifies queerness without engaging with the reality of such things as, say, AIDS or trans issues or anal sex or people of colour. The world is willing to accept the clean side of gay life: namely white, beautiful, successful, healthy men. And if the straights love anything, it's a drag queen: one who is fab, pink, and glam—never filthy, political, or intelligent. It makes them feel transgressive by proxy.

It's a hard line to prance because with this shifting lens of "tolerance" also comes the aforementioned pay cheque. I have a friend who danced all night, for four hundred pounds, at a Morgan Stanley Christmas party. I have a bunch of friends who dressed as giant drag squares, crosses, and circles and bopped up and down on a PlayStation float for the duration of London's apolitical Pride Parade. Morgan Stanley. PlayStation. This is how a drag artist makes money, atop other means such as bar work or graphic design or occasionally, for the supersmart, having a sugar daddy.

The thing about these jobs? I don't know a single queen who can afford to turn them down. Better to pay rent and dance for Nando's and still be able to make your rad art.

That's why when a friend of mine called, offering me a job singing at the Royal Horticultural Society, hearing that I'd quit *Chic* (the story I told everyone, to make me look much more principled than I actually am), I accepted—for the princely fee of £350.

It was hell on earth. I assumed it would be a glamorous affair—"How posh!" I thought when I googled the society. I soon learned that that was merely the building in which the event was housed; the event turned out to be pokeryou.com's annual piss-up.

Imagine for a second, if you will, a room full of men who invented an online poker-playing site on which you can choose to have your dealer wear a bra and knickers while doling out your cards. Imagine for a second, if you please, being a drag queen in that space after they've all finished dinner and moved on to after-after-dinner drinks.

It's safe to say that some of the words uttered were

not words of praise for this queen singing her lungs out. I was an exotic fruit, a circus freak, an accessory ripe for the abusing—leaving with an arse so slapped by passersby it hurt to sit down in the Uber.

So, with the £450 cash (I demanded an extra hundred once I found out the real sponsor—danger money), I decided the only thing to rid myself of these dreadful ass slaps and the visuals of these clammy men creaming over Russian roulette tables was to book a flight to Berlin. Lily, whom I've barely spoken to since I left New York, is there for a month at the moment, and so again I chose to spend my money rather than save it—transforming the coins made from the bleakest gig into some solid queer gold, a kind of alchemy.

DRAG PERFORMANCE MEMO: There are two types of queer performance—one for straights and one for queers. Queers expect a high standard, but with straights, if you replace any lyric for something sexual—so instead of "I Was Here" I sing "I Fucked Here"—they go nuts.

28th May / le 28 mai

Berghain, Berlin. The eternal Mecca for queer clubbers from around the world. The ex-power-station turned impossible-to-get-into club. Filled with all the expected druggy techno world stereotypes: Rick Owens queers in black drapery thinking they're God's gift to creativity but who haven't done or made anything of note in the last five years and think a nose ring is queer activism; Berlin daddies with a European kind of intellectual masculinity, awfully dated nineties tribal tattoos, well-sculpted beards, and more leather harnesses and jockstraps than T-shirts. They often love G—the gay party drug that doubles up as alloy cleaner. There's the thirsty twinks, who finally, after five tries, make it through the door and up the stairs and into Panorama Bar, and somehow all have enough money to be wearing head-to-toe Vetements. Arty girls who adore techno and love that shop Weekday, who sport an array of haircuts composed of angular lines and are likely studying at the RCA and once modelled in a Doc Martens campaign. There's the old-school clubbers in their fifties who smell like sweaty tights but are really into the party and shout things like "Berlin nonshhtoppppp!" as you pass them. There's the very, very rare straight dude who sticks out like a sore thumb and for once has no traction in the space; and there's that one drug dealer in the second-floor loos who literally never leaves.

If you've never heard of Berghain, it's because, obviously, you're a loser.

No, I'm kidding. But among queer folk it's a place of legend, which opens on a Thursday night and doesn't stop until Monday. Queers in Berlin call Sunday-morning Berghain "church." One time I saw a fully naked woman being carried out of there by three bouncers into a snowy Berlin dawn and screaming valiantly in a thick German accent, "I was the Queen of Party!" And you know what? She was. Berghain inspires such devo-

tion in people that they move to Berlin.* I knew this
one quite niche girl from uni who disappeared into a
Berghain stupor for her whole year abroad and returned
shockingly skinny, hooked on gay party drugs, with an
experimental psycho-geographic dissertation whose title
was, no joke, "Berghain Has My Soul."

This is some strong shit.

Crystal hates it. She's more suited to the glam interi-
ors of the Polo Lounge, or her penthouse on the top floor
of Harrods, because she, you know, invented capitalism.
But I drag her along. Get her a little high and she'll do
anything.

"Never a truer word."

The queue has never been a problem in my experience, although Berghain is known as the hardest door
in the world. The key is to stay chilled. I have a friend—
the journalist one, Amelia—who once got in wearing a
top and jeans from Brandy Melville: not the usual look
of the Berghain set, but she's so chilled she just strolled
through. Another friend of mine, Jacob—an incredibly
beautiful, cool model and the perfect Berghain client—
was rejected because he was so nervous. It was fine,
though: the next night we walked him right in.

"Keep your cool," Lily and I whispered to each other.
Neither of us has ever been refused, but there's always a
slim chance. We got to the door.

---

* All while claiming to be artists while not making a single thing for
years because clubbing is their art.

"How many?"

"*Zwei*," I said in my terrible German accent.

"Go." The bouncer gestured with his hands for us to scoot through. And we were in: queertopia.

Inside, it's a cavernous, gigantic, loud place that sits at the intersection of brutalism, dystopia, utopia, and pretension. Take your eyes off your partner for a second and they'll be lost to a sea of ecstasy-jacketed dancers, clouded in the smoke from their thousands of cigarettes. There's the garden to relax in, the sofas by the loos, the two humongous, indescribably big dance rooms in which the floors bounce and at least one drag queen loses her wig. No other feeling is quite like how cool you feel when you're dancing all night inside the guts of Berghain. The sex rooms are decorated in that Berlin vintage butcher-shop way—all meat hooks, concrete, and plastic-flapped doors. Lily and I frequented them sporadically through the night, sucking the odd dick there, rimming the odd butt hole here. She's into gay men at the moment, "plus there's just so many more for the picking in Berlin, and they have a much more sophisticated view of gender here. All this for twelve euros? A bargain."

While the door policy sounds savage—I always feel so sad for the folks who spend months planning their trip to Berghain, some flying from as far as Australia, only to be rejected at the door—Lily reminded me that a ticket to utopia is not easy to get: it costs much more than twelve euros' entry and a choker from Urban Outfitters. She's right: "You have to have earned this experience, and our lives have been spent earning the privilege. We deserve something."

She's now sleeping on a mattress on the floor in our apartment for the weekend, and I'm sipping coffee, looking out the window as the sun sets over a slightly wobbly-looking Berlin—maybe that's just my hangover. Must get ready—another all-black outfit and a smudge of eyeliner, I imagine—we're going again tonight.

June / juin

1st June / le 1 juin

As we fly through the air from Berlin to London, the plane rattling through the clouds—Lily deciding to ditch her drug binge and come meet everyone in London—I can't sleep. I fucking hate flying, so I'm thinking about queerness,* trying to take my mind off impending death. I tried to ask Lily what she thinks it means, but she just told me shut the fuck up as she hadn't slept properly in over thirty-six hours.

It used to be an insult. It's also a term used to describe a huge, trendy academic subject—queer theory—and a lot of that is about subverting structures and questioning everything such as time and gender and our roles in society and binary modes and stuff. I was obsessed with the latter at university† and was a receiver of the former the whole time at high school.

But, for most of us (well, me at least), queerness doesn't live in lofty theory books or the vocal cords of bullies. It lives, instead, in everything we do and say and feel. For me everything feels queer because my experience of it is queer.

That feeling is especially recharged in a place like Berlin.

Now, nothing is worse than a stereotypical Berlin obsessor, whom you can often find in the corner of gay

---

* Lol, when am I not?
† No wonder I failed vet med: "Hey, I can't diagnose your gerbil but have you read Judith Butler?"

bars in Dalston wearing a mesh vest and sports shorts, devouring any and every chance to slip Berlin into the conversation: "I love your socks. They remind me of my fuck buddy in Berlin . . . Oh, you've never been? Berlin is like my spiritual home. I love its energy, the streets are so wide and the drugs are so pure and the history is so present and the men are so virile yet tender and everyone's an artist and I love how the brutalism of the East side reflects my inner brutalism and is the rectum a grave?"

All this crucially misses the crux of what makes Berlin such a queer haven. Which is that Berlin has a strong relationship with fun. So much value and sanctity is placed on partying, euphoria, and nihilism.

So many of Berlin's spaces are predicated on exploring and accepting pleasure that—in comparison to somewhere like London or New York, whose priority is success, money, capitalism—you are taken to places it's not possible to reach anywhere else.

When so much of being queer consists of things that are definitely not fun, it can't be emphasised enough just how liberating, powerful, and radical having fun can be. It's better than any drug, better than any drink, almost better than cigarettes, and definitely better than an unspeakably dull job at *Chic*.

3rd June / le 3 juin

"It was genius. I looked to my side and there's Lily in the same orgy as me."

Over dinner tonight Hatty and Ace laughed as I revelled in retelling Lily's and my outrageous sex stories from Berlin. We had gathered for impromptu family fajitas so Ace and Hatty could finally meet Lily.

"Honestly. It was so liberating: the boundaries between platonic and sexual love really fell away. Lily and I had never entertained the idea of group sex together before, but it was actually very, very freeing," I said.

"I've been saying for months that we should start a radical masturbation/pleasure group, once monthly, at Wally," Hatty chimed in, her eyes glistening as they do every time she hears a new, exciting depiction of how far the limits of queerness can stretch. "Would anyone else be into it?"

Everyone went a little quiet, then Lily said, "I mean we just met, and I do technically have a boyfriend. His rule is that anonymous group sex is fine, but with people I know it's not."

"But a group wank? Like exploring pleasure?" Hatty pleaded, desperately wanting her idea to take off.

More silence. I was into the idea, but with Ace in the room a somewhat awkward air falls whenever sex together, in any form, is brought up. At moments the option appears—like in kiss-chicken that time, or when we kissed on the last day in his parents' house—but most of the time even touching is out of the question. It's that thing when your legs meet under the table at a restaurant or your knees knock when you're in the cinema absolutely hating Wes Anderson's *The Grand Budapest Hotel*, and a surge of electricity and awkwardness zings through your body and you can do nothing but jolt away from each other. So, yes, the mention of sex is out of the question.

I decided, instead, to bulldoze the conversation by airing more extreme sex stories from my life of late. A Grindr guy wanted to rim my unwashed butt hole, so I let him but I didn't enjoy it. He did, though, which made me smile. "Bless him, I think he actually wanted me to shit in his mouth, but he didn't dare ask and I definitely wasn't going to offer; I'd had enchiladas for lunch."

Another guy was obsessed with my balls and spent an hour sucking them and sort of pressing on my gooch trying to find my prostate but missing it. "He did find it, though, when he fucked me. He just didn't know he had."

An Irish guy was unusually muscly—not usually my vibe, not usually a body type I could get. It became clear that he wasn't scoring most men and had settled for chubby me because he had about as much charm as tonsillitis, and he spent the whole of our meet with his phone on loudspeaker trying to get through to Hackney council because his central heating was broken. "And we both came in unison when the automated voice said, 'You are number thirteen in the queue, your call is very important to us,' and then he burst into heaving sobs and screamed at me to get out. I wanted to stay to see if he was okay, to coax some of his gay shame out into the open, but he was adamant that I leave, immediately."

This other guy I met in Berlin but lives in London. "His name's Peter and he works as a librarian at UCL. We had really beautiful sex, actually, like really pleasure-focused sex. I'm really into him, I thi—"

"That's the time, fuck, it's eleven, I have to go," Ace erupted, before leaving in a huge rush—dropping a tenner on the table for the dinner and drinks, then disappearing.

"Whoa"—as the door clicked—"he's clearly very hung up on you, queen," Lily advised, from her objective position.

"What? No. He just had to get home for work tomorrow," I replied.

They both looked at me, raising their eyebrows, as if to say, "Grow up and do something about this."

"Was it the sex stories?"

"No, it was the guy Pete. His face literally turned puce at the idea of you with someone else romantically." Hatty urged, "Go after him . . . now!"

I slipped on my shoes and ran, which I never do, out the door and toward the station. I saw Ace in the alleyway between Tesco and Efes Turkish Restaurant, standing still, evidently upset. I had been insensitive. Maybe sometimes I subconsciously speak that way in front of him to hurt him. It takes two to tango, and sometimes I just step on his feet.

We faced each other silently, momentarily lost for words. Then Ace took a deep breath, as if he'd made a decision to open up. "I know it's all my fault, I know that, and I know I backed off when you made yourself available," Ace explained emotionally, "but I just hate the idea of you developing feelings for another person than me. I feel like I've trashed all this."

"Well, do you want this?"

"I don't . . ." He paused. "I don't know." He paused

again. "I don't know if we should just draw a line under this."

We kissed. By a giant blue wheelie bin, on which someone had comically graffitied the Prada logo, in an alleyway that smelled overwhelmingly of piss. None of that mattered because we were kissing and not drawing a line under this.

I'd rather not know than draw a line. Purgatory is better than hell.

10th June / le 10 juin

Ace and I have these two genius friends who still use the term *fag hag*. Everyone else I know has ditched the label as offensive, degrading, misogynist, and predicated only on a woman's relation to a gay man. It's bleak. But these two, Laurie and Chelsea, adore it. They're like Patsy and Eddie—chain-smoking, glorious women who are killing their careers while also popping up in different locations every weekend on Instagram. So when Ace and I were invited over for dinner, we were incredibly excited.

I'm currently not working on any writing stuff, and I was in the throes of chasing four hundred pounds' worth of invoices from last month, so the promise of a free meal is like manna from heaven. So Ace and I took the train to Brixton. We've spent the week apart after I sent an intense text message to him the day after we kissed by the bin. I thought it was superchill, but when I read it back that evening with Cecily and Ellie and Lily, they all shook their heads in disappointment. Apparently it read as though I was asking for a relationship because I'd said, "Let's just see where this goes!"

I fucking hate texting.

Anyway, Ace and I were awkwardly moving around each other on the walk to Laurie and Chelsea's place, but after three courses of oddly paired foods and a shit ton of wine, we were a little more relaxed, able to look each other in the eye.

After dinner, in vintage style, we played this game we used to play at university all the time to legitimise our bogus decision-making—Consult the iPod. You ask a question you don't know the answer to—Will I ever find love? Am I going to be a successful journalist?, etc.—and press shuffle, the first song providing the answer to your unanswerable question.*

Laurie: "Will John ever find me truly attractive again, after my shit-and-menses extravaganza?"†

iPod: "Reflection" from *Mulan*. We all decided it must be a message about loving yourself in order to be loved by someone else.

Me: "Was I right to leave *Chic*?"

iPod: "Sisters Are Doin' It for Themselves" by Eurythmics. Frankly, a great answer.

Chelsea: "Was I right to end it with the giant duke?"‡

iPod: "Living for the Weekend" by Hard-Fi. None of

---

* Others would go to therapy, but I'm too broke for that.
† Earlier in the evening she'd recounted how she'd shat on the floor and dropped her full mooncup on top it, and her boyfriend walked in. And she was completely sober. Incredible!
‡ Chelsea had just broken up with an actual duke because his dick was too big.

us like this song anymore since we're no longer sixteen, so we shuffled again.

iPod: "Blue Velvet" by Bobby Vinton. Shuffled again. (Number one rule of the game is that you shuffle until you get the answer you want.)

iPod: "I've Got the Power" by Snap. Perfect.

Ace: "There's a guy I like, it's complicated, and I don't know what to do."

We all assumed he was talking about me, and the room tensed up as we waited for the iPod's choice.

iPod: "Young and Beautiful" by Lana Del Rey. Not sure what this meant.

But it was evident Ace did. Picking up his phone, he swiftly exited the room, uttering a firm "Right! Here goes."

All of us, somewhat baffled he hadn't planted a wet one on me, listened silently as we heard Ace making a phone call in the next room. We heard him coming back, none of us quite sure where he'd been and whom he was talking to. The door opened, and to make it look as if we hadn't been talking about him, Chelsea, best foot forward, asked, "Have you ever sucked a really smelly dick?"

But the conversation didn't flow. All of us were baffled, and we waited for Ace to explain his somewhat odd move.

"That was William. He's out dancing, over the road at Hootananny's. I'm gonna go meet him."

A palpable feeling of shock, a real blow, engulfed the room. Ace packed his bag; he left. Going off to claim his prize. I spent the next few hours weeping onto the

remnants of dinner while weaving through my humili-
ation, as Chelsea shook watery espresso martinis and
Laurie handed me cigarettes and lit them with her Zippo
lighter, which has a picture of her own breasts printed
on it.

11th June / le 11 juin

I got a commission today to write about being gay and
holding hands in the street. It's cash in the bank and it's
kind of aligned with my interests. It's also frustrating,
though, because I had pitched a piece about this community of late-teen fisting gays who live in San Fran-
cisco, but my editor thought it was "too much." While
I'm not a nineteen-year-old fisting bottom, it's baffling
to me that people would rather read an article about the
politics of holding hands in public versus taking a fist in
the ass.

Naturally, I'm feeling burned by Ace's slight last
night, so I started weeding out ways I've been too much
over this incredibly strange, and somewhat exhilarating,
time we've spent semicourting each other. Was the text
I sent after we kissed too much? Or is my big body too
much? Is the way I speak or dress too much?

Thinking back over past rejections, this was the main
theme.

Back in 2010, I went on holiday in Benidorm with
my girlfriends from school to celebrate the end of our
AS levels.

From my diary at the time:

17 July 2010, Benidorm

Hey guys!

I'm feeling fucking tragic after last night.

So, all eleven of the girls descended on the strip dressed to kill. Matt and I demanded we go to a gay bar because we were intent on finding some other gay guys somewhere on the face of the planet! And the men here are so hot, like so chavvy and muscular and have really sexy tattoos like the lion on the England flag and stuff. I just go weak at the knees for manly men!!

Anyway, when we got there, the weirdest thing happened: as we were going in the door, Matt grabbed hold of my hand, only for a second, and then squeezed it. We both looked into each other's eyes, both unsure what to make of it but defo feeling something. Half totally wanting it, half knowing that if people at school found out, it would be a mega problem.

Anyway, I'm not sure if it's a thing at this point, and then we started dancing together and Matt was wearing these shorts that made his dick look really bulging and he kept like pointing it at me. We were so drunk, and even tho we def know that we have weird feelings for each other, we never thought these were sexy feelings. He asked me to go to the loo, and we sat on a sicky-smelling leather sofa and I just decided to fucking tell him that I was looking at his bulge. He replied saying that he didn't think we would really work as a pair and that he just can't see us together. It's so embarrassing because I ran home crying even though I didn't even know if I felt it in the first place. Anyway now he's at the pool and

he's reading my Belle de Jour book and I'm too mortified
to go down and join them.

A side note—I am absolutely obsessed with my old diaries. They are the bleakest thing ever, and I open every paragraph with the word *anyway*. I especially can't believe I would use words such as *chavvy* and put a heart under every single exclamation mark and glorify manly men. When I look back at myself all those years ago, I don't remember what it felt like to be that person. Adore the "Hey guys!" opener. Stunning.

I do remember feeling chronically single and achingly desperate to find boys who, through their adoration, might prove to me that all that self-loathing and inability to see myself as worthy of romantic love was just your classic pubescent hormone roller coaster. I always assumed that all those problems would disintegrate the moment I found a relationship. By the time I was eighteen and off to university, I was the only member of my schoolgirl group—"the bezzaz" as we said then, in the north—who hadn't had a significant relationship. They were all coupled up, having sex, wondering about their futures together.

I left high school already feeling like too much. But, as one does, I stepped into my outrageousness, my too muchness. Surprisingly, this brought me some wonderful friends. But when it came to dating, while the best things about me were the big things, the too-much things, I spent a while after Matt working out how to be smaller in a relationship. That's how I met Jake. God. Jake.

Here's how that went:

4 December 2011, Cambridge

I have been dating this man called Jake. Thus far the men in Cambridge have either been science nerds who can't really speak but just look at you with a kind of intensity that either means they want to kill you or rim you, or Tory douchebags. Jake is a medic, he's from Kent, and he's camp and very sociable and votes Labour. It's all win-win.

Until Tuesday things were going great. We had been on a bunch of dates and he'd even changed his profile picture to one of us together at a club. After our seventh date, on Monday, he came back to my room and we had anal sex for the first time. It was beautiful and really intimate and, as we fell asleep and he stroked my hair, he whispered, "I think I'm falling for you." I reciprocated, and naturally was on cloud nine. I felt like I'd found someone who actually wanted to be with me.

On Tuesday I texted him to see if he wanted dinner. No reply.

On Wednesday I texted him again to suggest a drink. No reply. He changed his profile picture back to one of himself looking drunk in a giraffe onesie. For some reason my critical faculties didn't kick in at this.

On Thursday I texted him a third time to ask if everything was okay. No reply. I was so distraught I had to leave a neurobiology supervision and lied to my tutor that a made-up auntie had just passed away. I'm going to hell.

On Friday I texted him again, somewhat desperately.

No reply. I was going crazy. Crying all the time, half-hoping he was dead so then I wouldn't have to face up to the fact that a guy who would actively choose to publicise his ownership of a giraffe onesie had rejected me.

But tonight, Sunday, I decided it was time to take matters into my own hands. It was pouring down outside and I was in my room pretending to revise, in reality obsessively going over every single detail of what had happened on Monday night. Once more, I texted him: "Hey, I'm next door at Chelsea's, can I come over for a chat?" A lie.

A reply! What the fuck? "Sure. In half an hour?"

I got dressed, backcombed my hair, and applied some Benefit Hoola, and headed over in a cab.

"I'm sorry I didn't reply this week," he said. "I've just been thinking a lot about things and I don't think me and you are going to work out. You know, I'm a doctor—I'm clinical, I'm busy, I am looking for stability.

"You're just so much to take on, I just can't see you and me outside of our bedrooms."

Stunned. But oddly not surprised. Wishing he were actually dead. I got up to leave, when—

"But before you go, if you want to give me a blow job or something, that would be nice. For old times' sake?"

"Are you fucking kidding me? Go fuck yourself."

And so we're over. Another relationship in tatters because I'm too much for someone. I am enjoyed as an idea, but never as a reality.

In my late teens I was already internalising this overwhelming feeling that I was too much. I always prioritised the other guy in the conversation. I always dressed on the less outrageous side when I was with someone. I always agreed with his taste in music even though I think the Beatles are wholeheartedly dull.

It's not something I've left behind. I am always trying to reduce myself to accommodate the insecurities of other gay men. Ace was the first example of someone whom I didn't make myself small around. Then there was Ethan.

19 January 2012, on a train from London to Cambridge
I had an interview with a celebrity stylist, to assist her on her next job. It went pretty well. I facetimed Ethan, as he told me to call him once the interview was over, and he said he had someone to introduce me to.

That's funny, he didn't ask about my interview. He was in bed, early morning, and he was topless—looking incredibly sexy and smart at the same time, there in his flat in Kreuzberg, Berlin. He turns the front-facing camera to his side. "This is Phillip, my new boyfriend!"

"Hallo! How are you? I've heard so much about you!" Phillip is the last person I want to hear from right now.

"I'm good! But my train's here, I have to go! Call you soon, sorry!"

I then spent the next two hours performing my sadness on the train back to Cambridge, weeping gently as I listened to "Stay" by Rihanna, pretending to be in a movie of my life—that's a much easier way to cope with yet another round of rejection. This is what heartbreak feels like. Ethan, I think, is the one. Well, was the one. Whatever "the one" means.

This list isn't exhaustive—it doesn't include text break-ups, men who left during the first date, those who saw me and my false nails when I arrived at their door as organised on Grindr and said, "This isn't really my thing, mate, sorry."

And then, there's Ace. A rejection that has been more a work in progress—a slow chipping away at a block of marble until it's now formed something rather ugly and painful and full of confusion. I have repeatedly put my faith in the idea that someone's reciprocated love might be enough to excoriate all of the negative feelings I've internalised about myself, but every time I end up not only with more but with the old ones confirmed—tattooed over my insides like the big butt of a cosmic joke.

There's no hope for Ace and me anymore. We've both ensured in varying ways that there's no chance a relationship could work. Each time he goes back to William or I reach for Grindr and an outrageous dinner-party retelling, it's as if we were taking out the other's heart and tenderising it with a steak mallet. We've decimated any chance of a relationship: if it's this painful when we're not together, imagine what it would be like if we were.

But, funnily, every time it hurts a little less. I can't tell if it's because we're both becoming increasingly immune to the other's thoughtlessness—like how we're all hyper-desensitised to pictures of human atrocity in the news—or because we're slowly remoulding what was once a feeling of endless potential into a huge vat of bile and resentment.

14th June / le 14 juin

Thousands of people gathered in Old Compton Street, Soho, last night to honour the forty-nine people who lost their lives on Sunday morning in an Orlando night-club in the biggest mass shooting in U.S. history.

I was there with Hatty, Glamrou and the rest of the Denims, as well as Ellie, Cecily, Violet, Pak, and William.

For this night we were all family. Any dynamics dis-appeared as we paid homage to the queers our commu-nity had lost on such brutal grounds.

At 7:00 p.m. the sound of a single whistle pierced the tension, and a minute's silence fell across the crowd, which spanned the entirety of the street. Wild cheers, applause, and streams of tears followed as a rainbow of balloons were released into the sky, one for each fatal-ity. The sound of the gay men's chorus echoed off the houses with their rendition of "Bridge over Troubled Water."

"I have never been a rainbow kind of lesbian," El-lie said through tears, "but right now I feel like part of that rainbow." It is incredibly infrequent that so many people who fall under the umbrella of LGBTQIA+ have cause, and a space, to congregate. In a community that experiences so much continued oppression and can feel so fractured, last night's vigil felt like a moment of unity.

As queer people, our lives are a continual cycle of for-giveness against those who attack and oppress us. This moment was painful yet bittersweet: for once, we were allowed a space, to be at the centre of the conversation. It's tragic how it takes such violence to make people perhaps stop and think that life for LGBTQIA+ folk might not be all pink pounds and sequins. If London's vigil proved anything, it's that love, togetherness, strength in numbers, and forgiveness will help us heal after hate, as much as I hate to write such a fucking cliché. After our collective mourning is over, however, we must look forward and ask what changes have to be made globally to prevent attacks like Orlando from happening in the future. We need to mourn, but we also need action.

I was asked to write a news article about the vigil for an online media outlet, so I spent a while recording the feelings of people from the crowd. I want to write a few of them in here for safekeeping:

Akowsa: "We had to be here tonight, for the queer people who lost their lives in Orlando, for their families, to show that we care about ending hatred. We need to do more things like this, to show that we are here and we won't go away."

Alison: "It's scary, people are on edge, and it did cross my mind, is this the smartest thing to do? Do we want to congregate? But if not, when? We have to come together, because without that, there's nothing else."

Alice: "As a queer woman, I don't feel separate here tonight. Maybe just for tonight, but all the borders which separate us in the LGBTQ community have fallen away, and any animosity has disintegrated, which is amazing."

Tyron: "There's a sense from a lot of white queers that a lot of battles have been won, particularly for those from a middle-class background; and I think this has shaken a lot of people out of that view. It's really important now for the LGBTQ community to self-analyse. We are making things difficult for each other. Something which has been glossed over in the press is that this was also targeting people of colour, trans men and women of colour, Hispanics, black people. And you know there's still a lot of bigotry against our fellow queers within our own movement: 'no fats, no femmes, no Asians, no blacks'—we see that all the time."

Sarah: "In all honesty, I'm not sure why people are reluctant to name this an LGBTQ hate crime. I think people are reluctant to think that hate crimes still happen, but in reality more than a hundred LGBT people still experience a hate crime every week in the U.K., and many more go unreported. Violent hate crimes are rising, and they happen every single day."

16th June / le 16 juin

A phone call with my dad. Went something like this:

"Are you okay after the news about Orlando?"

"I'm finding it all quite overwhelming, actually."

"Sure, but remember that the world isn't out to get you guys all the time. This was someone who was very unwell."

"I know it was someone who was very unwell. But—and this is very hard to communicate to you as someone who's heterosexual—this does confirm our worst fear as queers. There are people all over the world who actually want you dead, believe you should die, because of this thing inside you that you can't change. And every time someone says or does something phobic, we are reminded that we are despised and hated. So while I agree the world isn't out to get us all the time, it feels like it's a pretty common dynamic. And that makes me feel so, so sad, in the pit of my stomach, and I can't stop crying and thinking about all the injustice done to people like us."*

Silence. I could tell he was crying along with me, having understood something I've been trying to articulate for so long, at other times in the past when he's told me to look on the bright side or to not worry about a potential Trump presidency or the murder of yet another trans woman of colour. He wants to believe those things don't directly affect us. But they do. Anything that's an attack on an individual member of our community serves as a reminder of the violence that's out there, waiting to happen.

"Sure. You're right. I can't imagine how that feels. I love you. I am here, next to you."

"Love you, too."

21st June / le 21 juin

I always stare at queer people when I see them—on trains, in coffee shops, on the street. I know it's hypocritical because I always talk about how much stares can hurt, but when I see a queer person, I'm still so excited that we exist. I can't help it. I try not to, but I always find myself craning to see, half-hoping they'll notice me so

---

* Poor Dad, he was just trying to help.

we can exchange a knowing, coded glance like queers of the sixties used to exchange conversation in the secret language of Polari, half-hoping they won't notice so I can bask in all the glory of their visibility, overjoyed to be associated with them above anyone else.

Right now I'm waiting in a café before a Denim rehearsal because we've been booked for a fucking gig at Glastonbury, and after we all died and were resurrected I started writing this, and I've just spotted someone staring at me. They look like a queer person, and it's so warming to smile back and take a moment to appreciate an understanding of another without even saying a word.

Okay, so I smiled back and he got up and left. Savage.

PERFORMANCE MEMO: While not a performer per se, my friend Otamere pulls a kind of wild performance with them wherever they go. They make every conversation full of life and drama and glamour and politics, and I find this commitment to everyday life invigorating.

22nd June / le 22 juin

Every year, towards the end of June, all the queers I know start talking about Pride. I can't go this year because of Glastonbury,* and when I discovered the clash two days ago, I felt absurdly relieved.

---

* Ugh, even I'm jealous of me.

A part of me feels bad for being relieved to miss Pride, our annual day to protest for our right to exist*—but it's just become so centred on money. It's become a huge event where loads of straight people go to get wankered and wear glitter and say things like "God, I love Pride, it's just like so fabulous!" Yes, we need allies—but we don't need them to claim Pride as their own.

It's also become pretty militarised and corporatised. The army marches, BAE marches, the Red Arrows are even flying over all in a bleak attempt to normalise war and warmongering institutions, which both kill LGBTQIA+ folk in other territories and persecuted them here for decades. Last year at Pride we saw an armed police officer, and my friend who's considerably less bothered about shit and just wants to have fun, was like "Oh, well! In a crowd of this many we need some security!"

But that's the point: it's not security. It reminds me of masculinised violence and is definitely painful and triggering to queer migrants who have come from places where war and gunfire are a lived reality.

On the minor side, it always makes me feel shit about my body. It feels like the one day a year that every muscle gay has trained for and is there to let you know about it. What's with those vests that are just a flap of cotton? I can't even imagine how it feels as a queer person of colour—the Pride rainbow looks like a sea of white.

---

* It was originally called Christopher Street Liberation Day, and it started in 1970. It was, apparently, pretty rad—but it also had its problems centering on racism and trans exclusion. So not all rad.

I'm off to Glastonbury. Which is the radical anticapi-
talist bastion perfect to replace Pride.* Better get packing.

30th June / le 30 juin

I'm sitting, covered in make-up and mud, speckled with
faeces, outside the front door of Wally, waiting for Hatty
to come home because I lost my keys. I left her having
sex with two girls in a floating pod full of rubbish above
a pond in the Healing Field. I was going to wait there
for her, but she wasn't even packed and I wanted to beat
the early-morning rush. So I'm sitting here diarising in
the sun, surrounded by a wet tent and two suitcases,
drinking a warm can of Aspall cider—"the champagne
of ciders," as my northern friend Chris always says—
smoking and realising I hate cider.

I feel I must preface this next entry by saying that
I was in such a haze of escapist euphoria that I do not
know exactly when or exactly where everything that
follows happened, but I know that all of it did.

We arrived on day one, the day before everything
kicked off, on 23 June, and before we could take a sip
of that first stunning summer pint, mass devastation
swept Glastonbury's liberal fields, as it was announced
we would be leaving the European Union. Brexit had
happened. We had all postal voted and had been desperate to remain.

---

* Ugh, I'm such a walking contradiction.

It pissed on the week but didn't totally ruin it, which says something about the class of liberals who occupy the fields of Glasto one week a year, and after Crystal persuaded me to take a pill, I didn't think about politics for another second.

"Such privilege," I thought.

"Shut the fuck up."

But coming back to London today, you can feel the tension thick in the air of such an unknowable future for so many.

So there, among herds of performatively heartbroken music fans, we decided that from our position in a field nothing could be done but for us all to collectively mourn, and collectively escape.

On night one we did what all the gays do—arrived at NYC Downlow early to beat the queues of straight folk desperate to eat up a slice of what every mainstream publication has dubbed the best club on earth.

There, in our circle made up of the Denims, Hatty, and Pak, we drank and danced and smoked. Some popped pills and floated around another dimension for the duration of the night. To keep us going, we all ate pita breads that Hatty had stored in her trusty festival tote bag. Hatty and I both got fingered by the same guy but in different holes. He had a handlebar moustache and was wearing a PVC butcher's apron, steel-capped boots, and nothing else. It was the first time in six years Hatty had made sexual contact with someone of the opposite sex, so we found a quiet place by a bin between two clubs where the fantasy stopped and you could see the inner workings of Glastonbury, where we downloaded on what Hatty's developing sexual fling meant. Both absolutely wasted, we decided we were both desperate for an orgasm, and so we lay down side by side and had a wank, comically waiting for the other until we were ready to come. Which we both did in absolute unison. We embraced under the stars until the sun crept up and injected its pale rays into the sky, and for a moment being in the world was as good as being in any fantasy.

The next day, we repeated the same thing—music, dancing, drinking. Afterwards, we dragged up in the back area of the Downlow, as Denim had been invited to perform a set on the stage. We had a secret weapon up our chiffon sleeves to make our presence unforgettable.

> *"God, we look horrific. Call my agent, I need a heli out of this shit-hole."*

After wading through mountains of drag detritus to get to our seats, we sat down among glorious queens such as Scottee, Ginger Johnson, and Rodent DeCay. These queens are all very different, but all equally influential on the East London drag scene. They throw nights that explore everything from fat drag to sissy scumbags, and Ginger has even written a panto for Selfridges for the past three years, which they all star in.

Nervous about our performance, and whether our amazing guest will turn up, Glamrou drew on comically humongous lips. After we held back the tears forced out by the laughter, so as not to ruin our make-up, we five sisters along with Scottee and Ginger crowded around their mirror and advised them on where to draw her lips. There, in the middle of the mass migration from London to the countryside, we'd carried with us our wonderful queer bubble.

Five minutes until we go on and there's no sign of our guest star.

Two minutes, nothing.

Thirty seconds, and just as we were handed our mics, Florence Welch, wearing fringe everything from head to toe, perfect for a set with a bunch of drag queens, arrives in style in a golf cart.

The rumour had spread: the Downlow was now full to absolute capacity, and the crowd's drug-powered roar vibrated so loudly the stage physically wobbled. I was so drunk I had to cling to Aphrodite for support.

After our triumphant set, press queued up to speak to us and take photos of these five misfit queens and a Glastonbury headliner.

High on the atmosphere, Ace and I decided to take up the offer of this girl we'd met who turned out to be a lady of a neighbouring manor and split an ecstasy pill. I was terrified, and even though I know so many people who take them regularly, I wondered if tonight would be the night I lived my hardest and died my fastest. But before I knew it, Ace had taken his half and was kissing my half into my mouth, pushing it down with his tongue.

We were both in full, somewhat busted-up drag, and we wandered around feebly holding each other's hand, being swayed from location to location by an overwhelmingly huge crowd that didn't in any way overwhelm us, pulled with its movements like a fish swept by the current of the ocean.

We found the group, but stole away to behind the Portaloos as these magic pills started to release their wonder on our bodies. I couldn't breathe. This half a little blue thing pushes you to that euphoric state just before orgasm, where every touch makes you feel as if you might shatter, where you have to place a strategic breath between every word because even the bodily vibrations from talking release too much pleasure and serotonin to handle.

I said I needed the loo, pacing up the stairs of the compost toilet, trying to keep my balance, and as I went to close the door, Ace's hand stopped me from doing so. He had brought in water, which we ended up drinking by kissing and pouring it into our open, connected mouths like in *Fatal Attraction* when they fuck on Alex Forrest's sink.

We kiss, unstoppably, somewhere between rage and literal ecstasy. Spurred on by this chemical, we step into our feelings for the first time ever and decide to choose pleasure over responsibility.

There, in a Portaloo, we had our first sexual experience together, and perhaps our last. Who knows? But it lasted for about half an hour, which felt like a lifetime, which felt like a nanosecond, which felt like the most absurd amount of pressure and tension being released into the atmosphere, like spraying a can of deodorant into the air and watching the particles gradually settle. The rest of the night we spent dancing and touching and loving each other and our friends, and anyone we encountered, in a way not possible when bound by reality.

As with anything that's meant to happen at some point, the next day there was no awkwardness or immaturity or stunted communication. Ace and I spent the weekend rolling through Glastonbury towards each other and away from each other, finding ourselves in the strangest places alone together. Like in the hardcore techno area sharing balloons with five straight guys who'd flown over from Jamaica just for this patch of techno somewhere in the middle of a field some thousands of miles away from their starting destination, as fire breathers unfurled from silks above us like tacky butterflies from chrysalises; like watching Lily Allen's dad sing an acoustic set in a little tiny bar built into the side of a hill; like in the stone circle as smiling crackheads asked for money, which Ace and I didn't have.

He left a day early, he had to get to work. We didn't kiss goodbye or make any promises, but we left with a new level of comfort with each other. The litmus test of whether we could do it—the sex thing—passed with flying colours.

I danced with Hatty and Glamrou all through the night, before packing down and heading through various dimensions—a train, a bus, a tube, an Uber, a comedown—and back to here, on my stoop, in an entirely different world to the one that I'd left.

I've just checked my emails, to affirm I'm still attached to the real world, and I've seen two exciting things: a job offer as a contributing editor for *Love* maga-zine, something I applied for on a total whim before I left, and a commission to write a hot take on Brexit from a working-class perspective.

I'll deal with them tomorrow.

July / juillet

Having sex in drag is popularly termed a *kai kai*. Derived from the term *to kiki* (verb): when two queers chat, laugh, giggle, and gossip. The kai kai takes that a step further and into fucking.

It's never been presented to me as an option. Since I was attacked, especially, I avoid going anywhere publicly in full drag for safety's sake, so it would mean fucking in the club toilet—and 99 per cent of gay club toilets are not my desired space for such activity. But the other night with Ace marked my first kai kai, and it was in a toilet worse than that of a gay club. That's growth.

Doing stuff in drag was not much different from doing stuff out of drag. All the parts work the same, and it's quite fun messing up your make-up for such a good cause. I was tucked, so I had the awkward part of peeling off gluey duct tape layered over my genitals as my adoring lover patiently watched me accidentally yank out the few patchy pubes I have left after years of this shit.

I have a friend, James, who only fucks in drag. "Well, the men I like also like me better when I'm in full drag. We call them chasers—we dropped the *tranny* bit because that word's offensive."

I invited James for dinner while she got into full face to go meet a client. I'd asked her over to catch up, but also to seek advice on the Ace situation that I am currently shockingly relaxed about. James isn't so good at talking about others, something I always forget until she's settled in for the night and we're discussing whether she needs to change dentists, so we never got to the topic of Ace and me.

"Some are clients, some are lovers, some both at once—they're the best ones. I enjoy sex work in drag, actually quite a lot, more than when I did it as a boy. It gives me permission to act in whichever way I please—you know what I mean, the Queen!—and also punters pay more. I've found the richer they are, the dirtier the stuff they want. Perhaps it's a chicken-and-egg situation—they can pay for anything they want, you know? I had one guy who wanted me to shit on his suit in his office somewhere in Canary Wharf, and I did it, after I watched him wire me fifteen hundred pounds."

Fifteen hundred quid? To take a dump in drag? It's so tempting.

> *"Honey, I've done it for free. How else do you think I scored with the whole of the Scottish Darts team?"*

5th July / le 5 juillet

I have texted Ace every day for the last three days in a row and haven't had a single response. I haven't yet called. I'm currently surprisingly calm about it, but I'm giving myself one more day's grace period before that's no longer the case.

Have, naturally, turned to Grindr and have since met:

- Guy, thirty-eight, who sensually fed me a curry, then dipped his erect cock into raita before slowly walking towards me, pointing it at my mouth, while making an aeroplane sound; I received his Concorde, which was great after I plucked up the courage to ask him to stop making baby noises.
- Couple, twenty-six and forty-four, who wanted to Eiffel Tower me—which they did. An Eiffel Tower is when one participant fucks you in the bum and one in the mouth and they high-five/lean their hands in a diagonal position above the fuckee, thus taking the shape of the famous French monument.* I stayed a while with them, and we watched *Will & Grace* and ate poached pears and yoghurt, then they gave me a tag-team blow job while the Amy Winehouse documentary was on mute in the background. That bit was weird—watching this tragic story while I got a double bj.
- Guy, thirty-five(ish), who only wanted to gently suck my toes. Imagine a little lamb suckling at a mother's teat.†
- Guy, twenty-nine, drunk, came to my house and asked me to treat him like a sex slave. I find the terminology there problematic so I said no. Instead I ended up making him a cup of tea, and he wept while explaining to me he thinks he's developed

---

* *J'adore la France!*
† Thank God I've sorted that athlete's foot.

a meth addiction and that he has a wife and a child at home but can't stop going onto the gay sex scene. I gave him some numbers of groups to call and services to access, because he said he wouldn't even know where to look for something like that, and he gave me a hug before he left and seemed relieved to finally have someone to talk to.

- Guy, forty, Russian and virile but not too masculine. This was the fuck I'd been looking for, and we did it in the street by my house, in the stairwell, the shower, Hatty's room, and on the kitchen floor, where, halfway through, I clocked that there was a thin slice of red onion stuck to my forehead.

6th July / le 6 juillet

I've been asked to write an article called "How to Be a Real LGBTQIA+ Ally" and have been keeping a list of my/my friends' thoughts.

1. Please don't tell me about the one time in high school you thought you had sexual urges towards your friend / PE teacher of the same sex but never acted on it then or since.

2. Please don't try to outdo me on Madonna trivia. You might indeed know more, but she is like 70 per cent of my identity,* so it gets too emotional.

---

* I'm also 40 per cent Celine Dion, 12 per cent cigarette smoke, and 0.5 per cent water. That's more than 100, but I'm more than 100.

3. Queer people have differing views on things; we are not a monolith, so each and every interaction with us might require you to learn something new.

4. Don't question people's genders. They are what they told you they are. And if they haven't, try not to assume. Unless you're in a straight bar, and then you can assume most people are awful men.

5. Try to avoid telling queer folk what is and isn't queer-/homo-/trans-/biphobia. You might see it, but we feel it.

6. Be cognisant of your privilege.

7. Don't worry about getting things wrong, now or in the past; just admit it, accept it, apologise for it, and move on. We all get shit wrong.

8. That said, if you're going to ask questions about anal / how lesbians have sex / where the poo goes / what it means to be a top or a bottom / who is the girl and who is the boy in the relationship / whether a trans person has had surgery—please google it. Remember we have spent years answering these basic questions, for which we had to find the answers ourselves, once, some of us before Google! You can very much do the same.

9. Don't think that our only goal is acceptance and assimilation. We want much more than that.

10. I'm happy for you to come to (some of) our spaces as long as you remember that while for you it might be a party without the sexual pressure, for us it's an emergency room and one of the only places we can go to feel our oats, feel safe, and feel sexual. Good allies don't invade space; instead they

move over in it, they open it up, they decentre themselves and listen rather than talk about their experiences.

11. Watching *RuPaul* doesn't make you an ally.

12. If you come out as an ally, don't just say it—don't think rocking up to Pride or being chill about going to gay bars is enough. Challenge your colleagues, platform LGBTQIA+ people, unlearn unhealthy phobias. Try to prioritise those who really need it in our community—not simply fab gay guys who lend you sunglasses.

13. Listen; that's the first thing to do. Learn, the second.

14. Be like my brother Harry. He is the most wonderful ally. When I first came out, there was no such thing in my world, but he didn't bat an eyelid. He would be the first to my defence at high school and would laugh in a supportive way when I did anything outrageously camp or queeny.

He was the first in my family to see me in drag, and even at his work—a bigwig solicitors' office—he sends around my articles and publicises my shows and says things like "My brother is an amazing drag queen."

It doesn't sound like much, but in a world where your worth is often predetermined on how well you run in the dick-swinging wolf pack, it takes a lot of bravery to fight in someone else's corner. He reads, so much, more than I do, and will send me links saying, "I'm sure you've read this, but I wanted to send it in case you missed it!" Every time Harry gets drunk when we're together, he leans in, wobbling on his feet, and gurgles into my ear something about how he couldn't be prouder of me.

Sometimes I find it hard to say something back that doesn't just sound as if I'm returning the compliment. But I couldn't be prouder of him. Harry's support has lifted me up too many times to count.

That's not just tolerance, it's the celebration for exactly who I am, who my friends are. That's the mark of a good ally. I love you, Harry.

7th July / le 7 juillet

No reply from Ace other than:

> Sorry I haven't got back! Have been super busy! Promise I'm not ignoring, we will see each other next week at Denim? Xxx

He's definitely ignoring. Will continue Grindr binge.

9th July / le 9 juillet

I was walking home when I noticed two other queers walking in the same direction. It was dark, the kind of orangey dark of horror movies that makes your heart beat faster by association. My journey is down a twisty pathway, then via a wide-open, dark market street. The kind of twisty pathway and open market street that would be the perfect scene for a true-crime-style attack.

But there, unlike most nights when I break into a light jog, hot on my toes ready to sprint beyond my bodily abilities at the sound of something as minor as a moth hitting a lamplight, were two other queers on the exact same journey.

We didn't speak. We just put our headphones on, blasted our music up, and walked home how those unafraid of violence are allowed to walk home: my heart slowing, my Kylie blasting, a feeling of relief akin to that when someone you know has a big piece of spinach in their teeth but you don't dare say anything, then they finally go to the bathroom and remove it and you can breathe again.

15th July / le 15 juillet

As a perpetually single queen, I've always loathed couples who share on social media pictures of themselves kissing, the caption always reading "Cuddles with this one" or "Date night with the boy."

But recently I've succumbed to the lowest of the low, the pits of the human race, and I, too, have just posted a smugly captioned, semi-elusive picture of my (maybe) boyfriend on social media. I hate myself.

The funny thing is, my recent Grindr binge has, for the first time, speedily inclined towards an actual meaningful connection with someone.

We met on the seventh and have since spent every day over the last week together. During week one we did a ton of anal, and by yesterday we'd both been checked for STIs and have been doing it bareback since— something I consider sacred, and something you have to be incredibly careful with. I've slipped up a few times, although rarely intentionally.

He fucks me, I fuck him, we swallow each other's cum, and cum in each other's assholes. We even tried felching, which is where the cum recipient essentially farts out the cum into the cum giver's mouth, the cum giver swallowing their own cum now infused with the inside of the cum receiver's colon. Sounds gross, totally, but something is super-intense and connective about sharing all parts of someone else's body—be that fluids or toe jam or sweaty pits. It's completely freeing to be in someone else's physicality so deeply.

Shag numero uno—which was about a week ago—was amazing, but I kept my T-shirt on and left at 3:00 a.m. to take a cab back to East London (from southwest London, which is where Dom—which is his name—lives).

The second time, I took my top off and he came in my eye. Instantly guards were down, and he—as he's a doctor*—cared for my red, stingy eye. We laughed, chatted about coming out; he told me about the racism he's experienced on the gay scene; we postured over whom Beyoncé's most recent album is really for; and he daubed at my eye with a wet tissue, both of us naked, penises flaccid, me sitting on the loo, him facing me on my knee, chatting through the night.

---

* Finally, the big money.

He went to work, and I stayed at his place upon his invitation. That afternoon he texted me, "I've just got us tickets for Beyoncé at the O2 tonight—can you come???" I cancelled on my friends Ellie and Cecily, choosing Beyoncé and all-night sex, knowing they would understand a queen's need for a much-deserved Bey and lay.

Three days in, he told me he wants to marry me. The usual cynic in me would retort that gay marriage is a repressive, deradicalising tool to make queer people think that we have "equality" when it's actually just putting our sexualities in a context that heterosexual folk can understand. Instead I whispered, "I want to marry you, too." And I think I meant it, even for a second, which is fucked up.

Crystal was screaming, *"No,"* through tar-filled lungs, as if she were in severe pain. She's even more anti-marriage than me, and she says things like "The only good thing about marriage is when he finally dies and leaves it all to you," which makes no sense. She misunderstands so much because she's the lost Romanov daughter, so didn't have the whole family unit to learn from. Bless.

Then Dom and I both cried as Queen Bey sang "All Night" because even if this was it, it was the first time anyone had ever reflected our irrational need to be loved back. Shortly after, he gave me an emotional wank job, putting his big hands down my culottes, me climaxing in the middle of the crowd as Beyoncé belted out "Freedom." Freedom it was.

This weekend Denim has a gig—not a big one, but a paid one at a new club night in northeast London.

Oddly, I'm not so broke at the moment so don't need the money, and when Dom found a nine-pound flight on Monarch Airlines, he asked if I wanted to go to Budapest, and I—to the dismay of my fellow queens—didn't hesitate, sending over my passport details, unashamed about the hideous picture, for Dom to book the flight.

The queens are pissed. But they can do it without me.

The thing is, I've been in love three times, and every single time it's been unreciprocated for one stupid, made-up reason or another: "I don't want to jeopardise our friendship" or "You're too amazing for me" or "Fuck off, fatty."

There was Matt, there was Ethan, there's Ace.

There's Ace, who I'm probably still in love with, who still hasn't been in contact since we left Glastonbury.

But this potential love with Dom, fast as it is, this fourth attempt at what might be the first long-term relationship I've ever had, will not be put on hold for a random gig and eighty pounds. Denim can wait; true love cannot.

Now it's Friday, of "week two," at 5:00 a.m., and I'm writing this on my phone as Dom sleeps next to me on the coach to Luton. I fucking hate Luton.

But even Luton doesn't feel so bleak with Dom next to me. This is utterly maniacal, but I think I know that I already love him. It doesn't feel like lust, and it's totally unlike me to misread my own feelings* and overattach at the early stages of any interest, but, genuinely, I feel

---

* Lol.

magic. A new kind of magic, which must basically be what it feels like to have someone, for the first time ever, like you back. I'm not going to diarise this weekend, at least until I'm back, because—much like those trash people who post pics of their SO* on social media—I'm going to actually do what they are perpetually hashtagging and I'm going to #liveinthemoment. I just took a crafty snap of half of Dom's asleep face. I posted it on Instagram, captioned "Budapest with this one." If to be in love means to be human garbage, then love can come and collect me, crush me whole, and dump me in a landfill. I'm done being recycled.

18th July / le 18 juillet

We'd booked an apartment in District VII, in the Jewish Quarter. We spent the weekend back and forth between weird techno clubs and our bedroom, in this beautifully stark flat that housed nothing but a single bookshelf loaded with Hungarian books on labour theory, a mattress on the floor, and a gentrification-esque lamp that kind of springs in five directions when you try to reposition it, probably sold as a feat of minimal design, a simple pleasure, but that's just capitalism eating itself in the form of a lamp. Together we explored the depths of

---

* *Significant other:* wanker phrase for boyfriend/girlfriend/partner that removes any agency one might have in being significant in one's own right. Same goes for *other half* or *better half.*

the gay sex scene across the city, from the tame to this underground club that runs a poo party once a month.*

We liked that one. It's much like Lab.Oratory in Berlin, the sex club beneath Berghain. Once you arrive through flappy, fake-blood-covered plastic curtains at the unimaginatively named CoXx Club, the bouncers slide open a slat of steel in the door with an echoey clang. A glance up and down, surveying whether you're the right kind of clientele for this very specific establishment. Turns out we were—probably because we were wearing tiny little sunglasses at night—then the bolts ring open, and you're in.

Once inside, you're told to strip off all your clothes—"You can keep the shoes"—before they're taken away and a number is written on your hand, the idea being that on entering the space you become base, anonymous, a piece of meat—a touch I thought was a bit on the nose.†

We took a self-guided tour: St. Andrew's crosses spun to the left, tiny narrowing alcoves to the right; rooms purpose-built for fisting and more extreme sex acts peppered the perimeter. In one room a man lay on a gurney, tailed by an orderly queue of other men patiently waiting to sound this slung kinkster.‡ Glory holes, prison rooms (which Crystal and I both agree

---

* We didn't go to the poo party, sadly; that was next weekend.

† Or very *Les Mis* 24601, which is way more my brand.

‡ In *sounding* you take a thin steel, or sometimes rubber, rod and slowly insert it into the urethra. It must be sterile, and my friend Jeremy—who loves it—told me that if you time it just right, you can both orgasm and urinate at exactly the same time. Jeremy told me, with pride, that it's the most pleasurable sexual thing he's ever done, "and, honey, I'm in my fifties!"

are problematic and class touristic, and she should know—she once served a full life sentence), a smoking area where everyone was sucking dicks, fags in hands.*

After a little discussion, Dom and I decided to split up. He went off somewhere to explore, as did I. I always thought I'd be terrified of openness within a relationship, but not only did it feel fine, it felt full of trust and understanding. I had no doubt that Dom liked me better than all these men, but this was about having different experiences.

I spent the night in CoXx doing a lot of kissing and touching of other men, consensually of course. When a bald German guy with a head tattoo tried to put a finger in my bum without asking, I grabbed it and pushed off. Just ask first.

Funny, though, I wasn't in the mood for anything to go up there. A side note here: Dom is the first person I've topped. Until then I was your simple, run-of-the-mill bottom—constantly dodging burritos or avoiding one too many coffees in a row if even a sniffle of dick was on the horizon. Prunes were good on off days, but with so much food monitoring on "on" days, bottoming was bound to never last beyond my midtwenties.

"Unless the dick is worth the diet!" Crystal reminds. ⧏

Later, as we left a neighbouring club, where we went for a prolonged, sweaty dance, I counted that I'd had sex

---

* Obviously this was my favourite.

thirteen times in this one night. Not every single time
featured climax, but they all contained a sensation on
the edge of that—drawing me closer and closer to one
maximum climax with Dom at the end of the night,
during which my ejaculate flew so high it cleared the
wall of a bathroom stall.

As we walked home through that genius Budapest street, which houses all of the politicians' super-
Hungarian-looking houses, we ate late-night lángos and
kissed all the way home. In bliss, we were kissing near
the flat when Dom told me he had something to say. I
knew what it was, I was feeling it, too; I had been since
the moment our flight took off. There, in a Budapest
dawn, my first mutual "I love you" was about to be ex-
changed, a week-and-a-bit in.

Maybe I need therapy?

The air was febrile with potential, silent for a second,
and then: the bleepy, grotesque shrill ring of my iPhone,
in my pocket. The moment was gone, but I kissed Dom
and told him to hold that thought while I checked who
it was.

Ace. Calling me at 4:00 a.m. from London. I tried to
justify not answering, and Dom was begging with his
eyes for me not to. "But what if it's an emergency?"

I answered the phone. "Hello, Ace, what's up? I'm in
Budapest."

"I'm lost." He was wasted. "But I just called to tell
you," he spluttered, and it sounded as if he was falling
onto a wall, "that I ended it with William. You're the
one." He hung up.

Everything slowed down for a second, and I couldn't

pinpoint my feelings in the run-off of all the booze and the sex.

Dom asked what Ace was calling about. I paused, constructing a lie in my head, something about Ace losing his house keys.

"Where were we?" I looked up at Dom, the atmosphere totally swiped by this firework to the guts.

"I was just saying that . . . I think I'm falling in love with you."

A pause.

"I think I'm falling in love with you, too."

We buzzed home to bed, high off each other and the way our armpits smelled and the way our body hair was curled with dried sweat, while our veins swelled with MDMA, which has become much easier for me to take post-Glastonbury since I didn't die and had the best time. Full beginnings of love. As I watched Dom fall asleep, I nipped to the loo, my mind darting between Dom and Ace, snakes and ladders. In a 5:00 a.m. haze, I sent Ace the following, I couldn't resist:

> I love you, too. I'm sure we'll be too embarrassed to talk about this tomorrow. See you when I'm back. Get home safe xxx.

Does that make me a terrible person? I can't quite cope with the irony—although I'm never quite sure what irony means because apparently there's no irony in "Ironic" by Alanis Morissette, which is where I first learned the name for the concept—but this feels like irony. But I feel oddly totally fine about my double admission of love. Either Dom will fizzle out—"I mean it's been less than a month, this has messy divorce written all over it," Crystal says as she ashes a Sobranie into my glass of water—or Ace and I won't ever speak of this night again. So I hedge my bets, go for both, in the hope that one will come through.

I hope it's Ace.

Poor Dom, and the dick's so good, too.

20th July / le 20 juillet

Fucking hell the gays. You wait a lifetime for one to unblock you on Grindr, and then two come along at once. But, no—not for dating, or casual sex, or good conversation, or to put their card details on your Deliveroo—for actual love.

23rd July / le 23 juillet

Enough about love, I've got to work. I've been asked to write an article for a magazine about how you become a drag queen. Sure, it's easy to be like "Buy the make-up, you queen! Don't forget highlight and get a good wig and work, diva!" But, in my opinion, make-up, looks, lip-synching, are some of the least important things to learn. I think when you're born gay, you're also born with the impulse to be wildly famous—something about money and mass adoration and our legacy and as a tonic for all the shit you go on to get in high school—but as the hope of conventional stardom dwindles because of your difference, the answer is to find a space that might celebrate your difference, your femininity. Painting and dressing, I learned that at the stilettos of my sister Dinah, or Jacob, and Ellie, who put me in drag for the first time.

Jacob is a model who once had mumps so bad his face doubled in size. We went to university together, and after meeting at a particularly heterosexual gathering, we got to talking about how we were both dying to do drag—proper drag. We then used honing our craft as a means to escape further hetty gatherings. We'd found our thing, our hobby, our baby.

Drag is about both sisterhood and stardom, and those two things require respect: for each other and for yourself. As queer people, we are taught to disrespect ourselves because we're constantly disrespected, and so becoming a drag performer is so much about unlearning that: by respecting yourself enough to spend time on your appearance, to build a character to surface all of your wildest desires, to take up space onstage the ways you were never allowed to at school, to create a family who love you.

Dinah and I spent nights in her room drinking shit tons, doing no work, smoking a billion cigarettes, and pooling make-up kits—each of us attempting different techniques, Jacob endlessly more dexterous at this than me.

A lot of drag performers become enraged at the sight of stag-do blokes who dress as sexy nurses and run around Krakow, or gays who think putting on bad drag one night a year is funny. And for good reason. First, it's misogynist. Second, it disrespects a craft that is about honour and history, into which we pour countless hours, carefully considering how to bring to life these characters who are often the key to the stardom we always dreamt of.

24th July / le 24 juillet

Ace and I have been texting a lot, but we haven't seen each other once. Dom and I have been seeing each other a lot. I have one boyfriend URL and another IRL. One of them sends me funny memes and asks me how my day is going, while the other shares his food with me, a bed, bodily fluids, and sometimes some choice opinions. Like how he thinks identity politics are a waste of time, for example.

I love them both differently and am annoyed by them both simultaneously. Ace is noncommittal—we've planned to see each other twice since I got back from Budapest and he's bailed both times—probably because he knows a big conversation is coming. Ace and I can have productive conversations about what needs to change in the world, about climate change and social media and rising fascism and colonialism and gender, but we can't chat about some texts and our feelings. Very Gen Z. Dom never bails—he's there even when Ace cancels and makes me dinner without even asking. He listens to the boring bits about my day but avoids any "big" conversation, claiming he's too tired. This annoys me hugely—if we can't talk, then all we can do is fuck and eat, which is what we've been doing for the last week. The descent into a bedridden relationship was comically fast: the moment he told me he loved me, it was as if I were money in an ISA, sat there, secure, accruing weight instead of interest.

People call this a conundrum. What Miley calls "The Climb," what Crystal calls Wednesday (even though she's unequipped to help with this one—"Fuck 'em both, rinse 'em both" is as far as her stellar advice goes).

While Ace and I haven't promised each other anything, I have officially promised myself to Dom—when, last night, while eating leftover lasagne, we agreed to be monogamous for some stupid reason. So, because every time I'm texting "someone" (it's always Ace) he tries to look at my phone, already mistrusting me—which offends me greatly even though he has total cause to—I decide to broach the topic of an open relationship before the concrete of our monogamy sets. ("Concrete never actually sets . . . I know because I got bukkaked by a bunch of builders and they told me so," Crystal argues. "Fuck off," I reply.)

Open relationships, to me, have always seemed like a minefield of hurt. Yes, we fucked a bunch of guys in Budapest, but I knew that at any point I could run and find Dom and make it stop. But if you're open, you can't keep tabs on someone all the time. I've always felt prime for a swindling, and opening up a relationship just feels as if you're asking for it. Strange that now I'm asking for it. Maybe I'm becoming an adult, or maybe I just want to have my cock and eat it, too.

Now, we all know "the one" is a myth, like the moon landing or democracy. It implies that all relationships last happily ever after, when the truth is—most of the time, at least—they don't. No one ever said, "It just works," "We never argue," or "We still have sex twenty-five times a week" without it coming back to bite them in the coochie when they, inevitably, part ways. Today, finding "the one"—by which I mean a single, lifelong, dedicated love—seems unlikely. What if there's not one, but four ones, and what if they all come along at the same time? I feel somewhat manipulative coercing Dom in this way, like a Cersei Lannister type.* To clear this up: I'm not planning on sleeping with Ace; other people maybe, but not Ace. I just want to feel a little less guilty if Ace's and my texting becomes a little flirtatious from time to time.

"Sure, we can always close the relationship if it doesn't work?" I reassure, after Dom absent-mindedly agrees, his focus more on the screen than on the conversation.

"Sure. Love you. Now watch the telly!"

As simple as that, I go back to watching *Six Feet Under* in the crook of Dom's warm, hairy arm, while sending memes of Bree from *Desperate Housewives* to Ace.

---

* Which is actually every goal, so I've decided I'm fine with it.

25th July / le 25 juillet

A list of rules Dom and I agreed upon last night re our open relationship, after I woke him up in the middle of the night feeling worried and demanding we set some parameters.

- No sex with other people in either of our beds.
- No sex with exes / previous romantic conquests. (We never discussed texting . . .)
- Sex with condoms when sleeping with other people.
- No sex with the same person more than twice, unless there's a significant time gap.
- No telling about who/what/where/when unless asked.
- Do tell when it's happened, however.
- No cancelling on plans with each other to meet other guys.
- No choosing to go home with / get with other guys in clubs when together unless agreed upon.

I always felt that an open relationship wouldn't be the right thing for me: I'm much more monogamy-centric, and I didn't think my history of extra-relationship rejection would prepare me well for intra-relationship rejection. But with Dom it feels easy. I don't know if that's because it's convenient for me, or if I don't truly care about Dom, or if I'm neurotic, or don't know what love feels like, or love him so much and trust him so much that perhaps I'm ready to enter the world of the alternative relationship.

"You could just be dead and not know it?" **Crystal adds** ⪉
into the mix, even though we've sworn we're
both *"off the booze until this embarrassing mess*
you're making with Dom and Ace is sorted."

I always felt less queer because of my desire for monogamy. All the best, most radical queers I know practise
polyamory, group love, and at minimum open relationships. When I tell these people I'm into monogamy, it's
often met with a momentary look of pity, of condescen-
sion.

It took me a while to realise that there's no way to
be the most successfully queer person in a room. When
I pondered on it, I concluded that monogamy, in a scene
that's harsh and unforgiving, where intimacy is scary
and oft wrapped in barbed wire, might well be a radical
act of care. The queers have rejected it so hard that it's
become queer to be what was once deemed not queer.
Or am I rationalising?

After years developing a queer justification for my
monog obsession, at the sight of two men who want me,
just like that I take it all back and am first on the open-
wagon. Here goes.

26th July / le 26 juillet

Okay, so in other news—we have a new flatmate in
Wally. Hatty and I met her at a club, where she was
dancing from only the head up—rolling her head, her
neck, flipping her hair, but static throughout the rest of

the body. Hatty and I were hammered and we decided we wanted to dance like that, so we went over and asked if we could join in, and it twigged, after about five minutes of head dancing, that she was my best friend from my early years of high school before she was moved to a private school by her Catholic parents because she'd come out as gay. She'd recently broken up with her girlfriend, who wanted to move to Bristol to take up pottery. "Such a dyke cliché," Leyah said insultingly. "And now I'm looking for a place to live."

Leyah isn't like the rest of our friends—she's kind, funny, queer, attractive, and stylish in the way all my friends are—but she's less outwardly political and doesn't necessarily lead with her trauma. In conversation so many of us showcase our validity at being included in the things we talk about by recounting our traumas first: kind of like a ticket into the debate. But Leyah is relaxed; she listens and avoids revealing too much.

Meanwhile, I've also started and then left a new job at *Love* magazine. I liked it for the two weeks I was there, but working there meant that I was unable to do any freelance work or paid drag jobs, and when I summed it together, I would earn more in a month doing that than I would in three at *Love*. It's not that I earn good money freelancing and dragging, trust; it's that the pay at these magazines is obscene.

At home, my grandma is getting more and more unwell. I don't know how to cope with that, and I don't ever talk about it, even though Hatty does this annoying thing where she says, "Let it all out, baby," when I don't want to. That's the only annoying thing Hatty does. But it was my grandma who bought me *Chic*, took me shopping, told me I could be anything I wanted to be in the world. When I call her, she says brightly, "Oh, I'm ticking over! How are you?"—even though I know she's not. The women of my hometown are so fucking hardy, and I drink in Grandma's words as she lies there, legs in bandages, and try to hold on to her sense of fight, knowing that I might not have her to provide her "Fuck 'em all, you're a star" wisdom in the future, knowing that soon I'll have to give it back to her. I push the idea of her being sick out of my head, imagining her still as the broad, kind, direct northern woman with big boobs who taught me that waving at strangers, and making them wave back, would make them talk about you. "And there's nothing better than being talked about," she would say, smirking. Funny, that's one of Crystal's mantras, too.

August / août

1st August / le 1 août

Over lunch today Ellie asked me what I want from my life, and I said, "Safety." That's not fun, is it? I used to want fame, and now I want safety? She said she wanted to be pounded meaninglessly, which is a far superior answer because in our friendship group you get points for outrageousness, and safety is definitely not outrageous. Although perhaps achieving it is a more outrageous proposition than getting pounded hard.

DRAG PERFORMANCE MEMO: Finn Love dances all night. I don't know how the fuck they do it. But she dances from 10:00 p.m. to 6:00 a.m., and she loves it. It's so joyful to watch someone get their whole life, to live for themself, while in front of hundreds of people. Nightlife performers are amazing—dancing all night, pushing off dick punters, making the whole place feel queer and safe because of their visibility.

DRAG PERFORMANCE MEMO: Oedopussi Rex set fire to their fake beard onstage in a small football pub in New Cross. It was genius, supertransgressive, kind of visually stunning, while also burning down masculinity. Even the men watching the football couldn't look away from this topless drag king on fire.

5th-10th August / le 5-10 août

The human brain makes thirty-five thousand decisions a day. Bafflingly, this means that somewhere within the tangle of my routine, I made the off-piste decision to take a nine-hour flight across the Atlantic to visit Fort Lauderdale: the place where spring break used to happen.

> *"Ahh, the good old days. That's where I got* 〈
> *my first implants."*

I was asked to go for a travel feature (my first ever) for a niche magazine to whom I lied and said I'd done loads of travel writing.

In truth, I was looking to leave London for a bit, on my own. The situation with Ace has been getting weirdly complicated, intensified by his turning up on the doorstep of Wally four nights ago, after nearly three weeks without our seeing each other. Standing outside in the pouring rain, he asked if he could stay for a while, and I said yes, thinking we were going to have sex and then go full monogamous. We spent all night awake talking in the same bed, not kissing or fucking, but definitely in some semblance of a pair who were way beyond the line of the platonic.

On the other hand, the situation with Dom is seemingly circling the drain, and the guilt I'm feeling about Ace is probably exacerbating things. Dom has become incredibly contrary and argumentative, and I've become incredibly noncommittal. Last week he came to a night Hatty and I threw—under the guise of our budding pop band, ACM (A Cinematic Masterpiece, because that's what we, obviously, are)—at the Royal College of Art. We killed it—we've been working on the songs for a while on nights when we stayed up late, making joke lyrics about positive consent and grotesque Barbie girls, which somehow translated into possibly the most radically queer art we've ever made. During our set, Hatty and I covered each other in Nutella and eggs, and the crowd were living for it, but Dom stormed home, leaving only a text on my phone:

"When are you gonna grow up?"

"If growing up means not being able to express myself—then never," I replied.

I was hesitant about taking the trip, but I thought it would be the best for everybody. It's only five days, and the grown-up thing is to run from problems, right?

Day 1

The flight—terrified of dying. When I do die, I want it to be glamorous. Perhaps in a gruesome onstage-leading-lady-style disaster, or by crashing my cheating ex-husband's yacht on the Côte d'Azur in a lavish rage. Not in TAP Air Portugal economy, fogged on three zopiclone and a Jameson's.

Arrived. Suitably wan after all that in-flight agitation and self-medication, in the Sunshine State, the home of the homosexual, the place Edmund White in his 1980 gay travel guide described as the place to pick up a hustler. Rare is the moment when one is stunned by the beauty of American cities, but as the nefarious clutches of medical sleep wore off, I came to in a Marriott hotel room resting on the edge of the Atlantic. I grew up by the sea, but the view of a boundless sapphire ocean blurred into creamy-blue sky was a new kind of sea view, one thankfully lacking the more familiar bobbing, empty cans of Tennent's Super and floating used condoms.

Evening. Dinner in the new hotel restaurant because I'm a stunning glam VIP. I put on my best heels, a pencil skirt, and a giant oversize hoodie and sat down to dinner alongside some rather remarkable guests: Kellie Maloney, former boxing promoter since famed and unfairly shamed for coming out as trans; my online friend whom I was finally meeting IRL, Shon Faye—the funniest person I know and a rightful internet sensation; and Will, the editor in chef of the *Gay Times*. This was the first time I felt that I'd journalistically "made it" because the wine was literally on Fort Lauderdale, so I didn't have to order house white!

Alexis, the president of the Southern Comfort Conference, joined us. We had all come for the twenty-sixth annual conference, one of the largest gatherings of the trans community in the world. My entire stay in Fort Lauderdale was geared towards this event. One of the only of its kind in the States, and probably the world, the conference has become an incredibly popular destination for (mainly older) trans women from all across the world. There are nail salons, surgery workshops, "how to dress" forums, dinners, karaoke, drinks, dancing, live music—all by and for the trans community.

Day 2

In a winey stupor last night, I requested a tour of one of only two AIDS museums in the world. So today I was whisked around the museum by Ed, a handsome daddy type, and a self-confessed "theatre queen" who used to live two floors below RuPaul back in New York—"I was in the original chorus of *A Chorus Line*," he said, and there I died and went to gay heaven.

Broward County—where Fort Lauderdale is situated—has the highest prevalence of HIV-positive people in the entire United States. This is the right place to have a World AIDS Museum.

After this, a driver who was like a butch version of Dolly Parton took us on a minibus to the biggest archive of LGBTQIA+ memorabilia and literature in the States. Deep in the archives we rooted out games with such names as Twinkies and Trolls (Snakes and Ladders but with much more dick), Gayopoly, Gay Dream Date, and Gay Trivial Pursuit. Next, I'm handed the first-ever piece of published gay press in the United States, entitled *The Gay Blade*, distributed around Christopher Street in 1969, after the Stonewall Riots—detailing news stories about police raids and tips on how not to get busted for hustling. We unpacked the snake-print jacket worn by Carson Kressley on *Queer Eye*, which led me to rudely laugh over the tour guide's serious analysis of the importance of the jacket. But it was just so comical: *The Gay Blade* next to early circulars detailing tips on how New York "cross-dressers" should present themselves so as to not be arrested, next to this snake-print jacket, all venerated with same level of importance.

Back at my hotel room, I am now sitting on a shady balcony chain-smoking Parliaments* and trying to deconstruct this day. An intensely gay day,† but not overwhelmingly so—which is strange for me seeing as I feel a fair amount of anger towards the Londinium gays who frequent the gentrified streets of Soho. What is the reason for this lacuna separating me from my boy-loving brethren, despite our common lust for dick? Racism, femme shaming, transphobia, and misogyny currently feel endemic in my community.

But today also made me remember that gays are actually hilarious. Only a gay archive could feature a feather boa next to thousands of pages of gay and queer political press and view them with equal importance.

Day 3

I was treated to dinner at the Hard Rock Hotel. It's monstrous, but you can smoke inside, so it's an instant jackpot. I was told that this is the very hotel in which Anna Nicole Smith passed away, and I was surprised when I suddenly welled up. Hers is a story of tragedy you would only find in that late-noughties celeb-shaming press. It epitomises the demise of someone who was continu-

---

* The only straights I like. Pun intended.
† When's it not, though, henny?

ally shamed for being brazen about who she really was, something that rings true for so many of us queers.

Day 4

Bonaventure Resort & Spa, the day of the conference, most of it spent dashing between buildings dodging raindrops the size of rabbits. Everyone in the main bar was dressed to kill. I'd decided to don a T-shirt and fashion joggers, and now wished I were in something way less low-key. This incredibly glamorous social was populated with trans women and men who all sat and had dinner, drank wine, ate spinach with cold raspberry dressing, and prepared for karaoke (annoyingly I missed it). The attendees of the conference were mostly women over forty, and a lot of them seemed incredibly at peace with themselves and their lives back at home; they were just here to let their hair down.

The hotel in Fort Lauderdale was booked out entirely by members of the trans community, some seasoned attendees and some first-timers. To paraphrase Judith Butler: you come out of "the closet" only to find yourself in another one—being trans constructs another closet that wider society boxes you into, a closet that is often hellishly more dangerous than the one in which you previously existed.

It struck me that this was the first and only time in my entire life I have seen trans people prioritised; the need to say "I'm trans" fell away, that second closet disappeared, and people were free to remove politics from the discussion and instead talk about shopping, gambling, Justin Trudeau, their children.

I spoke with women from all over the United States, from Venezuela, Australia, the U.K. Waiting for another chardonnay, I got chatting to Diane, who had red eyes from crying. When I asked her if she was okay, she told me that today she had lived her lifelong dream, and that she was a little overwhelmed: "I went to all the designer stores with a new girlfriend I made, and I bought myself an expensive purse! I never go out like this." Diane presents as male back in Washington, D.C., and Southern Comfort is the one time of the year she stops being a doctor, a father, and a husband and flies away to her real life, here in Fort Lauderdale.

Nicole, who was telling me about winning nine hundred dollars on the slots earlier, eventually shares that she lost everything in her life when she revealed her desire to transition: job, children, partner, family, everything. She wasn't sad anymore, though; in the same breath, she explained that she was happier and freer than ever before, and that if she had to shed a skin to be herself, then the skin perhaps wasn't worth having in the first place.

Day 5

Flight home. On the zopiclone. About to pass out but need to write diary before I do. The getaway wasn't just needed; it was totally perspective altering.

I've decided that I'm done obsessing over the two

men in my life. I've frittered away countless, untraceable years obsessing over men and maleness. I've decided it's time to end it with Dom and look beyond my dependency on Ace.

11th August / le 11 août

Spent £230—all the money left in my overdraft, bar £16.54 for the tube home and a Deliveroo—on some Gucci sunglasses. They're pretty hideous, but after Fort Lauderdale I was in the mood to re-embrace my more gaudy side, which has faded since I got beaten up and stopped having a job at a fashion magazine to dress for.

> *"Finally. Plus I deserve a treat. That conference was*
> *fucking snooze-a-palooza. More dull than when I spent a*
> *weekend unable to move from beneath my ex-husband's*
> *corpse. The coroner thought he'd been poisoned, but I—"*

Fuck. Out of the gate and there was Dom. He turned up at the airport, waiting with a sign that read THE QUEEN. It was touching. But while I was away, I got a Facebook message from a friend of mine telling me they think they saw him at a gay sex club with his ex, Pete. I had ignored the message even though I'd been waiting for something to exonerate me of my guilt for my interactions with Ace, and it gave me a reason to chuck Dom and rediscover life outside of a double bed in South London.

So as soon as I saw Dom waiting for me, I decided to

ignore him. Quite harsh, but I needed a Costa* before I was going to pull the plug on our relationship. It didn't last long, as he spotted me in my hard-to-miss Guccis and started shrieking my name across the Arrivals forecourt, so he joined me in getting a coffee.

"Okay, it's true, I spent the whole weekend with Pete, but before you choose to leave me, can I just explain why?" he said, before I even had a chance to talk. "I've been thinking a lot recently about how much I love you, about how committed to you I am. And while you were away, I got scared that you weren't feeling the same for me, that you were becoming distant. So, when Pete messaged me to go down to Fire with him on Saturday, I was planning to go to just let off some steam with some random guys. But I got more and more drunk and took more MDMA and everything started to blur and I started to feel overwhelmed without you there, so I turned to Pete for comfort. But when I woke up on Sunday in his bed, I could only think of you and how much I want to be with you in all your femme, queer glory. And so I wanted to ask you . . ."

And before I'd even had a sip of my frappé, he was down on one pissing knee.

In Costa, in Heathrow. At 7:00 a.m.

"If you would do me the great honour—" Every dick I've sucked flashed before my eyes. He reached into his back pocket.

Everybody was looking.

---

* Hate Costa. Favourite is Nero, then Starbucks, then Costa.

"—of being my husband."

The whole of Costa's breakfast clientele were smiling, as if I were going to say yes.

Dom was still on one knee with a ring in his hand, a fixed, quivering smile held because I was taking my sweet time.

And there in Costa, via my stupid mouth, which was evidently unconnected to my brain, I said yes.

I am not fine with gay marriage. I am definitely not fine with this marriage.

And, today, I went from being cheated on to being engaged.

19th August / le 19 août

Yesterday was my birthday and all my friends were busy.

I haven't yet "found the time" to tell a soul about my engagement to Dom, except Ellie and Violet, both of whom I asked to be my maid of honour, in a kind of manic attempt to see if they might say anything to stop me or question me. Ellie is my most marriage-critical friend, but she was just excited, and Violet is into marriage (and divorce) and she just screamed about the clothes. Fuck. I couldn't quite muster the conviction to tell them I was in utter physical shock and wanted to break it off with my accidental fiancé because what if I was wrong and this was my one attempt at real love? Frankly, I don't think Dom was up for getting wed either because he hasn't mentioned it since he asked eight days ago and has also pointedly been watching videos in front of me of weddings gone wrong and this all feels like a strange torture routine, through which he might absolve himself of his guilt for cheating.

In the past—what?—five weeks that we've been dating, not one of my friends has taken to this man I'm supposed to be marrying. He's said some pretty shitty things to them—such as the time he told my friend Rina, who's Japanese, that she would be good at making sushi, or the time he told a rape joke at a party, then shouted at me in front of everyone because I said that rape is never funny. While my friends diagnosed our ill fit for each other early, I protested so much at the beginning of the relationship that it was "so amazing" and that we were just "kindred spirits" that admitting I want to run for the hills would give them the grounds upon which to say I told you so.

Looking back on this whirlwind monthlong relationship, I'm severely baffled at myself.

I just keep telling myself, "This will make a hilarious story." That always calms me down.

But, save for anything better to do, I ended up having a birthday dinner with no one other than Dom. He took me to a fancy restaurant in Soho and then to see an all-gay contemporary-dance troupe where muscular white gay men with septum piercings in all-beige outfits sort of jump about to bad white-people spoken word. He chose a birthday perfect for him, not me—an all-gay dance troupe? Really?

And the worst part? I hate my birthday and the attention it brings. No, it's true. I'm a drag queen who hates attention. An oxymoron, I know. To clarify, I don't hate well-deserved attention from large groups of people—*j'adore* the sound of a Denim audience, yelping, fainting, and screaming when I hit that high note. But I feel that birthday attention is unearned, forced.

And birthdays always bring with them a huge amount of guilt. Growing up we didn't have much money, so every time a birthday rolled around, it always brought with it this horrible feeling that your parents had spent a fortune on you, even though they couldn't afford to, and you wanted them to even though you know you shouldn't have. This guilt continues today because, as a drag queen, I often demand that my friends show me attention and adoration during my shows, so it feels excessive to ask for it on another day when I've done nothing special.

Back to last night. Dom had, sweetly, planned a surprise party at a bar. Perhaps the only thing worse than an all-gay dance troupe.

Every one of my friends, my whole family, and some totally random people I've never even seen in my life.

I burst into tears. It was so sweet. It was also a living, breathing nightmare.

My sweet, wonderful parents had come all the way from Lancaster, my brothers and my sister organised childcare and made me a photo album of all of us when we were young. All for my twenty-fifth birthday, hardly a big one.

The Denims had all pooled their minimal cash to buy me a wig—flame red, set in a 1920s style.

Ellie, Hatty, Leyah, Violet, and Cecily bought me a bottle of wine from the bar.

Pak gave me a book of Avedon photography. Pak knows I love coffee-table books because they signify a kind of cultural and economic capital I could never justify both now and when I was growing up.

Ace's family gave me more drink.

Then. Dom made a toast. I knew exactly what was about to happen.

"And speaking of changing worlds, I want to announce some news we have been sitting on: we've been waiting for just the right moment to reveal that we are engaged! I asked, it was a total surprise, and they said yes! And, yes, I'm the happiest person in the world! I'm so glad we can all share this moment together. To the love of my life! Cheers!"

"Run, bitch! This dude's crazy. Let me call the heli."

I took brief comfort in that this moment, like my KFC mishap or the time I got fucked on broken glass and had to dash to A&E straight after climax, will eventually be added to that glorious collection of stories that detail just how unstable all of our early twenties were, to be rolled out when we're all desperate for a bit of nostalgia as we approach a life more settled.

The crowd was naturally baffled. Glamrou left, Pak laughed, Ace locked himself in a loo and cried and then left. My parents were half-happy, half–unable to speak.

Then, as we walked through the streets of Soho, after saying goodbye to countless friends who didn't know how to look me in the eye, Dom started to complain about the negative ways my friends had reacted to our news. I couldn't listen anymore, and I snapped, cruelly.

"I can't do this anymore. I can't. My friends are the most important thing to me, and they've all proved repeatedly that they're not these things you say about them. I don't want to marry you. I don't want to be with you."

He said nothing. He looked, for an instant, like the man I'd met and adored a month and a half ago and swept through the sex dungeons and melancholic streets of Budapest with, and I wondered if I'd made a grave mistake.

Then he walked away, and I was left with my one birthday wish having come true: to be left alone.

"Come on, old girl. Let's get fucked up and go suck some *dicks."* **And off we went.**

22nd August / le 22 août

Breaking up with Dom has blown my calendar wide-open. Instead of throwing myself into emotionally exhausting back-and-forths about where we went wrong, I've thrown myself into work.

Because of this uptick in productivity, work is going well. Denim has scored a residency at this niche café-bistro-bar-whatever called Brasserie Zédel, where rich people come to gawk at you while eating French onion soup. It's absurd; we're like queens for hire, and a lot of these posh people don't have the spine to be openly homophobic, so instead they offer words of encouragement to prove to the rest of the room that they are fine with the gays: "Aren't you splendid!" they say through gritted teeth. The money is outrageously good, though. *The Guardian* accepted my fiftieth pitch to them—I'll be tracking down and interviewing every Sugababe ever, thus meaning I've hit my journalistic zenith and will never again produce anything as important. Hang on, that's a lie, because just last week I interviewed the Cheeky Girls, who likened the U.K. music charts to Romania under Ceauşescu's communist dictatorship.

Hatty and I have been working in all our spare time to perfect our music, too, because we've been asked to play at a showcase for Columbia Records. And I've been asked to cover fashion month for one of my favourite magazines—which means I'll be going to Paris for the first time, as well as Milan, London, and, quite terrifyingly, back to New York. I still have no money to buy new clothes, so I'm going to have to go on a borrowing binge before I leave in early September.

Turns out, when you take your eye off obsession with men and thrust all your energy onto creating positive visions of queerness, the world gets a whole lot bigger.

31st August / le 31 août

It's fucking grotesquely hot in London. Like the kind of hot that makes you sweat through your backpack and worry whether your laptop's going to break from water damage.

When I look around on the tube, it always feels as if I'm the only one dragging a used napkin across my forehead, bits of tissue sticking along the way, to rid myself of the beads of sweat that have pricked through my now-obsolete make-up. Hatty, as she sits there sweat-less in a floaty nightie, tells me it's because I wear too many layers. I always reply that I feel too self-conscious to expose my fat body in any way—layers are the best way to camouflage.

But she's right: looking around the tubes and the streets and the buses, everyone's in teeny-tiny tops and I'm soaking through all four layers I'm using to cloak how much space my big, wobbling body is taking up.

My body, my most time-consuming obsession.

When my mind is free of other anxieties, I land right back to base, to my body, and my constant obsession with covering it. If I'm on a deadline, on a stage, or on a dick, I don't consider my body or my hatred for it.

It disappoints me, constantly, that I preach body pos-itivity, fat activism, all the buzz words that populate our feeds and then get sucked into nothingness by brands wanting to profiteer from another unflattering, terribly made Curve collection, while internally I only ever pun-ish my body, which works so hard for me.

So each year as the summer rolls around and 90 per cent of the population reveal their gym-toned arms and wardrobe of teeny-tiny clothes, I start to torment my-self over what my body looks like, taking on unhealthy modes of consumption, wearing a jacket in thirty-degree heat so I won't have to expose the piled-up rolls that make up my torso.

I recently met a friend, through Twitter would you believe, who's a vehement fat activist. She's fat and rad and very much practises what she preaches. While it's evidently a lifelong process, I've been trying to shift my view of this body that I have deemed wrecked for so long, into one of gratefulness, adoration, power.

But it's hard to stay constantly in power over your fat body, and in love with all of it. *Fat* has been deleted from public discussion. The word, the people, and any positive associations with fatness simply do not exist. The only time we see, or will talk about, fat in public is to state a negative. First, there's the classist kind of fat shaming: on those dreadful morning talk shows where the male presenter will shout a fat person down for spending their benefits on fried chicken. Then there's the patronising kind of fat shaming from random TV doctors: "Are you not worried about your health? Look at all the terrible food you eat." There's the coercive kind of fat shaming: all that "summer body" / "Can you keep up with a Kardashian?" / "Lose those extra pounds or you'll die alone" crap. There are magazine covers, and sales techniques, that punctuate our lives everywhere we go, telling us, "If you're fat, you're gross."

All my life people have pussyfooted around my being just a bit fat. Often the confession of my awareness of my fatness is rescinded with a retort that goes something like:

"No . . . you're not fat, you're beautiful."

"You just have a massive ribcage, you're built stocky . . . it's not fat!"

I would be lying if I said I didn't have a massive ribcage, sure, but that doesn't explain my double—sometimes triple—chin, and my party pack in place of a six-pack. These statements allow me to be either fat or beautiful—but not both, which I am.

Despite the fact that advance-stage capitalism is designed to ditch the weak, to dump the chubs in the trash alongside people of colour, poor people, queer people, trans people, disabled people, immigrants, and women, it is possible to be fat and happy and, as afore-mentioned, beautiful.

So today, on the Central line, I took off all my layers and stripped down to my T-shirt, shoving the jacket and the oversize shirt in my already overfull backpack. It was terrifying, and I felt as if people were looking at my jiggling boobs and my back rolls, snickering like the kids at school. But I did it.

It's my new mission. As I lie here single, I will not think of the men I can't get or the diet I need in order to get them. Instead, I'm thinking of how I want to order a Deliveroo for dinner, how I know that will make me happy, and how that is surely better for my health and well-being, and my overall attractiveness, than chuck-ing up another McDonald's in the same bush in your back garden three times a week like when you were a teenager prescribed weight-loss club by your doctor.

My body isn't seasonal, nor is anyone else's. It's my vessel through which to experience pleasure: of eat-ing, of sex, of smelling, of doing an amazing shit. So this time when I start to obsess, I've decided it's high time to obsess over the pleasure I can experience in my body, not the painful ways in which I want to, and have tried and failed to, change it to take up less room in the world.

A KFC it is.

September / septembre

I've been commissioned by a bunch of different fashion magazines to go to the international shows and give my opinion on the clothes. I can't get my head around my being flown somewhere for work. You don't know dreams coming true is happening until it's happening, and then it's happened and, somehow, you're the same person. A year ago I would have wept at the thought, but perhaps becoming more fashion-industry critical since *Chic* means I'm less invested. Which means I come off cooler. Perhaps to make it in fashion, you have to be over fashion.

This is bonkers because I have no idea what the difference is between chiffon and taffeta. I've always been more drawn to the meaning of fashion, for its ability to allow one to transform entirely. The fabric isn't what's in my heart, what you can do and say with it is. This is my fashion-journo beat, working out the "political" message behind clothes. Sometimes it's bullshit, sometimes it's deeply moving. Watch this:

> DIOR: Raf Simons, in his final outing for the storied French house, gave actual meaning to the seemingly oxymoronic idea of maximal minimalism. Yes, the lines are clean, the cuts are direct, the colour palette consists of four main hues, but the pieces are bold in their presences and make. A thigh-high PVC boot, a knit sweater with giant shoulders, a classic trench with a statement sleeve.

In these tumultuous times Simons's proposition speaks to big ideas communicable to more than just those in the know.

See—absolute bullshit, but sounds like I know just what I'm talking about.

> ASHISH: A rainbow spectacle where every outfit came in a single colour, from head to toe, complete with matching giant Afro. It's an ode to brazen queerness, to committing to standing out, and Ashish's use of sequins in a distinctly sportswear market offers a glint of light in these dark political times.

And now you want to buy sequins, right?

"Forget the environment! Global warming's a myth!"

What does one pack for a month's worth of fashion weeks? In New York it'll be the tail end of summer, in Milan it'll be classically sultry and all I'll eat is flattened crumbed meats, and in Paris the world will have tipped into autumn and a PVC rain jacket will protect the underlayer of an outfit from the torrents, but see it soaked through with sweat. Sweat isn't very front row.

I'm finding this whole thing absurd—hiking up a humongous carbon footprint to go watch clothes and then write about them is hard to get your head around when the political, social, and environmental climes are as tumultuous as now. But I've always believed in the

power of escapism through fashion, plus I need the cash.
I always need the cash.

Plus it's glam.

Plus I'm on the front row at Raf Simons. And Dior,
lol.

Hope I'm not too sweaty.

4th September / le 4 septembre

Before I left for New York, Glamrou asked if Ace and I
wanted to go out clubbing for a rare night away from
Denim-related stuff. I was packed; all my tickets, money,
passport were in order.

We started the night as all classy girls do—two-
for-one cocktails, which we call cocks because we're
all homosexuals, at this bar with Barbies on the roof,
which was where I had my traumatic birthday. I'm trying to reclaim those spaces from their association with
that savage night. We then swung by the Med Café for
a quick coffee and a glass of wine at the same time, and
Ellie and her dad were there—they're always there, they
call it "the front garden"—smoking and giving us free
drinks. We laughed for a little too long, while Bob (Ellie's
dad) serenaded us with stories he'd collected from his
decades working as a theatre director, which we'd all
heard before but were happy to hear again.

Glamrou checked the time, and it was nearing 1:00
a.m.; our only option was to hit XXL—the big bear sex
club in Blackfriars. We had a shot of tequila and jumped
into a black cab, which we never do but we were already

quite smashed and thus had no qualms about chucking a tenner away on what could be a simple tube journey. Out, into the queue, and Ace, Glamrou, and I were already sizing up the clientele. It's the first time I'd ever been to a sex club with Ace. Before, the idea of my going queer clubbing with him inspired huge anxiety and pre-rejection feelings of rejection, but last night I was feeling nothing of the sort. I still felt very much emotionally in love with him, but the usual unhealthy crippling jealousy was nowhere in sight. I don't want to plumb this too much, for fear of undoing it, however, I think the key lies in my failed attempt at monogamy with Dom, and also a newfound belief in myself that I'm more lovable than a guy Ace will find in a sex dungeon at 2:00 a.m. on a Saturday night, whose face he can't see. If Dom taught me one thing, it's that someone could be in love with actual me, romantically, and not just the idea of me, and I'm grateful to him for that.

Pak joined us in the queue, with his flatmate Isaac and Isaac's new boyfriend. Things are still somewhat tense between Pak and Isaac, but the new boyfriend—a big, lovely bear—is sweet. It's hard not to feel a little movie-of-the-week warm when someone finds gay love.

We got to the door, and it was the same guy as the last time Glamrou and I were here. We laughed that we weren't sure if I did end up sucking his dick that night, but his wink at my heels and his air of sex was confirmation enough. "See you later, boys," he said, tapping Glamrou's ass as we walked in.

"Ugh—boys—that's ruined," Glamrou glumly remarked as we paid our entry fee and the lights switched from street orange to seedy red. "I hate it when people just assume you're a boy."

"Well, this is a male-only sex club," Isaac's boyfriend piped up. At that, we all jerked our necks around in unison, offended by his gendering of space but aware he was totally right, thereafter questioning our patronage of a place that's so restrictive and so anti-us.

> "... but we're going in, right? I didn't come out of cryogenic freezing to go home at the door. I need my face sat on!"

After Crystal's loose moral compass pointed us inside, we lost Isaac and his boyfriend fairly quickly, and for the following two hours Glamrou, Ace, Pak, and I pushed and pulled together, each time in different pairs, exploring different parts of the dance floor, the bar, the loos. After too many Red Stripes and countless rubs from topless, sweaty bears whose collective odour takes me back to my childhood garage (which had a damp problem), we made a group decision to have a look in the dark rooms.

As we all approached the back of the club and walked through the greenroom, we became an unstoppable force, our imaginary wigs flowing in the cum-scented air.

I'm Samantha: slowly unbuttoning my fly, sliding off my top (which I never do unless I'm at a bear club, specifically in the sex room), pushing my fingers through my fringe to make sure the curls have extra bounce. I say something too filthy for words and disappear into the dark.

Pak is Charlotte: prudish, shy, but desperate to find a husband. We've suggested that a dark room isn't as effective as places in which Pak might be able to, say, speak to someone, but instead of listening, Pak points to his ring finger and says excitedly, before he steps into a sea of anonymous semen, "See you at the wedding!"

Glamrou is Carrie: sexy, coy, a writer, and a former smoker. Before we part ways, they make their T-shirt into a sort of fashion crop top and mutter a sentence perfect for any Carrie B cutaway: "If sex with strangers is more intoxicating than a dinner date and a DVD, why are we so obsessed with finding true love?"

Ace is Miranda: clever and practical. "Has everybody had enough water?" Bless him. I love him.

Every dark room is the same. Not architecturally, or in clientele, but every single memory I have of being in a dark room may as well be the same one. It's quiet—quiet enough to hear an orchestra of groans and moans and whispers and, if you're lucky and listen hard enough, the pattering of a vigorous hand job. You can also always hear the faint throb of Kylie or house music. It's initially a daunting prospect: upon entry, a sea of shadowed bodies in various states of undress and pleasure greets you; some people on their knees, some in a circle looking down at one hardworking blow jobber sucking eight to ten dicks, some sitting on dicks, some fucking the person sitting on their dick. Until you're inside it, it all appears as one big, beating mass of flesh: pulsating with an intimidating, arousing mix of shame and sex and pleasure and power.

*"All key ingredients in my skin care line. It was
huge in the eighties."*

Once you're in it, it's like being absorbed into a
sponge or being on a water slide: you lose all idea of space
and time and dimension and spend hours being carried
around the room, from dick to dick, without even realising it. It's not uncommon to suck nigh on thirty dicks
and not say a single hello. But sometimes you connect
with one person so intensely that you spend the whole
night together, talking, kissing, maybe having sex, and
feeling as if you were going to run away together, as
if someone finally "gets" you. In hindsight all of those
guys were just heavily on drugs. But it was nice while
it lasted.

Last night was the former—no talking, just anonymous pleasure, circling round the room barely catching
glimpses of the other queens, a few of whom had left.

As the night drew to a close, I took one more gentle
tour around the room, landing on this guy whose face
I couldn't make out, who just pushed me down to the
ground, incredibly hot. Only after about three minutes
and an increasingly audible groan did I look up as the
light caught Ace's face. I stood up slowly and revealed
myself, and we spent the whole journey home in hyster-
ics but also deconstructing the cosmic meaning of what
this chance encounter had meant.

When we got back to Wally, we finished what
we'd started earlier, eventually falling asleep next to
each other, naked. As I arose this morning to head to

Heathrow, where I write from a Burger King, I found a note left by Ace on my pillow, which said the same thing I had written on a note when I left him for New York a year ago now:

"When you wake up, when you go to sleep, and every hour in between, I'll be thinking of you."

A nice note on which to leave, I think. I've learned, however, to leave expectations to a minimum. So I do just that and focus on the task at hand: fashion.

8th September / le 8 septembre

CRYSTAL'S GUIDE TO FASHION WEEK PARTIES:

- You're on the list. Even if you're not on the list, you're on the list. At no point should it ever be revealed that you were never on the list. You invented the list.
- To confirm you're on the list you work at only the most important magazine / fashion house / PR firm in the whole of fashion. Make it up, or lie and say Chanel.
- If you wear sunglasses and get your tone right and turn up looking frantic but in control, like busy is your forever mood, and act as though it's the person holding the list who's responsible for your not being on it, your chance of entry will increase fourfold, at least. If it takes physical violence, get one of your security guards to rough up one of

theirs. You don't want to be caught fighting by the paps—that's cheap!

- Either dress way way up or way way down. No in between, no "nice." It's either a head-to-toe archive Miu Miu fluffy four-piece suit sent to you by Miuccia herself (stolen from the fashion cupboard at work) or banged-up trainers, a white T-shirt, and grey sweatpants. Anything in between and you won't look suitably over it, or suitably under it.

- Once you're in, use the coat check. Rich people and fashion people are the only two types of people who won't chuck their coat and handbag on the floor, and the initial entry is all about looking both rich and fashion.

- Once you have a complimentary glass of champagne, take your pick between the four sub-moods of a fashion party and stick to it:

   1. FUCKED. This is 90 per cent of attendees; too much coke, too much chatting, but you'll fit right in, and maybe Marc Jacobs's boyfriend will follow you on Instagram once you've made a point of telling him you follow him.

   2. BORED. This is a hard one to get right, but it will guarantee you ten points in cool rating. You must not smile, remove your sunglasses, talk to more than three people, all of whom you know very, very well, take any photos, or insinuate that you're happy to be where you are even though you spent a week planning your look.

   3. FUCKED AND BORED. This will eventually be 90 per cent of the attendees. Conversation

has gone dry, your boozy, friendly countenance has dissolved, and your shoes are hurting. No more is to be squeezed from the lemon that is this party, but Gigi just arrived and you want to wait to see if you can befriend her for the Insta followers.

4. YOURSELF. A hard one to pull off; try it at your peril. One time when I was myself at a fashion party, I ended up weeping on Rita Ora, telling her she'd saved my life. It's not even true. I then tried the same with Halle Berry and was forcibly ejected from said party.

- Never, ever, look the following people in the eye: Naomi Campbell; the door girl who knows you blagged your way in the moment she let you past; any of the big models except Poppy Delevingne, because she's not quite made it and needs a friend from time to time; the famous female rapper you just met in the toilet; and the two girls you know but, if you do, will only talk to you about iPhone cases and what the *Vogue* party was like last night, and the Calvin Klein party was like the night before that. They will talk to you for three hours, and every time you think the conversation has dried up, they will bring up a random mutual social media friend whom you absolutely despise because the person is a proud Tory, but you can't say anything because one of these girls' dads is a director at Condé Nast. They will likely corner you by an outdoor fire or a speaker, and either you will be too hot to concentrate or it will be too loud to hear them.

- Try to get into one official photograph taken by the guy with the swept-back, curly grey bob who takes every photo. While posting about your party presence on social media has become unsavoury in the fashion-party world, there's nothing wrong with showing up unwittingly on Getty Images looking great and then posting on Facebook, "omg lol last night."

- Do not, under any circumstances, stay until the end. You'll look desperate. Get out of there, preferably with a few friends, and act as though you're heading somewhere glamorous and not straight home to order a Pizza Hut and stream episodes of *Real Housewives of Cheshire*, which you're rewatching for the fifth time.*

10th September / le 10 septembre

I was nervous to come back to New York. Not that it had ever done anything to me, other than been a harsh mistress, an unconquerable thirteen-by-two-mile island that saw me sext for my boss and shit.

When I moved here last year, it was the first time I'd ever been. I wandered around for the first week, waited

---

* Hands up, who misses Magali?

outside the *Vogue* offices to catch a glimpse of Anna Wintour, spent sixteen dollars on a cocktail at the Bowery just so I could say I had, all while fantastical Carrie Bradshaw monologues, quote for quote, raced through my head.

But it turned out I wasn't Carrie Bradshaw. Nor was I Samantha, and I definitely was never going to be a Miranda or a Charlotte. When I arrived into JFK this time, I was nervous. I had shed all my cultural touch points, my lenses through which to see the city, them having not quite fit the last time: I wasn't Patti Smith, nor was I Andy Sachs from *The Devil Wears Prada*. I wasn't Lady Bunny or RuPaul or any of the queens who invented Wigstock and performed at the Pyramid Club. I wasn't Marsha P. Johnson or Stormé DeLarverie, nor was I Amanda Lepore, Joey Arias, or Penny Arcade.* For me, the idea of New York was this—a fantasy lived through obsession with these figures and the way they had lived New York. New York in reality was anything but a fantasy. Even Crystal was bored of it, and she owns half of downtown.

> *"If you ask me, New York's been over since the end of my film career in the sixties. It's all about small seaside towns now, honey. That's where the big bucks are."*

As my taxi made its way towards the centre of Manhattan, I stopped and got out on my old street and

---

* If you're unsure of these names, it's time you used Google properly!

decided to walk* from the Lower East to where I was staying in midtown (what a blow).

Perhaps because I was back here on my own terms, or perhaps because I wasn't longing for somewhere else, I stopped being nervous and just felt that I was seeing New York. And you know what? It's pretty grey.

11th September / le 11 septembre

Got fully fucked up with Lily and Cora last night, and we all ended up making out. We were bought shooters by some random banker dude who was obviously into the spectacle, and eventually he pulled me over to him, handed me another shooter, and told me he wanted to pound my queen hole in the bathroom.

I was thinking of Ace, but we're not exclusive, we're not even official, and I needed to get some in if we were going to go the whole hog and go monog.

He was fancy—well, he was wearing a custom Armani suit, which is code for money no style—and as we slammed the bathroom door, he got his cock out and started calling me "bitch," which I told him to stop: "It's misogynist, you idiot." I gagged as his precum snail-trailed on my glittery beard.

I was on my knees, his dick at eye level, and he was moaning and sort of heaving with delight. Crystal was in her element: performatively choking, making potentially

---

* Which is unlike me. I hate walking.

problematic porn noises, thinking of the divorce settlement and defying my gag reflex.

> *"You like that, big boy? You gonna buy me diamonds, big boy? I want a nose job, baby, you get that for me?"* she whispered into his dick, as if it were a microphone.

He was loving it, heaving with pleasure. Then his heave turned to a gyp—which I still assumed was an (albeit weird) moan of pleasure. Until a gyp turned into a bigger heave, his dick still in my mouth, and a heave turned into a full stomach of rich food, red wine, and probably three grams of coke chucked up all over my head from the bird's-eye position.

Imagine that feeling of disappointment when a bird shits on your good hair. Then multiply that by a thousand times the volume and make it human sick and make it a club where a bunch of your editors are, the same one where Solange kicked Jay-Z in the lift. That's how my night ended—bathed in the worst of the six bodily fluids in the epicentre of fashion week's afterparties.

13th September / le 13 septembre

This morning, post a dance at one of Susanne Bartsch's parties in order for me to resurface on the nightlife scene post-vomitgate, Cora, Lily, and I wandered off to buy apple doughnuts from Dean & DeLuca and sit in the park and catch up properly, before I had to go to shows.

I was reminded how lucky I am to have made friends such as these in a city where so many feel lonely. Certain prevailing memories flooded me from my first time here, but they only served as comparisons to demonstrate how much one's life can change in, what? Eight months?

I also managed to skim through this diary. I tried to mark out a specific point when the tide changed, when I became a person looking back on a series of diary entries feeling like the same person who wrote them, but not remembering what I actually felt like writing them.

I landed on the entry from the day I quit my job, then checked my phone and saw a follow on Instagram from none other than my old boss Eve. I spent a moment considering whether she was a ghost sent from hell to haunt me for some bad shit I did in a past life when I was a butterfly, or whether my suspicions were true all along and I am like Jim Carrey in *The Truman Show* and Eve has a recurring role in my life so the real world can see how I react within an emotionally abusive dynamic. Great TV, to be fair. But then I stopped this mad narcissism and just blocked her (without even stalking her), which to me feels like huge growth.

I feel like a different person in New York now. Might be the attack, or Dom, or Hatty, or like not being broke, alone, and sexting a man I don't know against my consent. I like myself more now, perhaps. I know myself better, for sure. Although if a text from Jared were to swing by my phone, I'd be all ears, but this time he'd know about it.

"Hmmm, he was hot." ⧩

He was.

But I don't think there's a singular, definitive answer to looking at yourself and liking yourself. There's no definitive stop, no point where you've worked on yourself totally and arrived at a place where you're happy with yourself: the choices you've made, the way you treat others, the way you allow others to treat you, the things you do for money, and the way you uphold systems that both hurt you and benefit you.

It always felt important to me to work hard to be the person I "wanted to be." I used to think this would happen overnight, as if you eventually save enough money to tip from overdrawn to drawn.* But I can't see that happening—at the end of all the work there's no final eventuality other than an acceptance that my queerness, my fatness, my drag, my class, all my identities, my relationships, my love life, are all messy, rolling, fluid. There's no turning point into stability, there's no end to the learning, and there's no one conception of yourself that you'll one day land on and be happy with. The person I'm working towards doesn't exist because they're always changing.

---

* Is that a thing? I've been in my overdraft since I opened a bank account.

15th September / le 15 septembre

Back in London, and so many of the runway shows are referencing drag. Some are doing it well, some are doing it flimsily. I ran into an editor friend and we spent a lunch discussing the appropriation of drag culture by the mainstream.

"We're all assigned a gender role, so is gender not anyone's to mess up? Is drag itself already an appropriation of femininity or masculinity? And what about drag lexicon?"

She was asking me a bunch of smart questions, and I was just sucking the dressing off salad leaves because I hate salad but that's all there was left at the fashion week café.

Yes, drag is appropriation. We've taken a lot from working-class black women, for example. A lot of the words I once bandied about, thinking I was getting the whole being-a-drag-queen thing right by screaming "slay" and "shaaaade" and "oooh, girl" and "you better work, bitch" and "henny," I later realised weren't my words to use freely, even as a drag queen.

Of course I didn't say that, I just stared blankly and said, hoping to get paid, "This would make a really interesting feature?"

"Doesn't drag get a free pass, though, because it exists in a neighbouring realm of oppression?"—her next question. Again, I said I didn't think so, but I was nervous and was thinking of the pay cheque.

What I really think is, no, it doesn't get a free pass. It does get things wrong, but that's okay as long as you're willing to work hard to put it right. Drag thrives on the incorporation of aspects of different cultures—but I think where you fall on the race, class, gender, sexuality, ability hierarchy within society has to matter when deciding what cultures you can draw from. Can drag offensively appropriate? Yes. Can drag also undermine and put right that kind of appropriation? Absolutely, by presenting the powers in femininity or the weaknesses in masculinity, by allowing artists from those different backgrounds to make work that actively critiques appropriation by parodying race and class and gender in humorous or honest ways. The best queens will do the latter. Such as Glamrou, or ShayShay, who's a veteran on the London scene. Such as Sasha Velour or Bianca, or Bob if we're talking *Drag Race* queens. Or such as Chiyo—probably the best drag king I've ever seen. They'll entertain and aggress at once, they'll use camp to critique.

The editor and I talked some more, and I stumbled over answers, trying to be as impressive yet chilled as I could.

"Why is there such a fuss about drag?"—her closing question.

I spluttered out some shit to do with building power in failure.*

But why is there such a fuss about drag? I've never thought about it other than just saying, *"RuPaul,* obviously." Is it the sequins? The wigs? The make-up?

---

* I really need to read another book.

As I packed my suitcase for a Denim gig we have to-morrow, laying the sequins over the chiffon, encasing the wigs and the heels, I felt an overwhelming joy, a sense of completeness, bundling Crystal into a bag.

"I love to travel in style," she says, as I curl my wig into a pillowcase and sit on the little case to close it.

It's not just the sensory elements of drag, even though they are absolutely something to make a fuss about. But drag isn't simply the buying and wearing of these fabulous, subversive, glittering markers. It's not about what these markers are; it's about what donning them means.

Drag forces you to question the world as it's been presented to you. It asks you to step into a world of radical history, broken-down gender systems, and acerbically critical wit. Drag allows you to create a self from scratch, to amplify the things you want to be.

That's why people who come to drag often devote their lives to it. To a precarious pay cheque, a rota of late nights and pricey costumes; to damaged skin and cracked nail beds; to bouts of scary homophobia and blistered feet. Because, beyond all that, drag allows you to become the kind of superstar you never thought you were allowed to be. It allows you to transcend this terrifying plane. Drag is radical. Drag gives you new perspectives, allowing you to pull back the curtain and glimpse a world where you're free of all the restrictions that cause you pain. It's a healing aid, it's a therapy. It's an antidote to all the terror outside.

While drag is probably the most fun you can have with your clothes on, the fuss is about more than just fun. It's about love—for yourself, for your siblings. It's about giving back to people, and saving a bit for yourself. It's about being the most glorious person in the room, while pulling everyone else up to your level. It's about proving that, while you might be an outcast, you're quicker, cooler, funnier, than the people on the inside. It's about proving that being a misfit is the best place to be. It's about showing there's hope, and that happiness and power aren't the stronghold of those at the top of every structure. We have it, so much of it, in abundance. And we deserve it.

I decided to email my editor most of these ramblings. She replied, "Yeah cool can pay u £45 for 1000 words?"

Gorj! So glad years of my intellectual life are worth forty-five pounds! At least my Ubers for tomorrow night are covered.

17th September / le 17 septembre

Speaking of drag, last night we had a Denim gig—a thirtieth birthday for Glamrou's housemate, who's a really attractive twink. Can you be a thirty-year-old twink? A contradiction in terms, surely, but he pulls it off.

It dawned on me only when I arrived in central London for the day of shows that I'd forgotten the suitcase I packed, so I ran over to the costume shop where my northern friend Chris works—So High Soho, an institution—and together we constructed a look that was half-Shakespeare, half–"Sissy That Walk." Think an oversize, foppish shirt, a wavy red wig, and some thigh-high boots.

Had lunch with Ace. We discussed how it burned when we went for a wee and blood came out, too, so we booked in to have a speedy STI test before the gig tonight.

Gig went fine. Ace flirted with an annoying cool guy from Berlin who makes short films about contemporary dance or some wanky shit, so I went to leave—a looming flight to Milan—but Ace asked me to wait: "Two mins! I just need to say goodbye."

Forty minutes and thirteen cigarettes later, I was furious—a mug once again, standing there looking like a Shakespearean jester, ready to draw a line under it. As I turned toward the corner to find a better Uber spot, I heard Ace shouting to me.

"Stop! I have something to tell you. Well, ask you. I don't know."

I looked up, leaving my Uber pin floating in midair.

"I want to be with you. Not just like the way we are. But I want to be with, with you. Together. I love you. I just told Glamrou, downstairs, that's why I was taking so long, and they told me I have to say it now or I'll regret it forever. Why just be best friends with the person everyone wants to be best friends with when I can be the person, your person, and you can be my person. You're already my person. Stop me, say something, oh my Go—"

"I told you so, you fucking loser. You're beautiful!"

Both of our phones picked up a text.

Both of us received a message from the sexual health clinic. Both of us have gonorrhoea. Team.

"Wow, the most romantic moment ever ruined by the most unromantically named STI ever," Ace sighed.

We got in the cab. Went home. I asked for some time to think, while I'm away in Milan at least. He obliged.

The usual me would immediately have said yes. But I'm trying this new thing where I think about the things I need, just briefly, before I jump straight into a decision. While the fantasy of jumping into a relationship with a best friend sounds just dreamy, de facto there's much more to consider.

I need to sleep. And get my clap treated.

19th September / le 19 septembre

Do I want to be this man's best friend or partner? If we go for it, there's no going back. No matter the amount of froufrou well-intentioned promises we make each other about "working hard to maintain our friendship if we were ever to break up" or "having an open and honest communication channel re our feelings," there's absolutely not a single speck of hope that once you have moved through a relationship together, and then a break-up, things can ever go back to the way they once were, when you were simply best friends in the magical, hurricane-like place where you're on the brink of falling in love.

If we don't go for it, there's also no going back. First, there's no way to re-create the way we were when this all began. That incarnation of us, that simpler, more naive version of us, is over—dead in the water. We've changed, both individually and with each other: we've inflicted scars and hurts that weren't there when the seeds of this thing were so greenly planted. Besides, all friendships change—especially the intensely unsustainable ones you desperately want to keep preserved forever. No way can those huge, wonderful thunderstorms that some new friends bring into your life last. So while we talk about "risk," about "losing what we have," it'll never be the same forever anyway. It might grow into something better or healthier, but it won't be what we have now. Beyond that, the what-ifs would always slightly encumber our ability to be best friends—seeing each other with other people, always wondering if he was the one that got away, as cheesy and delusional as that sounds.

I thought this would be easy. I dreamt of this moment in times when I felt particularly lonely or melancholic, and now I have fewer answers than I had before all of this started. I worry, for a moment, that I've done that awful thing where all I wanted was the amateur dramatics of the chase, the rush of the turmoil, and now that the outcome is positive, it doesn't get my rocks off the way emotional torture does.

But now, sitting here, when I think about Ace, I feel full, happy, warm, and understood.*

---

* And I have an erection.

And that's the only answer I need.

Of course I'll wait a few days to tell him—let him sweat—plus I have a Philipp Plein show to go hate on.

Ciao!

24th September / le 24 septembre

So I slept with someone else. A fashion person with whom I'd bonded over the preceding international weeks as we were both equally out of our depths. He's hotter than my usual one-nighter scores, and he wears loads of Louis Vuitton because he once had sex with a famous designer.

This was the first time in years I'd met someone organically and had sex with them, not via a hookup app or in a sex club, except Ace (who, by the way, hasn't responded to any of my messages since I arrived in Italy), and I enjoyed the process very much. The slow build, the flirt, the eye rolls across the runway at Dolce & Gabbana as they sent yet another bunch of irrelevant influencers down the runway.

I don't think I'll see him again, though, because he did that annoying thing where someone forces your head repeatedly onto their dick. Usually I'm into this, so I couldn't put my finger on why I wasn't. But I wasn't.

This was the first time I couldn't make particularly bad sex work for me. It just was bad and there was no fixing it. He thought it was great.

> *"That's men for you, baby. Like when I fucked Rasputin,*
> *he just didn't know how to make me cum. Tried to his*
> *dying day, bless him, old Razzy, and that's what finished*
> *him off in the end. He was just so exhausted."*

At uni Crystal and I used to say, "You can polish a sexual turd"—which meant that even an unsatisfying sexual situation was guaranteed to always become a story and therefore have a happy ending. But this wasn't even funny or outrageous, and the happy ending came after he came and he spent the next—what?—twenty minutes lying there tired, giving me a hand job as I slowly went soft at the sight of his evident apathy. In the end I thought about my rugby coach* from high school, which always does the trick.

Perhaps my inability to turn this sexual frown upside down was linked to my already feeling committed to Ace. But, before this whole relationship thing kicks off, I'd told myself that having one final blow was going to be much needed. While there was indeed a final blow, it wasn't really a blow at all; he just kind of gummed it like a baby with no teeth gums a banana.†

---

* Lol, me, rugby.
† I should mention that I had a jab in the ass for my gonorrhoea the morning of my flight to Milan. It had been approx seven days, all good.

26th September / le 26 septembre

Fashion shows are hectic: it's all about keeping face, an art wherein one must act angry at everyone until you're let in, and then, upon sitting down, you must be on your phone and appear not to care. Maybe people don't care, maybe all these editors and writers and buyers just want to sit down and chill for a hot sec.

But this means being on your phone a substantial amount, pretending you're on email or posting on social to a million-plus followers. Sadly I am doing neither. Instead I'm slowly tipping over the edge into severe neurosis and paranoia. Ace hasn't messaged me back for six days, and so instead of messaging him again, I'm just spending my pre-show phone time noting down when he was last online on WhatsApp.

Such as today: 8:34 a.m., 9:12 a.m., 1:36 p.m. He's seen and not responded, and tonight there's a Wally party—the theme is Strippers in Paris, iconic—and loads of hot tops will be there propositioning him, and I'll be here alone in a hotel room irrationally imagining him meeting the love of his life (and probably wanking over it).

It's just after 5:00 p.m. and I'm at the Versace show, which is running late, writing this on my notes, trying to distract myself from those two blue ticks and no "Ace is typing . . ." at the top. I have to leave. This is absurd. This is ridiculous. I can just google the images. I have to go back to London. Yes, every piece of feminist literature would tell me not to jeopardise my career for a man, but I'm on the third row, which is hardly good for my reputation anyway. I absolutely have to go, right?

"God, I live for this drama. Go get it, queen!" ⟨

I'm doing it!

27th September / le 27 septembre

A car.

A flight. A wine.

A train. Another wine on the train.

A foot tapped in anxiety nigh on a million times. A cigarette.

A tube. A walk.

Torrential rain.

A key, a door, a flight of stairs: a massive party. Wet. Dripping wet.

Ace.

I saw him in a see-thru shirt dancing with the lights behind him—beams shining through his outfit, a cut-out of a glorious body of a person I love.

I dropped my bag, walked across the warehouse, and stepped right in front of him.

"Yes, please, can we do this?"

"You're home!"

"Is your offer still valid?"

"It is!"

We kissed in front of every one of our friends.

We were there together, in the same place, wanting the same thing, for the first time.

We both laughed as we started to use tongues, unable to control ourselves, as we heard every one of our

friends who has lived through the confusion of our situation cheer and clap in celebration. Savannah, Ace's
sister, was repeatedly shouting at the top of her lungs, "It
was inevitable!" and "Euphoria" by Loreen played over
the amp Hatty had stolen from our local rehearsal room.

It was the most romantic three hours of my life. And
the little queen inside me, who has been so bound in
nets of rejection for so many years, was temporarily set
free—and she sang all night.

October / octobre

3rd October / le 3 octobre

For the first time I feel that I don't have to diarise every detail of my interactions with Ace to prove they're real, to take them from a jumble in my head to a tangible, organised thing on the page.

It's jumped out of my mind, where I'd assumed it was partially made up like so much of my love life past, and into reality. Into kissing without spiralling out or needing to be high, into talking without an awkward feeling of there being so much unsaid, into touching without flinching after that electric zing—instead feeling it, leaning into it.

I had to go to Paris,* and Ace surprised me the day after by coming, too. I'm not so fussed about writing about what Paris looks like in love because everyone knows. Why waste time writing about Paris in love when I could be in Paris in love?

> *"Honey, we're literally Carrie.* <
> *'An American Girl in Paris: Part Une.'"*

"'A Northern Queen in Paris: Part Deux.'"

---

* When did I get so glam? Ugh, capitalism is so irresistible, goddammit.

4th October / le 4 octobre

Been asked to write a non-binary how-to, which I'm unsure about because there's no real way to how-to this.

Thus far, these are my notes:

- *They/them/their* is the most common pronoun used among non-binary people. However, countless other words and pronouns are also used. I know someone who uses *Miranda* instead of *he/she/they/ze* and it's amazing. Don't question someone's definition, just accept it and try to get it right.
- Non-binary folk are often seen in relation to binary cis gender, but we exist outside that in our own right, not in relation to. Try to reposition your view; it's way less hard than other things straights do such as going to the gym or years of unhappy marriage.
- Don't conflate or compare gender and medical transition. There are endless ways to transition.
- Gender is often contextual; it changes for everyone. My gender changes a thousand times over the course of a day. There are endless genders, and I have been, like, six while writing this.
- We're learning, too, experimenting with our presentation until we learn what's right for us.
- Non-binary genders aren't a millennial fad. We have existed for centuries. We just had different names.
- To that end, gender is a Western and colonial construct. Think of the hijras of India, the two-spirits of indigenous Americans, the waria

of Indonesia, the māhū of Hawaii, the muxes of Juchitán, Mexico. We didn't invent non-binarism.

- We aren't just words or online ideas—we are human and very, very real.
- We're fun, just like you. Please don't tiptoe around us. Unless you're a transphobe: then tiptoe. Tiptoe like you've never tiptoed before.

Trying to add something in about nail varnish, but it's just not clicking.

5th October / le 5 octobre

No other sex is quite like new-relationship sex. I've read enough pop-feminist online literature to know that new-relationship sex will most probably dwindle into three-times-a-week sex after a month, once a week after a year, and once(ish) a month, with slightly more regular pre-bed hand jobs, thereafter until you break up or die.

But new-relationship sex seems much like a recipe. Not that I'd know because I can't cook. But I reckon it goes something like this:

NEW-RELATIONSHIP SEX
Ingredients
    1 year of yearning looks, to grease the tin
    11 months of casual flirting disguised as best
        friendship, at near boiling temperature
    10 years of romantic rejection, finely chopped
    1 guarantee that new-relationship person is into you /

won't reject you mid-sex (the worst), for the topping

1 new body to explore, whipped until smooth

100 per cent actually wanting to pleasure your partner, rather than just get your own rocks off with a guy on Grindr, to season

80(ish) sexual partners with whom you've learned some pretty impressive tricks, to finish

A pinch of desperation to show your new partner your best bits, to help the relationship rise successfully

A dash of whipped cream, because it's hot

Method

Take all ingredients and mash them together into a stiff aromatic mix where pleasure is the optimal consistency of the final concoction. Bake/fry/spit-roast mixture in interesting settings: club toilets, the back of a taxi, a bush, under the table at a fancy restaurant, a bush again, sometimes in bed but more likely on the floor next to it, in the kitchen, the bathroom, the hallway, the hallway, the hallway, in your flatmate's bed when she's out, in a dog park in the morning, on a tube late at night, and one time in the deep end of a kids' swimming pool after hours.

6th October / le 6 octobre

It's every gay kid's dream to be a pop star. Yes, I know it's harmful to try to work out the causation of gayness—like the whole dreadfully dull, pointless debate about "nature or nurture" and "genetics or environment"—but there's defo a gay-boy-pop-star gene. I've seen enough wannabe fag performers with no talent to know this to be true. No matter how far you move away from that childhood dream—some gays are now allowed to play sports and be builders and stuff—every gay kid dreams of pop stardom.

It's something that I still want: to be as culturally agitative as Madonna, as mainstream yet transgressive as Gaga, as wildly talented and politically empowering as Beyoncé, as important a lifeline to people as Liza or Judy. For me it's always female pop stars.

Well, today, Denim got the news that we had been signed by an agent who wants to put us on stages everywhere. I'd always been baffled that I wasn't yet famous, but turns out it was just a matter of time (and six years' hard work, late nights, bad gigs, and no money). We all calmed one another down, not wanting to get our hopes up.

So, diary, let it be known that on this day—6 October—I started to become famous.

7th October / le 7 octobre

Three people. Three people are all it takes to make the perfect drag audience. I learned this, officially, this weekend, when Denim hosted a gig at this shambolic festival in Southampton, at the end of which I stripped in a trite ode to body positivity to a grand total of three people.

In a giant tent, I'd say capacity 350, three people

watched me strip. And it was the most joyful moment, full of failure and transcendence and queerness where we, the four of us, had found a place free from external pressures and just were. Afterwards we all embraced, and one of the women watching wept, then stripped for us, too.

DRAG PERFORMANCE MEMO: I never know if it's okay to invoke images of pregnancy as a drag queen. But Aphrodite does, and it's all about her relationship to her mother. I think it works because she's talking about the mass cultural ignorance towards female and feminine labour; it's not just like "Waaah, look at my baby, I'm a woman."

9th October / le 9 octobre

This afternoon as I was grumbling around the house, working out what food I could reasonably steal from the fridge, my phone rang.

"Are you sitting down?" It was Beth, one of my best friends from high school.

"I can be. Should I sit down? Are you pregnant?" I said, totally overexcited.

"No. I didn't want to call you out of the blue, but you're so far away and I didn't want you to see on Facebook."

"You're engaged! Oh my God, I knew it! Although I thought he would be asking you when you went to—"

"It's not that either, let me finish."

I hear her intake breath, like the sound someone makes when they're trying to pull themself out of heaving sobs. When you went through teenagerdom with someone, you come to know their version of this sound very well.

"Wait, are you crying? What's up?" I sit down.

"I can't believe I'm saying this, but . . . Ben . . . It's Ben. Ben's just been in an accident and he was found dead on arrival."

"Ben who?" I knew exactly which Ben, but I was clinging for one second more to the idea that it might be another Ben, a more distant Ben.

It wasn't, though. It was our Ben. One of our best friends from high school. He had been driving characteristically fast down a country lane near where we grew up and had crashed into a tractor. Had died on impact.

"I'm coming home. Should I come home? I'm coming home," I say coldly, not sure how else to respond.

10th October / le 10 octobre

I hadn't visited my hometown in over a year and a half. I speak to my mum every day on the phone, and my dad three times a week, my siblings, too. I whatsapp with all my friends from school on a group called Slags (No Lauren)—a name made up when one of our girls, Lauren, beat up two of our girls on a night out and we decided we should make a group without her. We've never changed the name back, but we've all lost touch with Lauren, except when we happen to see her on a night out and there's a red alert. Then the evening is spent skilfully dodging her. There's also the terminally misogynist issue of the word *slags*. But it's a funny word, we were all pure slags at high school, and my friend Beth named the group, so I feel that I have permission to rejoice in its reclamation.*

Anyway, slags, I used to go home all the time, back when I was at university, and the years following that. But over the last year and a bit, I've developed a more complicated relationship with where I'm from, and I've been putting off the work it might take to go back there.

It's a relationship I've rarely thought about. I didn't know about my class until I was grown up—because when you're in it, you don't see it. It's not something I had to deal with until I moved to university, where class difference played out everywhere.

My relationship with Lancaster stretches across a complicated nexus of strings that I've pulled to near breaking the more I desperately tried to assimilate into my new life in London, a life that I thought had more meaning.

At Cambridge I met a group of people who expanded my worldview so shockingly, so irrevocably, that I constantly felt simply grateful to be allowed to go along for the ride. I was desperate to fit in with my new radical group of friends: confident, cool, political, and with endless amounts of knowledge and critical thought I didn't

---

* It must be noted here that communities reclaim lots of words that are not yours to use if you don't belong to that community. *Faggot* is one, the n-word is most definitely one.

even know existed in the world. I just thought criticism meant, like, criticising someone's outfit, because did you see what Charlotte wore to her wedding? Seriously pure tack, who wears a short dress to their wedding?? Omg and him with a tribal tattoo???

My friends from Cambridge knew all about criticism— they went to Eton, St. Paul's, Ampleforth, Westminster, Harrow, St. Blah of Blah where Daddy and Daddy's daddy went. It's not fair to upbraid these friends for where they were sent to school, but it is fair to talk about the vast differences these types of education proffered.

I've benefited from their education hugely. I've invested the way I talk about my queerness or my work with the way they were taught to talk and think about this stuff: with confidence, entitlement, knowledge, and a vigour that allows them to take up space.

Until recently, I thought that where I'm from, and the culture that resides there, had nothing to offer: I can't explain gender theory with my rough state-school education; I can't offer advice on poststructuralism when I've only known what it means for a few years and still don't know whether I understand it.

And I think about my friends, and my family. My girlfriends who say things like "Yeah, feminism and stuff, but some women are just fucking dicks."

And: "Okay, explain this to me: Why do we need gay Pride when you're, like, out and stuff? We don't get straight Pride!"

And: "I'm not voting. I'm just not into voting."

These statements go entirely against my worldview. Often, when challenged and offered other viewpoints, my friends will be the first—quicker than any of my friends in London—to admit they "didn't think of that!" Sometimes, when we clash hard, they'll call me a snob and I'll call them offensive, but we'll quickly be laughing and agreeing that we were perhaps both wrong.

But then I really think about my friends: the friends who stood up to playground bullies, my ten best girl-friends, who collectively beat up a guy in my year because he'd pinned me against a wall and repeatedly kicked a football into my face, over and over. I think about how so much of our youth was filled with getting fingered in parks, stealing booze from Amy's mum's booze cabinet and getting so pissed we all snogged and cried, always prioritising laughter over whether we might be perceived as smart enough, cool enough, well read enough. We didn't ever read—I can't think of a single close friend of mine who had a bookshelf growing up. While I might later have been publicly humiliated for having never read Oscar Wilde—"But you're gay?!?"—I can guarantee my best friends can tell a story with as much life, vigour, humour, and knowingness as Wilde ever could.

It would be naive to claim that class difference doesn't matter. But, as I think about the class I've tried to distance myself from, I consider how much of me it has produced and how grateful I am for what it's given me. While public perceptions might be that the work-ing classes are stupid yobs, my experience couldn't be further from that. Here, in Lancaster, I was shown the ropes on how to live a fuller life better than any book or lecture or artwork might teach me. I was taught the importance of hard work, of accepting others around you as long as they're "sound," of having a fucking brilliant time. I was taught the importance of family and about committing to your friends. I was taught how to tell a story and laugh about the impossibly hard things in life. I was taught so much that is valuable to who I am now.

As I pull into Lancaster, Beth is waiting for me in the car park with Matt, Hannah, and Sara, and I get a text that reads:

> In car park! We can't wait to see you, baby. Meeting Becky and the baba at the Sun for a bottle of rosé—I think we all need a cry. xxxxx

11th October / le 11 octobre

Last night we sat at the pub until it closed and shared stories about Ben. I didn't have so many stories about Ben. We were close-ish in high school, we were in the same group, and he was one of the only straight boys who wasn't homophobic towards me. My other friends, the ones who had stayed here and stayed much more in-tertwined with his life, were grieving for a Ben-shaped hole in their lives, singing odes to his loyalty, his quiet-ness, his simple goals for good fun and a good drink. I couldn't help but feel like a bit of a grief tourist, but Ben would have told me to get on with it, and not to worry so much. It's strange grieving for parts of you that exist in the past, and it makes you feel selfish because Ben was not in the past for so many people. Crystal was loving it. Offering up monologues in my head as if accepting an Oscar.

DRAG MEMO: In London I don't know if it's super-radical to just put on a dress and face anymore. But here in Lancaster I think even the slightest transgression from binary gender—like an earring on a dude, a crop cut on a girl—is radical. It's like "the geography of radicalism" or some shit.

12th October / le 12 octobre

Being at home is a strange thing for someone who's currently trying to prove to their family they've forged a successful adult identity. By this I don't mean that dreadful verb *adulting* when used in relation to such things as doing washing. I find that millennial trend particularly bleak, one trying to make baby people of us all.

But no matter how good you've become at being away from home, in your own context, making your own money, forging your own routine, the minute you step over the threshold, into Mum-and-Dad land, you become the baby again—your siblings ribbing you because you're the spoiled one, the one who always gets their own way, the one who always "goes on about politics"; your mum practically forcing you to the ground so that she can cut your nails, squeeze your spots, and feed you vitamin tablets.

My dad is the exception to this rule: he and I have

always had a specific and sensitive bond. We would, and still do, have long conversations about things like the stars and family and mental health and what the provisos for success are in a rapidly changing world or just how Rachel Dolezal could've gone that far on her quest into postracialism. My dad is a special man, and he's also wonderfully strange—I credit him totally with my love of a good shit story, and my often irrationally romantic side. While the world plunders what it means to be a man, my dad taught me early on—as he lay on the floor next to my bed and made up stories about boys who were mermaids—that being a man wasn't half as fulfilling as being yourself.

My sister is one of the most memorable people I know, even though she's the furthest from a show-off you could find. She says the most inopportune or hilarious things as if she were looking for trouble. She taught me the power of the outrageous story in effectively breaking ice.

My brother Harry is a show-off. Just like me. Together we get into huge fights as my mum yelps, "I can't cope," at a louder and louder pitch, which only drives us further. He's also a wonderful person who is constantly trying to understand others around him.

My other brother, James, taught me how to party. Not like a soft-core drinks thing, like a blazingly wankered four-nighter at a festival. He's famously "chilled," although since he had a baby, he's become more serious (until the baby is in bed, wherein James brings out mental stories of what he and his friends got up to all those times I was too young to go out and party).

Then there's me. While I don't want to sound full of ego or self-obsession, I often think that our collective openness comes from there being a queer person in the family, a person who cracked open the normative dynamic and asked more of us all. I write this having been told this by them. While we're just like other families in my hometown, a get-together will so often consist of a conversation that flits from drag queens to childcare, dresses my mum asked our lightly homophobic next-door neighbour to make for me to stories from another stag do my brothers went on. When I visit friends' houses, their parents say things to me, with a knowing wink as if they've got the measure of us gays, like "Oh, there's a new gay couple living two roads over!" or "Oh, your mum says you have a partner—she's so amazing about it all!"

But my family doesn't say things like that, not anymore. In a decade we went from fighting to discussing fisting. While that kind of candour, and the humour and love with which we all now approach it, journeyed via some dark pits and scary cul-de-sacs, we all emerged from the other side with an understanding that more is to be gained by speaking about our differences than by trying to go through life smiling on the outside but wilting within. As I looked around the dinner table, I couldn't think of any other biological family I'd rather have, and they've proved time and time again that what they need isn't a façade or distance: it's honesty and a chance to prove that they're always willing to learn.

13th October / le 13 octobre

A map of Lancaster is imprinted in my head, the land-marks not historic nor of public interest, but instead the various sites of the attacks I underwent in my early life. As I drive past my old school, I remember the ache of a stream of Bibles being launched at me by two boys who were telling me to die; as I drive past my old bus stop, I recall the sting I felt after five men on the bus strad-dled me, pinning me down, squeezing lemon juice into my eyes as they shouted "faggot"; as I approach home, I remember the darts in my lungs after sprinting there from a nearby petrol station, fleeing from three men who threatened repeatedly to kill me, over and over, in the most violent of ways, because I was wearing pink flip-flops. I was heartbroken the way a fourteen-year-old should never feel as I threw my favourite pink flip-flops away that same night.

Foremost, I find these memories upsetting—for the little, confused boy I was then who never knew every-thing was going to be all right. I find it more upsetting that I still don't know if it is now. I also find these mem-ories sickly rewarding, that I'm thankful they happened to me because they armed me with a quicker wit and a more advanced danger detector than most people I've ever met.

But today I went into town to buy a shirt for Ben's funeral. At university I was, for want of not trying to sound like a big-headed asshole, kind of known for the way I dressed. It wasn't always good—in one phase I wore teeny-tiny dresses held back by body harnesses to my veterinary anatomy practicals, where I'd use my acrylic nails to slice muscles of deceased animals for laughs. But that was my thing: for as long as I can remember, I used dress as a means of provocation, as a means to show, maybe scream to, the world that I exist.

I was thinking back to the way I was at university when I was in Topshop in Lancaster, holding a blue-and-white-striped women's shirt with floppy cuffs. Old me would have snapped this shirt up, along with a ton of other things that I would wear once and then exile to the back of my ethically questionable overflowing wardrobe. But holding this shirt, I was having a block about buying it, and it dawned on me right there in Topshop that I'd been having a six-month block, a block since I was beaten up outside Wally by that rogue asshole who never got his comeuppance. Over the last six months my wardrobe had become monotonal: all-black everything, oversize if not drowning, and zero accessories. I'd even let my hair grow back to its usual mousy-brown shade.

It seems blindingly obvious now, but there by the shirts in Topshop I let out a load of tears: tears that represented not only years of deep fear for my physical safety but also sadness that this punch to the right side of my face banged into me what the less violent of the daily attacks on my person were trying to do for all those years. To make me invisible, silent, unchallenging, ashamed, covered up.

I felt momentarily guilty that I wasn't crying about Ben, but the funeral's tomorrow so I'll do that then.

After about four minutes at the shirt rail in Topshop, a sales assistant came over and offered me a tissue. I

said, "No, thanks"—and while wiping away the tears—
"but I will take this shirt."

The irony of this being a shirt is not lost on me: I
am a million miles away from where I was. But in that
choice I decided to make a further choice to chip away
at that internalised self-loathing and fear, and to rebuild
both the confidence and the wardrobe that will get me
noticed once more. People often say, "They'll spot you
for the wrong reasons," but there are no wrong reasons,
just wrong, homophobic people.

14th October / le 14 octobre

Today was Ben's funeral, and it was a peculiar day for
us all. I loved Ben, the way you love the person you're
most distant to in a close circle of friends, the one you
wouldn't necessarily want to spend a day alone with,
but value most highly in the well-oiled dynamic of an
inseparable friendship group.

The way different members of the group, the Slags
(No Lauren), went through the day positively correlated
with how close each of us was to this wonderful friend
of ours, the guy who had at one time or another, despite
being a man of few words, said something more profound to each of us than all of us collectively did in our
constant, brilliant buzz of manic conversation.

When I was outed at school, Ben was the first to find
me, to check on me. I still can't fathom how he, a heterosexual boy of thirteen, worked out what to do. But he
found me, being hounded by bullies from years above

and below, and took me behind the drama block, put half a Lambert & Butler Blue in my mouth, lit it, and said, "Look"—his feet shuffling, shoulders raised—"I don't want you to think that I'm gay and stuff, but I just want to tell you that . . . I love you and I'm very proud of you. In a place like this it takes way more courage to be you than it does to be me, mate. I've got your back"—eyes shifting—"now pass that fag."

I remember hoping so desperately he would kiss me— that would've been romcom worthy—but I don't think I ever received a more beautiful reaction to any of my comings out. Today I didn't cry. I didn't post a long eulogy on Facebook—I hate that performative grieving so many people do on social media; already I've seen nigh on a hundred posts on Ben's wall from people who had no clue who he was. I didn't even feel that sad.

My grandma said to me after the funeral that grief is like a tiny pebble you carry around with you wherever you go. "It might start like a boulder or a bullet, but eventually it turns to a tiny, beautiful pebble that takes pride of place on your inner mantelpiece. You carry it everywhere, never forgetting but eventually moving on. You must treasure the pebble, because while it's there for a greatly sad reason, it's better to have had a reason to put it there."

I kind of understood what she meant by the last sentence, but as I tucked my grandma into bed because she can no longer get there herself, I took a little pebble and placed it there for Ben, and a little one for my grandma, too, who had changed beyond recognition from a bird of paradise to a real person who was ageing so quickly, and a little one for parts of myself that I'd lost along the way, too.

I spent the night in bed, on the phone to Ace until it was late. We know each other so well, but we spent nearly the whole night drilling down into the parts of our past we both had left behind when we arrived to university. This is what it must feel like to have a boyfriend—someone who spends the night on the phone with you even when they're yawning through it, still desperate to know you better.

While some friends had wept and wailed at the funeral, I found it hard to believe that I would never see Ben again. For me, that's my grief, my little pebble: a life lived forever in slight disbelief, wondering when he'll poke around the corner, asking me a slightly nonsensical ontological question I'm not quite in the mood to answer, telling me drunk on Jack Daniel's that he'll buy me this one, but the drinks are on me when I'm famous.

20th October / le 20 octobre

Until you've been on a night out in a northern town, have you ever been out out? When you grow up outside a cultural metropolis, with one dodgy cinema and a bowling alley that stinks of piss, the Night Out becomes religion, the centre of the week about which everything is planned. It's like a debutantes' ball—everyone's opportunity to debut their newest, shortest New Look purchase and to showcase the progress their Dove gradual tanner had made over the week.

A usual northern night out is full of unspoken rules and regulations:

1. Flat shoes? Are you fucking kidding me?
2. If you're bought a shot, you fucking drink it.
3. "Why the fuck you going home early?"—never go home early.
4. Predrink minimum a bottle of wine or 0.75 litres of vodka.
5. Arrive at Lancaster's only cocktail bar for strictly one cocktail. After that Emma gets mad because a cocktail is a fiver and she's famously tight.
6. Proceed to Wetherspoon's or Walkabout (closed down now) and purchase bottle of wine to consume for self.
7. Have a fight with Beth/Hannah because one of us is being "peaky" about something totally illogical.
8. Fall down stairs in Vodka Revs in front of everyone you know because here in Lancaster you know everyone, and they all go to Vodka Revs because it's the only place that doesn't have a sticky floor.
9. Cry in loo because you "just love each other so much" and make up from fight.
10. Dance for a bit, demanding the DJ to play song after song and getting visibly pissed off when he declines.
11. Drink more, dance more, and watch as Beth keeps revealing her tits because she wore a particularly chesty playsuit.
12. Take off heels and walk down to takeaway barefoot screaming about how much your feet hurt. "It feels like daggers are goin' in me feet!"

13. Get takeaway.

14. Eat takeaway while covering yourself in mayonnaise and garlic sauce, ruining an outfit you'd spent all week planning. Matt, the guy I was in love with for years, still eats mayonnaise with a spoon.

15. Sit in takeaway for at least an hour saying, "Hiya, hun!" to girls from school and then rolling your eyes at them the moment they turn away.

16. Fall asleep in taxi / cry in taxi about how much you love each other.

17. Don't take make-up off.

18. Text girls to say, "Love you gals best night ever!"

19. Repeat. Every single Saturday.

Here's the classic set of people you'll see on a northern night out:

The girls: Generally glam, loads of make-up, one or maybe two gay men in tow. One from the group will be limping from her heels, one will be so smashed she's kicked out of the club and will absolutely lose it with the bouncer, one will always get with the same pervy guy from two years above you in school, and another one will be jealous. They'll all fall out and make up minimum four times over one night.

The boys: I hate how gendered this is, but it's unlikely you'll find a group of non-binary folk on a night out in Lancaster. Anyway, the boys: The boys are fragile boys dressed in blown-up body suits—muscular, tattooed, shaded and faded hair, and they will all be wearing either Lyle & Scott, Stone Island, or Vivienne Westwood if they've got a particularly good job in Manchester. These ones tend to have quite shiny faces. They'll all drink in a circle and bop instead of dance. They, too, will get in fights, but they will be physical. I will at some point say something a little too over-the-top, and one of them will call me a "fucking faggot" every time he sees me thereafter. I will tell him I fucked his dad.

The old lady lushes: My favourite. They're all called Beverley or Linda or Kath, and they'll wear sheeny plum-coloured lipsticks called things like Iced Chardonnay or Cheeky Champagne. They'll have lots of old gold jewellery and will be guaranteed to be the ones laughing the most, their hair so lacquered you could crack a tooth on it.

The students: A much-disliked group among the townspeople, and you might encounter them on a weeknight. Once, I was challenged to a dance-off in Toast by a student from the uni, and the whole club—thus the whole of Lancaster—watched, enthralled. I was killing it, until I went for a high kick, fell over backwards, split my pants from waist to asshole, and lay there as my exposed genitals were presented for all to see. My friend Beth laughed so much she was sick in the club.

Your auntie and uncle: Related or not, they're fucking everywhere.

One of your friends' mums: She's wasted, and your friend has to leave early, hugely pissed off, to take her home.

Things you might see: A baby in a pram in the club, a person wearing flip-flops, someone trying to beat up a bouncer, boys lurking outside the club in cars playing music loud, a flirty teacher, someone in a Day-Glo ra-ra skirt who's just put an ecstasy pill up her bum.

You'll never see a drag queen (there are places, but these tend to be in the bigger cities such as Manchester, Newcastle, or Birmingham with a burgeoning drag scene). Blackpool has lots of drag queens, and they're iconic, rock-hard diamond ladies—the real old-school queens, the fascinating, hard-as-nails ones who are probably quite bitter, having lived a life of brutal homophobia. They're enthralling performers, and they definitely shave their arms. They're called things like Mercedes Bends and Miss Liza Garland.

Other things you'll never see: A busy gay bar, flat hair, subtle make-up, someone paying over two pounds to get into a club.

These nights are strict in their routine. They are a tried-and-tested method that guarantees maximum fun, in minimum time, on a minimum spend. They never change, but why should they? Because on a Saturday night in Lancaster the people who spend their weeks working to the bone—as nurses, on farms, as teachers for kids with severe behavioural issues, as carers for their elderly parents, as builders and hairdressers and nail technicians and cleaners—have a place where they are like celebrities. We know everyone, we look amazing, and we feel, for one night a week, absolutely, unstoppably joyful.

24th October / le 24 octobre

Tonight I was talking to my dad. We were walking our dog along the beach, dodging puddles and squelchy marshes that have eroded so hugely since my last visit home, and he recalled a type of nail varnish I used to wear, back in the days when my mum used to hate it.

It was when nail art was all the rage, when companies like Rimmel and Barry M brought out a new formula each week: matte, shiny matte, crispy seaweed.

"This one was a crackle one," my dad said, eyes aglow. "It was black, and you used to paint it over coloured polish and it would crack, like scorched earth, and reveal the colour underneath. It was beautiful, I loved it, and I was so jealous, because it was so detailed and I've always loved detail."

Blithely I told him he should wear it, that I'd dig it out for him. He told me that he never could: the world had come to expect him to look a certain way, and it would cause a stir among the people of our hometown if he started wearing nail varnish. "They'd think I was a freak," he worried, before going on to list all of the things he wishes he could adorn himself with but can't because he's a man and that's not okay.

"But I wear purple shoelaces," he concluded. "I wear them to remind myself that I'm colourful, that I love colour and small things, and pretty things, and nobody will ever know. That'll have to be enough."

Then, for all my complaining, for all the violence and all the difficulty, I thanked God that she'd made me queer, that I could wear whatever I wanted and didn't have to hide my true self between the rivets of my shoes.

I don't like many straight men, but for the first time ever I was stopped in my aggressive man-hating tracks and my heart broke for all the people like my dad who wished they could be a certain way, but can't because someone somewhere decided once that things should look like this. Yes, patriarchy affects men, too, sure, and I've said this loads in conversation, but I never felt it more than on the beach with my dad. There, at that moment, I had never been more glad to be different, to have been excised from that system by a process of gaylimination.

We came home and I painted his nails with the crackly stuff that I found in the back of my wardrobe. Despite our absences, my parents have kept all of our childhood bedrooms intact. An idea that makes me tear up to even think of it.

My dad loved the nails. Then we took them off. We'll probably never speak of it again.

26th October / le 26 octobre

Lancaster is a matriarchy. Never has the power of women been proven more than in the smoke-stained, sticky-carpeted pubs; than in the glittering, gossiping chairs of nail salons; than at the tills at Morrisons, where lads would try and always fail to steal bottles of piss-like cider. Hair piled high, lacquered so extremely you could crack a tooth on it, make-up caked on, lipstick bleeding through the wrinkled skin around a mouth carved from a lifetime of gossip. The women run this town like a well-organised Mafia.

These women—from my grandma, to my mum and sister, to the dinner lady who returned to work the day after having an eye removed—display power like thunder. They seem able to work an endless week, smoke interminable Lambert & Butler Blues, and keep a family of could-be disastrous men in full control, control born of both fervent fearmongering and aggressive love.

These women defy binary modes of gender and make the men who are, rightly, under their control do exactly the same. In my hometown the women wear the trousers; in my hometown the women take up the space; in my hometown the women hold court sat at the bar, telling story after story.

It's by no means queer, and I can feel the distinct lack of that when I'm here. It's often homophobic. But it was here, taking cues from these trailblazing, hard women, and the way they dominated men, that showed me ingenious ways to survive if you'd been dealt cards that put you to the bottom of the deck. When I look at these women as I walk through town, I can see every possible expression of gender—whether the brilliant butches off to a party in Manchester who will head-butt a homophobe at a moment's notice, or my auntie Andrea, who taught me the power of sex as a weapon and wine as a lubricant for laughing at it all.

In my first summer out of uni, I got a job at one of the nail salons in the centre of town. Called A Touch of Serenity, it was light years from serene. Here I would befriend clients and cosmetologists alike and would sit filing off and sticking on giant, weapon-like talons in repeat motion. I was presenting very much as gender questioning—big nails, dresses, long hair, high heels, walking along the pedestrian paths of town listening to Amanda Lepore as I had rocks hurled at me. The women of the salon—and their advice to "keep on going" and "get on with it!"—saved me.

For many of us we talk about finding gender nonconformism as the thing that saved our lives, and, yes, being able to explore my gender in safety, to present in the ways I feel most authentic in queer spaces, to have that golden feeling of finally being understood when someone gets your pronoun right, all of this not only saved my life but filled it with validity and power and brightness.

But before I was allowed to flourish, I first needed to find a way to survive. And the women of my hometown wrote the rule book, passed it to me, and showed me how to put it all into action.

30th October / le 30 octobre

I'm heading home to London today, having been in Lancaster for nearly a month. Denim has a Halloween gig in a bleak members' club in Mayfair, but it's good for the bank balance.

I feel the most upset I've felt leaving this place since I left for university. I don't know whether it's because Ben's passing made us all feel more volatile, or because I've become much more stable in myself, my link to home, and in what I want, but as the train rolled off, I noticed the absence of the usual relief I felt when leaving Lancaster and going back to my queer life down in London.

I feel that the stretch between where I'm from and where I'm going has vanished, that the same person is simply stepping between the two places, not flitting between two lives. There is no escape, no running from, just travelling between.

For the first time I don't feel desperate to get out.

November / novembre

2nd November / le 2 novembre

We've been kicked out of the warehouse because we are a "fire hazard." I didn't know until I returned because the Wallies didn't want to tell me while I was at the funeral.

Amazingly, they've found a house on the same street. I use the term *house* lightly. It's essentially a series of corridors in between two kebab shops (yes!) that has a basement prone to flooding and a terminal rat infestation.*

It's all we can afford short of moving to the Isle of Man, but our mantra is simple: "It's queer!"—"Rats are queer!"—"Floods are queer!"—trying desperately to polish this property turd as most young people who live in London trying to "make it" in the arts do. Unless you're one of those people whose dad secretly bought them a house, then you just have the stress of having to pretend to be stressed about money and living costs and gentrification.

DRAG PERFORMANCE MEMO: Boyz are a drag king band that Hatty and Savannah are in. They use the aesthetics and ramblings of teenage boys, instead of power and politics, to showcase how pathetic masculinity can be. It's funny, and dumb, just talking about girls and Green Day, and for a minute men become less scary. That's effective, too.

---

* So nice to find a rental that allows pets.

3rd November / le 3 novembre

People who say things like "I would genuinely rather have no money than ever work in that place again" have never known what it's like to have no money.

6th November / le 6 novembre

Every cigarette I smoke makes me feel invincible. My friends, family, articles, the government, they all tell me to stop.

They all show concern when I splutter midway through a sentence, or when I can't quite muster the energy to climb the stairs at a particularly stairsy tube station. But cigarettes make me feel invincible. They make me think I'm not dead yet. So I keep smoking—a lot—because sometimes I just desperately need to feel invincible.

7th November / le 7 novembre

I was scrolling through Facebook, idly, distracting myself from how little money is left in my overdraft, when I saw something that took the words out of my mouth.

*

There, on my feed, was Lara. Lara Cocks.

---

* This space symbolises my loss for words.

Lara Cocks, the new drag persona of Paddy, the ring-leader of the homophobic bullies at my school, now a fully-fledged, all-singing, all-dancing, all-dick-sucking drag queen replete with lace fronts, padding, and an actual Facebook page you could like. I was aghast, so I dug more: going into the profile, right back to the start, which was two years ago, when Lara was birthed. This was the boy who would ash his cigarettes in my hair and make whole groups of lads chant, "Puff, puff, takes it up the chuff"* when I entered the classroom or got on the bus. He always had a gay vibe, to be honest—his shirt constantly French tucked—but he was so terrifying that to even suggest a hint of faggery would see me battered worse than my butt hole after a night at XXL.

Dumbfounded, I was going to ignore the page, but then I remembered that while he caused me some severe pain, it was probably because he was going through it, too. So I liked the page.

I'm going to take my good karma and spend the day waiting on hold to Santander to request an overdraft extension. Gonna be gorgeous.

8th November / le 8 novembre

It's free to call Santander if you go in branch, so yesterday I made the trek to my nearest branch to make the call to get my overdraft extended. I thought about borrowing

---

* A catchy rhyme, I must admit.

money from Ace and/or Hatty, but they both extended their own overdrafts last week, which is where I got the idea, so probably a no-go zone, I imagine.

I thought about calling my mum but she's broke at the minute. I thought about asking Pak, but I owe him five hundred pounds because he lent me two hundred pounds for my flight from Reykjavik ages ago and also bought me a three-hundred-pound Marques'Almeida puffer jacket that I wore once and decided I hated.

So there I was, inside a packed Liverpool Street Santander, on hold as lunchtime bankers ran in and out to check their huge assets hadn't been, I dunno—what's the worst that could happen to huge assets?—taxed at a fair rate?

Anyway, thirty-three minutes in, Kimberley from Liverpool answered: the thickest Scouse accent you've ever heard. Having grown up in the north, I love hearing another northerner, so we got chatting in that northern way only northern people do, in that way southern people hate.

I asked her how she was, and she told me she was sad because her family dog had just been run over by a lorry—which her stepdad was driving. Tragic.

She asked me how I was, and I told her I was freaking out about money. I asked her about the overdraft and she said she desperately wanted to help but couldn't.

Crystal kicked in.

"What if I give you something people usually pay me for, and you, instead of paying me, extend my overdraft?"

She was laughing and asked what I meant, to which we responded:

> *"A rendition of Whitney's 'I Will Always Love You,' in dedication to your dog?"*

She jumped at the chance. "Okay, maybe, only if you're good."

There, in full view of lunchtime Liverpool Street, two doors down from where my shit had shat on everyone's fried chicken dinner, I started slowly, as Whitney does, eventually charging into full song as I heard Kimberley breaking into a gentle weep on her end of the phone. I was trying to avoid eye contact with everyone else, not wanting to wither from embarrassment, but after I'd finished the song—fake sax solo, key change, big drum et al.—at least fifteen people in the bank started clapping. As I took a mini-bow, those sweet, sweet words ran from Kimberley's mouth like honey from a bee, like cum from a peen: "I've extended your overdraft for you—another seven hundred and fifty pounds."

9th November / le 9 novembre

What's a relationship, really?

For my whole life I was fed an idea that it's movie-like, impossibly romantic, a cure-all for every insecurity.

But, as dating happened more frequently, I found myself changing in disingenuous ways just to match what I thought the person sitting opposite me at Las Iguanas sucking on a margarita would want.

But with Ace I'm trying to let all of me flow free.

It's easier said than done—the slightest signal of Ace's flirting with someone else at a party and I'm sent ricocheting back into my insecurity. Am I not masculine enough? How can a flabby, loud, northern drag queen ever compete against that muscular guy who's succeeded at the whole "being a man" thing?

I always assumed being in a relationship would fix me. But it doesn't. Oftentimes it reflects your worst feelings about yourself back to you when the other person doesn't say exactly what you want to hear or doesn't tell you they love you in exactly the way you need to hear it.

But recognising that a relationship is a bunch of failings and successes that snowball into a deeper knowledge of someone, a further understanding of who you both are together and separately, is what it's about. It's not about filling a hole or sacrificing swathes of yourself to fill theirs. It's about making a space where you just are. Ninety per cent of the time Ace and I are that. The other 10 per cent— the fuck-up bits, the flirting-with-others bits, the not-texting-back-for-hours-so-you-assume-they're-getting-pounded-by-someone-else bits—they create, paradoxically, a space to explore yourself and your worth. They give you a moment to reflect on yourself and remember that the grass is way pinker in your field.

13th November / le 13 novembre

Last night I had a horrendous nightmare that I was straight. I woke up in hot sweats, from a life where I had a wife and three children and was a wealthy vet who wore jerkins* and chinos and said things like "the missus" and "Kids, shut up, I'm watching the golf."

I opened my eyes, breathing heavily, and looked over next to me at Ace, asleep naked. He has the most beautiful body, as if it were carved from a chunk of soft stone you can find on the beach near where I grew up. He has two little dimples above his bum and fluffy hair all over it. He has a sprouting of thick ginger hair on his chest—which he hates, but I adore—and a dip in his chest at the bottom of his ribcage, which ripples when he breathes in and out. His hair is red, thick like a mountain pony's mane, and his nose is ever so slightly bumped at the bridge, and I thank God that she gave him at least one physical flaw so that I'm not constantly in terror of his perfection. There's a scar on his leg from where his cat attacked him when he was young, and his mum, dad, and sister always say that the cat was given to a neighbour, but I think it was euthanised. I think it's weird that I'm thinking about cat euthanasia as I write about my boyfriend. I replay the dream—the tidiest life, the loveliest family—and then I look around at the mess in our room: the ashtrays full of cigarettes, the clothes jumbled all over the floor, the fine sheen of black dust that covers

---

* Such a stunning and underused word. xx

our room from Commercial Road's constant traffic jam. A Volvic bottle full of piss because I was home alone two days ago and was too scared to walk down the stairs to the loo because I'm always convinced I'm going to be attacked by an intruder when I'm home alone.

I kiss Ace on the forehead, and his breath smells like stale lungs, and I wonder if it's possible to love someone more than I love this person, where even his smelly breath makes my heart beat faster. When I look at our life—mine, mine and Ace's, mine and all my friends'—so departed from what I once thought my life would look like, it makes me feel overwhelmed that I get to do it like this.

15th November / le 15 novembre

We were getting ready for a Denim gig last night, all sitting on the floor, squatting under blinky strip lights, in a loo that was overflowing with poo onto aforementioned floor. In drag, at so many moments you stop and wonder how all the choices you've made in your life led you to this moment as you're putting on layers and layers of make-up to go to your actual job while eyeing up a poo that is edging closer and closer.

I asked the girls what they think the most important thing a drag performer should know. The answers varied:

Glamrou said, "It should be silly; we all need to have fun in an increasingly angry world."

Aphrodite proposed that it should have something to

say. Electra agreed with Glamrou. Shirley said fervently, "That we honour our history." And I agreed with her.

"Why?" I asked, but then everyone descended into gluing their eyebrows down because it's an urgent and detailed art, which, if done wrong, could produce the hellish phenomenon known as Oatmeal Eyebrows.*

As I painted on the rest of my face, squinting into a tiny compact mirror, doing it section by section, I thought, quietly, about all the queens and kings and gender artists who came before us, who put us here. For centuries it was religious or ritualistic: whether Aztecs or Egyptians, kabuki or shirabyoshi, or the misogynist men of the early English church system who had to take the female roles because women weren't allowed. Dumb.

It kind of went this way for ages, and then Shakespeare and all that boring stuff. It was chill then, to be a man who dressed in women's clothing. Fast-forward a while and you've got the revue shows of the thirties, around the time sexology deemed drag kings and queens to be of a third gender, around the time straight culture discarded it all. It became a thing of secret gay bars and underground private parties in the days when being gay was illegal.† But, as is the way with history, it's never made by the legislators or the people in power.‡ It's made by

---

* Exactly as it sounds: when the glue on your brows becomes bitty and crusty, like dried, glittering oats, belying your true identity.

† It should be noted that it's still illegal in seventy countries.

‡ They just take credit for it.

the people who resist, who are active and who have had enough—and looking back on our history as LGBTQIA+ folk, it's drag queens, non-binary folk, trans women of colour, butches such as Stormé DeLarverie, who put us where we are.

Now it's big in pop culture but we're by no means safe despite new levels of notoriety.

Later, after thirty minutes of listening to Kylie's new album, which we all decided we think is a three out of five stars, I said again that the most important thing about drag is knowing our history—because without it how will we take back our future?

20th November / le 20 novembre

A note from an old diary, nine years ago today, a different me, pre-university and queerness and an expanded world.

> *I hate fanny. It's so scary and it makes me feel weird.*
> *That's why I told Beth she can't sleep naked! Eiw!*
> *I'm gay.*

Sometimes I shock myself when I look back at the ways I used to be. I also relish looking back over my diaries to see how far I've come—to glimpse all the things I've, thankfully, unlearned. I also love that at the beginning of every entry I would start by writing "Dear World!"—literally addressing the whole world, ready to go for whenever these remarkable works of non-fiction would be published in a smart move from a savvy publisher and I, with my witty childhood musings, would become a global superstar.

Nothing is more bleakly cliché than a gay man who flinches at any talk of vaginas. Hatty, Ellie, Cecily, Violet—all my female friends—have experienced this, and all of them tell me it feels deeply hurtful and, when it happens, only loads them with shame about having a vagina.

I complain when people shame me for the things I am or the things I've done, as do so many gays, so why has it become part of our cultural code to scream every time someone brings up vaginas?

21st November / le 21 novembre

I'm done with fashion—today I was asked to write an article called "This Year's Ultimate Accessory: The Hair Tuck," and it was, no shitting you, an article about how to tuck your hair behind your ears. It was "URGENT!!," according to my editor. I sat there wincing as I wrote 650 words about Gigi Hadid and Jessica Alba,* trying to make pulling your hair behind your ears a thing. I stopped for a moment, deleted the whole article, and with crystal clarity replied to my editor:

---

* I mean, you're flogging a dead horse if you have to use Jessica Alba in a trend article: she's done nothing of relevance since she launched that baby-food line years ago.

John,

I appreciate you have a content quota to fill but this is by no means urgent and I can't seem to find the will within me to pull some crap out of my arse to talk about hair tucking. I'm sorry, it's just so painfully inconsequential. I will pitch you some features tomorrow.

Now I'm terrified I've fucked the contact, but I felt that it was time to stop wasting my time for tiny amounts of cash and focus on something more important.

I'm going to watch reruns of *Desperate Housewives*. That's way more important. Such a shame Marc Cherry's a Republican.

22nd November / le 22 novembre

Yes, I fucked the contact. He replied saying that he was insulted that I couldn't get behind his editorial vision, which made me do a spit take of my coffee all over Leyah because to use the word *vision* for an article about hair tucks is worse than saying being gay is a choice.

PERFORMANCE MEMO: Kai Isaiah Jamal is a poet who writes about their body and its link to religion and masculinity. Was on a panel with them yesterday and they read a stream of consciousness and I wept. Queer people are so fucking talented, like prophets.

25th November / le 25 novembre

Something that always comes with the start of a new relationship is a moment when you consider that you might not have sex with anyone else again. Luckily for gays we can oft revert to the whole open-relationship thing, but Ace and I are currently attempting monogamy because it's still exciting to be exploring each other's body and we've both sucked enough dick to take a breather from others for a little while.

While our sex is wild in many ways, we have differences in our sexual tastes. I'm very "piss in my asshole and drink the contents," and while he's adventurous, he's not so into the more extreme sides of sex: punching, pissing, degradation.

With such different sexual tastes, one will have to compromise to accommodate the other. The one who does the compromising should be the one who wouldn't be in breach of consent if they were to make said compromise. Me asking Ace to punch me in the face would be great for me, but not for him—hence his consent breached. Him asking me to suck his balls in a stairwell—we're both consenting, everyone's a winner, and we teabag all the way home.

It's the first time I've ever considered this because before Ace my relationship with consent was very much based on, first, the fact I was looking for the wildest sexual anecdotes with which to shock my friends—this would often leave me exiting a sexual scenario wondering if I had really wanted to drink from the toilet like a "mangy little mutt," leaving a knot of discomfort in my

stomach but with a great story to tell. The second factor
was that I was never aware of what my limits were until
I'd crossed them, so I'd think, "Why not—he wants you
to dress up like a Disney princess and fuck you in his
daughter's bed—cool!" Turns out it wasn't, and thereafter I wouldn't ever be consenting to children's princess cosplay again. Not my thing. Ergo I only worked out
what I wanted after I worked out what I didn't.

Once, when I was at university, I had my consent
outright breached. It wasn't a case of working it out on
the job. No, this one was someone hearing me saying,
"No, I don't want that," but powering ahead regardless.

I'd been dating this older guy from Cambridge college, in total secret, for about six months. We would see
each other once, twice a week—for dinner, or cans of
Fanta on his lawn, or to look over his vast array of rare
butterflies, which were pinned inside dusty glass display cases across every one of his walls. It was a sweet
relationship—he was angry, odd, and he'd get frustrated,
but I found it endearing, and he cherished me and celebrated things such as my acrylic nails or my ever-changing
hair colours, giving out titbits of compliments such as
"Looks good," which would make me feel like a princess.

"God, you're cheap."

We had brilliant sex—uninhibited, vanilla, but with
pleasure at its gooey core—which is why we probably
worked for half a year. One night we'd gone out for
dinner and I was feeling unwell afterwards, so I declined
sex. He listened at first, but persisted in coaxing me into

a blow or hand job, his coercive language something I should have said no to, but in the moment I didn't see the harm in giving him a quick handy-j even if I was uninterested: at least one of us could get off. Now my lines on coercive language in a sexual, or any, scenario are much tighter.

After about six minutes of lubey hand sliding, he climbed on top of me. Fine—we were kissing, it was his way of showing how much he was loving it. He started to pin me down, which I was somewhat into, assuming he was just enjoying my handy work. Then he fucked me. I said no, both during and before. But he carried on, pushing deeper, holding me at my wrists, as I asked him to stop, kindly at first, then angrily, then worriedly, and the only thing he said was "Come on, you love this!"

In that second I became aware that my line of consent had been crossed—this wasn't an experimental face-sitting balancing act or fetishwear session that just didn't quite do it for me; this was what I was so reluctant to name, for so many years after, rape.

Eventually I got a wrist free and punched him over and over in the shoulder. He pulled out and I pushed him off the top of me—the first time in my life I'd used my strength and been so thankful to have a big body. I leapt off the bed and screamed at him so loudly yet articulately, it was as if it were perfectly scripted. Then I threw an unopened can of Fanta at his face as he tried to approach me, missing him and shattering the glass of his biggest butterfly case into smithereens, the wings of many of those precious butterflies chipped and crackled to pieces on impact. I walked home, weeping, in the late dusk, and all I could think about was the butterflies, and how damaged they'd been against their consent.

I've had a strange relationship with consent for as long as I can remember, a lot of it lying in what my sexual partner wants fulfilling, dictating the lines of my yeses and my noes. With Ace, consent is the beginning, middle, end of our sex—which some might think is boring or takes the sweating edges off the act, but I've never felt more considered or more safe, which has allowed me much more pleasure. For someone who has been seeking unsafe sex in various forms for a long time, I'm coming to realise that perhaps to feel fully consenting—and not like a trapeze artist treading a wobbly line—is more sexually satisfying than any of the radical, dangerous sex I've ever had. Perhaps eventually it will blossom into both, but this time it will start with consent, instead of ending with a question.

27th November / le 27 novembre

A message from Lily:

> So I have a friend who runs a record label in London and I want them to see ACM. How about I pay you a little yuletide visit? My family are in Guyana for Christmas (don't ask) and Jeremy is with family. A space for me at your table, perhaps? I might even get you something Balenciaga. Love you xxx

Me:

> Are you fucking kidding me? Book that flight now, my queen! This will be the best Queermas ever! xxx

Lily:

> Okay, amazing! Will let you know dates! By the way I said that Balenciaga thing as a ruse to get you to say yes—probably not gonna happen, I'm broke xxxx

DRAG PERFORMANCE MEMO: Saw Victoria Sin perform at an art gallery last night. Their performance is all about consuming space. So they put on their wig and their heels and they walk around the stage and talk about how their wig ate yours for breakfast. It's all about showing female labour. They make a cheese sandwich and make you watch them make it. They drink a glass of milk for three minutes and make you watch them drink it—celebrated for doing nothing, but being in drag while doing. Both critiquing the ignorance toward the labour of women, and how easily we'll celebrate cis male drag queens doing nothing. It's honestly brilliant, spellbinding. Saying so much while doing so little.

29th November / le 29 novembre

So I was in the shop over the road from our new house, and I overheard a kid, tugging their mum's skirt, querying, "Mummy, what's wrong with that boy? He's wearing a dress!"

It cut deep. It cut real deep. It cut even deeper when she replied, "Oh, honey, he's obviously just very unwell."

All I wanted was pita and taramasalata, and instead I got diagnosed by a mother and a sweet babe.

I turned around, removed my Gucci sunglasses like a character from *Dynasty*, and responded, "I'm beautiful!"

Crystal erupted into rapturous applause, a single tear wobbling from her eye.

"She's all grown up!"

December / décembre

1st December / le 1 décembre

Denim is hosting a World AIDS Day party tonight.

A party sounds like a strange way to honour the virus that's killed thirty-five million people worldwide, that saw and still sees the persecution and stigmatisation of those who live with it, even though HIV and AIDS don't discriminate.*

But that's exactly the point: it is a party to honour those living powerfully, and those lost who with them took so much talent, beauty, and love. A party is the perfect way to do this.

That's because a party doesn't always have to be wild or wasted or joyful. A party isn't always about getting pissed, but it's always about the collectivity of people, sharing an experience of—yes—sex, joy, love. But also grief, pain, silence, quietness, all soundtracked by booming music, which levels the playing field among everyone dancing. You can fade in and out, together and apart.

Those who were lost to AIDS-related illnesses, and those who still suffer today, must be honoured with action—and there are people working to make changes every day, from aid workers to councillors to hard-core activists who devote their lives to ending stigma, to finding a cure.

But on World AIDS Day it's a time to collect, look back, and celebrate. And so we keep dancing.

---

* Only people do that, which is worse.

2nd December / le 2 décembre

"Well," he says, "I've never really," he says, "been to a drag show," he says, as his hand slips down your back and onto your ass.

He's slurring his words, his breath so plump and hot with alcohol it instantly condenses on your nose, and he thinks you're his. He thinks you're his for the taking.

He's attractive, early thirties, long-term girlfriend, and he bought you a friendly drink after the show, which you accepted as a kind gesture in return for what you gave him while you were onstage. Now, a few drinks later, friends gone home, he commandeers you, tells you, over and over, how he's never been to a drag show, as he clutches you and another beer.

You don't want him to touch you. This strange, dissociative feeling isn't wholly of fear—though that's a part of it—but it's also of fury, of lack of surprise, of yet another night spent with someone unwanted who thinks, because you're in drag, you're public property.

Touches come all the time: people grab you on the arm, touch your dress, feel your wig. They are fucking magpies to shiny things, and when in drag you're often both aesthetically and metaphorically shiny while also appearing as debased, because you're probably desperate for their approval, attention. Because why else would you be a drag queen?

As drag performers we're used to fielding certain types of behaviour: the drunk straight man who's curious, the hammered hen party for whom you become the most glittery accessory, the *Drag Race* obsessor who pins you against a wall and tells you which queen you're most like. Even the kindest of statements can become grating: "We need a pic!" or "Can you do my make-up?" is like someone getting their accountant friend to do their accounts for them, for free. Yes, drag is my way of life, an emancipation, but it's also a job, a craft I have worked hard to perfect.

These people are all insidious. They're all a reminder that you're not necessarily human, that you're a totem for tragedy and triumph, for loneliness and love, for power and powerlessness.

I'm not saying the right response to a drag performer is to sit them down, make them a cup of tea, and ask them how they are. But it's to match their energy with yours. It's to respect their want for boundaries, even if, as a drag performer, they seem like the most boundless thing you've ever seen.

5th December / le 5 décembre

Today the news ran that Oxbridge accepts more entrants from Eton per year than there are kids on free school meals. Vile.

So a national newspaper asked me to write about class and going to Cambridge. I said yes and wrote a piece about how isolating it felt to be from a different world— the underworld, as a lot of people saw it—recalling professors telling me to change my accent if I wanted to succeed, or being told there was no culture outside

Zone 2. I didn't even know what Zone 2 was. One time I told someone I had never read a newspaper and they didn't speak to me for the rest of our time at university. I told them my family didn't have a bookshelf, that we weren't big readers, but that just made it worse.

I spent three years at Cambridge trying to climb the mountain of class difference, trying to reach the peak where the social, cultural, and financial elites live. I came from the bottom of the mountain, a place where I had never even known about class because the top was not in view. Maybe on TV, but that was TV, and so while it could perhaps be seen, it was never felt.

It took me a long time to understand the key to being posh.

As Crystal puts it, *"Once you do away with your accent and your lack of confidence in your own voice, class difference comes down to the fact that posh people wear a lot of clothes with holes in them."*

In my town you were not allowed holes in your clothes—you did everything to avoid looking poor. But rich people can pull off the aesthetics of looking poor because everyone knows—from their staff, to their colleagues, to their friends—that they're not. We all know the posh guy who just threw on this moth-eaten shit stain of a sweater while they were tending to the deer and writing their crap novel, before, in a jiffy, they'll dress for dinner.

I could never pull off the holes. Sweatpants now perhaps, but holes in them—absolutely not.

9th December / le 9 décembre

Today on the Bakerloo line I saw the man who attacked me. He sat opposite me, we caught each other's eye, and a shiver instantly went through me, like when someone says, "Oops, someone walked over your grave" or "Oops, that was a dick pic flying right through you."

For all these months I couldn't remember his face, which I'm glad about, and in recollections of the event—which would rush to me, vivid as an acid trip, when I walked home alone at night or closed my eyes when I was shampooing—he was a hooded figure with a booming drawl.

But this man was absolutely him. I heard him speaking to a friend, and it was his voice, and when he glanced at me in the eye, we connected in exactly the same way we connected just before his fist met my face. He knew it; I knew it. I spent the first two stops anxiously considering moving down the packed carriage full of December shoppers, as I could feel his stares passing over me while he probably tried to work out where he knew me from. Then, much like Harry Potter's scar when he's near Voldemort,* the scar on my nose started to crunch as it does sporadically from time to time, as if a chip of bone is obstructing a small blood vessel.

So I decided to stay where I was. I decided not to move an inch. I decided to sit and rub my scar and look him directly in the eye because I'd done enough moving

---

* I've never read it, does this metaphor work?

to last us both a lifetime. The moment he clocked me staring, he averted his eyes. But I kept on looking.

I grew ever more furious as the train whizzed through the tube tunnels, through decades' worth of dust and skin cells and breath from the lungs of Londoners and all its wide-reaching visitors. His included.

Most of my conversations, either the ones with myself or the ones with my queer siblings, are about analysing the world's structures to try to solve the mysteries of why we all behave in certain ways, why different people's situations and histories produce different types of behaviour in them. We spent months doing just that for my lovely attacker, trying to find rhyme or reason in his actions—"He can't take his fragile masculinity so he lashed out at you" or "It was a cruel thing that man did, but we must locate the problems in the structures, not in the actions, in order to really prevent attacks like this happening again."

I buy it. I believe it—that people's negative behaviour often stems from their difficult backgrounds. The tag line for my favourite movie—*Burlesque*, a masterpiece starring Cher and Christina Aguilera*—is "It takes a legend to make a star." Now that thinking can be transposed onto lots of things, and in the case of my attacker it would look something like "It takes a hard life, bad decisions, the plights of masculinity, and a lack of exposure and education to make a queerphobic attacker." Catchy.

---

* I've seen it fifty-three times, really proud, someone call *Guinness World Records*.

These deconstructions of what makes people violent towards people like me are integral in helping those on the receiving end of said violence maintain our faith in humanity.

But after a life spent locating these specific alleles on the helix that is social structure, trying to forgive my attackers, I'm sometimes pushed out of this mindset and simply cannot understand these actions no matter the circumstances from which they arose.

As I sat on this train staring at a man who transferred so much rage and fragility into my body that I still can't leave the house in full drag, that I feel like a trembling deer every time I hear a sharp noise, that caused me to mute and edit parts of my expression into obscurity, my brain can no longer compute these structures and all it feels is a lack of understanding brought on by clouds of scarlet rage.

In that moment I couldn't give one tiny shit that this man might have had a hard life. I don't have an iota of concern for his situation, the pain put in his body that he took out on mine. My community, too, has received so much of that pain, yet I can't name a single person in it who has replicated such rage and passed it onto others the way our attackers do to us.

In that moment all my interest in humanity drained from my body, and all I felt was an overwhelming desire to cause this man some long-lasting hurt. I didn't think to take a picture or report him because the rage was clouding my judgment, although my judgment tells me not to rely on any justice system for any justice.

He got off at Lambeth North, my eyes following his

red Converse to the edge of the carriage as he stepped out into the world. The rage drained, the desire to hurt someone disintegrated, and I clicked back into considering what caused his actions.

It's the right thing to do—both morally and politically. But it doesn't mean that sometimes you forget, even just for a moment, what's right. When some people in the world want you dead or hurt because of who you are, it's hard to always keep treading water, keep trying to find ways around their actions that somewhat absolve them. At some point, perhaps, people need to take fucking responsibility for their actions. I don't know.

But we've done it for centuries, and we continue to now. We've done the work, we know why we came into being in the all-sparkling ways we did. We see the power in rising higher. It's just such a shame that men like him can't do the same.

10th December / le 10 décembre

A call from my only friend from *Chic*, Amnah. She's iconic: I've never seen a better dresser, and I've never met someone with such an appreciation of style and aesthetic who desperately cares about the politics behind it.

She's a woman from Saudi Arabia who came to London and found her people. She's a laugh a second—like a tornado screeching through the bar in which we decided to meet for a long, boozy lunch.

"I've got a project and I thought you might be the perfect person to do it with."

"Sure, hit me!"

"You know how we always talk about the way fashion creates fantasy but excludes so many people from it?"

"Yes, and that if it's a fantasy, why the fuck can't everyone be involved? Are fat people, black people, trans people, disabled people, not allowed to fantasise?"

"Right, yes. Well, I got some cash to do something with this idea, and I wanted to start a publication. I can pay you a decent hourly rate, and we can just make a fantasy where everyone's in it?"

"I'm in!"

As lunch stumbled into dinner, we drank three bottles of wine, three tequila slammers, and ate a McDonald's. It was one of those afternoons where you feel as if you've fallen in love with someone from the moment you sit.

"We're having a Queermas at my house, on the seventeenth. You wanna come?"

She nodded.

"Amazing! Bring wine, or any booze, one item of Christmas food, and wear something show-stopping!"

11th December / le 11 décembre

At a conference about queer grief and trauma, a friend of mine and I got into a heated debate: he argued that most of our problems are over, and I said that we've barely begun unpicking the wealth of shit that has been hurled at our community for the past forever.

He cited that video series It Gets Better as a good example, but I just don't see that. Maybe I'm a fucking cynic, and while this drip-feed of information and advice, which can thankfully be accessed at the click of a trackpad—much more easily than when I was a kid—is vital for the survival and education of so many distressed LGBTQIA+ people out there, is its message true?

Yes, there are more movies, articles, political "wins," and more gay, queer, and trans people being granted a sliver of the media pie than ever before. But what does this all count for when life for us is becoming increasingly punctuated by verbal, media-driven, and physical violence,* erasure of our communal spaces, and the swift dismantling under a Tory government of the meagre legislative support we have? I'm constantly so aware of being grateful for what we have, on the backs of those that fought for us, but sometimes I just feel furious.

Next year it'll be the fiftieth anniversary of the decriminalisation of homosexuality in the U.K. Although we've made countless steps towards a better future for our community, the road ahead is still dishearteningly long. To tackle it, after a year of bad news upon bad news, in this new world of neo-fascist politics, we must seek to engage with the actual experience of LGBTQIA+ people, to ensure it does get better for ourselves, and for others, to make sure Orlando never happens again, to gain the rights we deserve.

I agreed to disagree with my friend on this one. We could agree on one thing, though: that our community is getting stronger . . . that our collective enemy in a

---

* Homophobic hate crime has risen by 147 per cent since Brexit, according to "The Hate Crime Report," published by Galop.

world leaning toward the right is sparking more political activism and unity than we've ever seen.

Gonna have a wank to take the edge off.

14th December / le 14 décembre

I've never enjoyed narratives. I find them suffocating, unlikely, linear, often missing key parts of the picture— rewritten to amp up or downplay the pain or the drama or the emotion we've decided that story will tell.

My best parts are in all the minging bits that would never make it into a book or a film. Like when you love the smell of a crusty new piercing or when you pick your earwax and eat it and realise it tastes horribly bitter.*

"I bet Kerouac never wrote about cheesy piercings," I said to a friend's boyfriend who idolises Kerouac (wtf?).

He said that Kerouac explored baseness in ways that could metaphorically mean that he was exploring those things.

Then I told him to fuck off.

15th December / le 15 décembre

I had my first argument with Ace today.

We were on Oxford Street, Christmas shopping, and I was talking about how different things feel this year

---

* Or when you wank over being gangbanged by the original cast of *Rent*.

versus last year: last year I was in New York swaddled in three duvets, seeing nobody, eating pita breads in bed, and wanking on a loop. I was talking about how much changes in a year for the individual but how so many parts of society that virtue-signal for change are actually the slowest to do the things they advocate. Journalism is a perfect example: it writes about us or asks us to mine our trauma to get the clicks, but it doesn't hire us. Same with publishing or making movies or theatre.

I was churning over and over how culture isn't deemed to be culture until some middle-class, highbrow man reviews it. I was getting louder and louder, angrier and angrier, and I accidentally smacked him in the face while I was violently gesticulating about men who violently gesticulate.

He got mad, which was fair, told me I was spatially unaware and inconsiderate; I said he was entitled; then we both walked off in different directions.

After he had a coffee and I had a full Five Guys burger and fries,* we met outside the flower shop at Liberty, where I'd bought him the most expensive bunch of peonies ever and he'd got me a can of Diet Coke, which, while cheaper, was much more thoughtful because, you know, it's the little things. As he approached, I inhaled sharply and was reminded, as I am every time I re-see his face, of the wonder of him.

I apologised, as did he, and we both admitted we were both wrong and then we kissed by the flower shop, the

---

* Eating my feelings as per, stunning. xxx

posh Tudor backdrop of Liberty illuminating the street, people looking—some in disgust, some in support, and I couldn't help but recall the Christina Aguilera "Beautiful" video, the one that had made me realise I was gay. It had all come full circle, without ever being a circle at all. I felt full.

17th December / le 17 décembre

Today was Wally Christmas, or Walmas, or Queermas— we never settled on a name, we're all so indecisive. But that's queer so it's fine.

Ellie organised it: she's a stickler for organised fun so, while we all tried to help, she got carried away and we let her run with it. We started out with a fashion show runway reveal at Stepney City Farm. Prizes were awarded for the best walk, the best look, and the best overall performance. Ace did a tri-reveal, unlayering three times, ending his sashay by sitting on a pig, as we all yelped in utter exultation, "Work that pig, mama!" He won, and prizes were doled out after we were forcibly removed from the property for our inappropriate pig use.

"But the pig loved it!" we protested. No luck.

After that we arrived home to prepare Queermas dinner. As can be expected when planning a dinner with nearly twenty queers, nobody brought what they were assigned by Ellie—which would have made for the perfect, all-rounder Christmas dinner. What was brought, in the end, by friends who'd rushed from all over town, some even from other countries, was far superior to any other Christmas dinner I'd ever had.

On the menu:

- Ellie's sweet potato with marshmallows. Two bottles of rosé fizz.
- Cecily's duck, which wouldn't fit in the oven, so we had to ask the kebab place next door if they could fire it up for us, to which they sweetly obliged.
- Lily's brick of Marlboro Lights from the airport: "Twenty packs of twenty—I want to get through them all, bitches, smoke up! It's Queermas!"
- Glamrou's inhaler.
- Aphrodite's homemade cheese sticks.
- Ace's stunning salad dressing, a Lady Gaga picture cake from Asda, and a cheese grater, because ours had been used (and subsequently broken) to support one corner of the washing machine as the floor had somehow become warped in the kitchen and the washing machine was moving about a metre and a half every time a cycle was completed.
- Electra's famous apple cake, which she buys from a bakery and takes all the credit for.
- Cora's news that she's moving to London!
- Amnah's magnum of cheap prosecco, some Patrón Cafe, and a dildo for Stick the Dildo on Dolly Parton— much like Pin the Tail on the Donkey, but queer.
- Savannah's whiskey and weed for everyone to share.

- Pak's disappointment at the lack of food, followed by twelve pizzas from Deliveroo, over which Cecily shredded the duck.
- Violet's boyfriend, who was dressed in a rugby shirt, which we all made him change for a glitter halter. "Much better!" Violet rejoiced.
- Allegra's copy of Susan Sontag's *Notes on "Camp"* with which Allegra posed like a seductive lecturer as she read a passage to us in place of grace.
- Jessie's camera and a bottle of Babycham.
- Hatty's decorations: the house was like a neon sex dungeon, plus tinsel curtains, and a homemade Christmas tree, made out of wire hangers, to which we made endless, obvious *Mommie Dearest* jokes.
- My make-up, and some bondage tape for lap dance hour.
- A suitcase full of Rina's beautiful clothes, which we all threw on and off throughout the day.
- Jacob's leftover spare ribs from a meal he'd just had with his dad in Chelsea, and his social media following.
- Chris's playlist full of niche Swedish dance tracks that none of us know, plus his iconic brand of Yuletide bitterness.
- Leyah's four pale ales and a bunch of petrol-station flowers: "What? I'm broke!"
- Shirley's high heels and wigs, for those who put in low effort on the costume front.
- Everyone's avid desperation to drench the holidays with as much queerness as possible.

And it was drenched. A tasting menu. A far cry from last year in New York.

The night rolled on, and we got through eleven of Lily's packs of cigarettes, all of the pizza, and every drop of booze. We rattled through games, sat around stewing in gloriously nostalgic stories from our collective years of friendship, and pulled queer crackers—just average crackers, but pulled with our ass cheeks, so that makes them queer.

We all began to drift off: strewn in full drag over mismatched dining-room chairs, covered over on the floor by thin veils of orange and green chiffon, five to a bed on the second floor, four to a bed in the basement, Amnah and Chris still smoking and chatting and cackling about being "overthirty" on the roof.

Collecting glasses from across the house, I thought about going home for Christmas and how full up that made me feel, for the first time in years. I wandered round the corridors of my big queer life, looking at my glorious friends and remembering the hunt I undertook to find them, for us to find each other. I heard shouting outside, but being in here gives new meaning to the term *safe as houses*.

I thought about family: my chosen family, and my biological family, and for a moment I stop and thank anything that is holy that I'm all the things I am, and that those things brought me to this day with these people.

In the middle of the night I was awoken by the drum of lorry hour outside my window. It wasn't dark in the house because it never gets dark from all the neon lights

of East London. I lit a cigarette and was standing looking out the window when I heard muttering from the
kitchen downstairs.

I padded down in the nude to find Hatty, Ace, and
Leyah chatting away, all unable to sleep, discussing
identity politics as per.

I sat down, and Ace and Hatty took a seat on each of
my knees, and Leyah sat on the washing machine. The
kitchen is so small that we were all huddled. We embraced so tightly.

"What do you want for Christmas, kids?" I asked,
like Santa.

A moment, the air becomes unusually sincere for a
bunch of nude queers at Christmas.

"This."

"This."

"This."

"This."

We all say it one after the other, glimmers of happy
tears in our eyes. And we all mean it.

"I want diamonds."

Acknowledgments

First of all, thank you for reading this. If you've got here, then I hope you got your life; if you're reading this in a bookshop, then please buy it.

First I must thank Zoe Ross, my agent: this book is in so many ways down to you and how fervent you are in your support and championing of my voice. You are a wonder, and I am so lucky to work with you. The same goes for Kitty Laing, who, when I don't feel it, reminds me that I'm a star.

To Jenna Johnson for being the most engaged, smart, challenging editor and for bringing Crystal to life. Your edits made me laugh, cry, but also feel seen. Thank you also to Lydia Zoells for the support, and to the whole team at FSG for taking me so skilfully through such daunting a task as publishing a book in the States. Little northern me is squealing.

Sara Cywinski, Michelle Warner, Chloë Rose, Emma Smith, Becky Hibbert, and the whole team at Ebury— thanks for taking a chance on the little book that could, and on me. I hope it does you proud. It has been such a pleasure.

To the editors who empowered my voice and told me my words were valid—Sarah Raphael, you are so deeply generous; Lynette Nylander, you were the first person who told me, and so many others, we could do it. Thank you.

My parents. Mum, thank you for teaching me how to love unconditionally, how to stand up for myself, and that the people in life are the most important. Dad, thank you for always telling me that it's the effort that counts, and for showing me that sensitivity isn't weakness. You are both the loves of my life. Danielle, James, and Harry: for teaching me wit and humour, strength in the face of bullies. I love you all so very much. Grandma, you helped me find glamour and beauty when I couldn't. You are an icon, and although you'll never know it, it was you who taught me to be gay. My nieces and nephew—don't read this till you're thirteen. Can't wait to give you your first cigarette. You're all amazing.

To Wally: for giving us a place to make mistakes, to love radically, and to ash on the floor.

My friends, my other family. To Shughie: you have shown me what it means to feel full, and to value myself by valuing me. You are the true queen, I love you. Hatty, you taught me queerness, and I am forever in your debt. Can't wait to spend forever with you. Leyah, for your patience and kindness, for your strength, and for always rolling me a cigarette. To Emily, for always giving your honest opinion, and for showing me gay culture. To Jacob, for being the best drag twin-baby ever, and for showing us all the radical power of glamour.

Amrou, you are a second mother/sister/daughter to me, and my world is expanded so greatly by your presence in it. I hope I can do the same for you.

Thurstan: thank you for always letting me be myself, for always being so proud of me, for teaching me work ethic, and for loving me when so many people love you. You are one of the world's real gems.

To Amnah, you always hear me and tell me my emotions are important. I fucking live for you.

To Emma, for always telling me my work is valid and for all our early-morning breakfasts and late nights falling asleep together.

Talia, thank you for showing me that weird is wonderful.

The Denims: you refashioned my idea of family, and I owe you, in so many ways, a lot of my life.

To Allegra, for teaching me how to write way back in my bedroom in Lancaster. Amelia—thank you for the brilliant advice, and for being someone to laugh about it all with. To Sadhbh, for always analysing the niche with me.

To my other friends, without whom this book, and this life, wouldn't be possible: Daphne, Rina, Jessie, Anna, Eve, Charlie H., Claudia, Decca, Ellie K., Chris, Harry P., David, Tamara, Harriet, Kai, Will, Sarah L., Sarah S., Nick, Lettice, Liam H., Theo, Claire W., Temi, Travis, Chiyo, Max, ShayShay, Margo, Megan, and Otamere.

To Sarah and Norman, for giving me a home to start in, and for being so constantly interesting.

To my bezzaz, you make me laugh like no other, and you pushed me through some of the toughest years of my life. You're all so, so iconic. I love you all so much.

To Celine Dion, for teaching me to be a queen.

To the north—for teaching me the value of kindness. To the drag community—for teaching me the value of community, of power, of self-love. To the LGBTQIA+

community wider—for teaching us all resilience. I am so proud, and so grateful, to be a part of you.

And, finally, thank you to my butt hole—you've really been through the wringer, yet you're the strongest thing I know.